Keeping the Red Flag Flying

KEEPING THE RED FLAG FLYING

The Labour Party in Opposition since 1922

Mark Garnett
Gavin Hyman
Richard Johnson

polity

Copyright © Mark Garnett, Gavin Hyman and Richard Johnson 2024

The right of Mark Garnett, Gavin Hyman and Richard Johnson to be identified as Authors of this Work has been asserted in accordance with the UK Copyright, Designs and Patents Act 1988.

First published in 2024 by Polity Press

Polity Press
65 Bridge Street
Cambridge CB2 1UR, UK

Polity Press
111 River Street
Hoboken, NJ 07030, USA

All rights reserved. Except for the quotation of short passages for the purpose of criticism and review, no part of this publication may be reproduced, stored in a retrieval system or transmitted, in any form or by any means, electronic, mechanical, photocopying, recording or otherwise, without the prior permission of the publisher.

ISBN-13: 978-1-5095-6095-0
ISBN-13: 978-1-5095-6096-7(pb)

A catalogue record for this book is available from the British Library.

Library of Congress Control Number: 2023946008

Typeset in 11.5 on 14pt Adobe Garamond
by Fakenham Prepress Solutions, Fakenham, Norfolk NR21 8NL
Printed and bound in Great Britain by CPI Group (UK) Ltd, Croydon

The publisher has used its best endeavours to ensure that the URLs for external websites referred to in this book are correct and active at the time of going to press. However, the publisher has no responsibility for the websites and can make no guarantee that a site will remain live or that the content is or will remain appropriate.

Every effort has been made to trace all copyright holders, but if any have been overlooked the publisher will be pleased to include any necessary credits in any subsequent reprint or edition.

For further information on Polity, visit our website:
politybooks.com

In memory of John 'Jack' Johnson
Teacher, Socialist, Grandfather

Contents

Figures and Tables viii
Preface and Acknowledgements ix

Introduction 1

1 In Pursuit of an 'Insane Miracle' (1922–1929) 9

2 A Battle Over Peace (1931–1940) 35

3 In Opposition to the Wartime Government (1940–1945) 60

4 'Fight, Fight and Fight Again' (1951–1964) 68

5 Yesterday's Men (1970–1974) 92

6 Impossible Promises and Far-Fetched Resolutions (1979–1987) 112

7 Thatcher's Greatest Achievement? (1987–1997) 142

8 In New Labour's Shadow (2010–2024) 166

Conclusion 198

Notes 206
References 227
Index 239

Figures and Tables

Figures

1.1	Number of votes cast for Labour, Conservatives and Liberals, 1922–1929	31
6.1	Constitutional reforms at Labour Party conferences, 1979–1980	118
6.2	Polling during the short campaign of the 1983 election, with trendline for Labour (8 May–9 June 1983)	127
6.3	Polling during the short campaign of the 1987 election, with trendline for Labour (2 May–11 June 1987)	130
8.1	Average left (–100) to right (+100) ideological placement, according to Labour members, 2010	172
8.2	Results of the 2010 Labour leadership election, final round	177
8.3	Breakdown of voter types in Labour leadership elections, 2015–2020	179
8.4	Labour Party membership, 1997–2022	181
8.5	Labour's share of eligible voters and total votes cast, 1997–2019	190

Tables

1.1	Growth of Labour candidates in the 1920s	31
6.1	Total votes cast in the 1981 deputy leadership election, indicating the number of abstentions in the second ballot	122
8.1	Ideological placement of Labour's manifestos	186
8.2	Class voting in the 2015 and 2017 elections: Support for Labour	191

Preface and Acknowledgements

The plan for this book was conceived while two of its authors travelled to an event organised by the third. On 1 October 2022, the 70th anniversary of Labour's notorious 1952 party conference was marked by an event held at the original venue, Morecambe's historic Winter Gardens. Thanks to the catastrophic Kwarteng/Truss mini-budget a few days earlier, an opinion poll lead which Labour had held consistently since December 2021 inflated into the kind of advantage enjoyed by Tony Blair's 'New Labour' in the run up to the party's landslide 1997 election victory.

The Labour Party delegates who met in the Winter Gardens in 1952 were coming to terms with rejection by the British voters, having finished their first of thirteen years in opposition. The activists who gathered to commemorate the occasion seventy eventful years later could allow themselves to dream that another protracted period of opposition would soon be over for their party. In an insightful and often moving address, the keynote speaker at the Morecambe commemoration, the former Shadow Chancellor John McDonnell, emphasised the importance of party unity despite the promising electoral outlook. The remaining question was: unity on whose terms? It was by no means the first time that the party had had to confront this dilemma as a party of opposition. The authors left the Winter Gardens with a reinforced feeling that a full-length study of the subject was sorely needed.

The authors are especially grateful to those who read and commented on particular draft chapters: Bernard Donoughue, Lee Evans, Bryan Gould, Conrad Landin, Colm Murphy, Kate Williams and Lewis Wormald. The two anonymous scholars who reviewed the whole manuscript provided many constructive suggestions.

Although the book was a collaborative endeavour, each chapter was assigned a principal author in initial drafting: Mark Garnett (chapters 5 and 7 and the Conclusion), Gavin Hyman (Introduction and chapters 2, 3 and 4), Richard Johnson (chapters 1, 6 and 8).

Introduction

In June 1971, the BBC broadcast an infamous documentary – 'fast moving and irreverent' as one commentator called it – on the Labour Party in opposition.[1] It was entitled *Yesterday's Men*, a mischievous turning of the tables on the Labour Party, given that they had adopted precisely this phrase in their electoral advertisements in the general election of 1970 to refer to the members of the previous Conservative government. The documentary broke new ground in that it shed some of the deference which political interviewees had hitherto been accorded, and asked questions that until then had been considered taboo.

It also broke new ground in its very focus on the Labour Party in *opposition*. Media attention has for the most part been lavished on governments and their doings, and opposition parties have tended to be left in the shade. At the beginning of the programme, the presenter David Dimbleby muses as follows: 'Labour has now been a full year in the wilderness. Perhaps the worst is over; the harsh rediscovery of what it means to be out of power. It was a year to be got through rather than lived, a year when the other people made the running. Politics is severe on those who fail. They're left to kick their heels and wait, and watch the others have a go.' But is this all that political opposition is about, kicking one's heels, waiting and 'watching the others have a go'? The programme asks and seeks to answer this question, although it focuses more on the fate of the senior former Cabinet ministers and their personal fortunes rather than on the party as a whole and its work in opposition.

In books and studies on the Labour Party – both scholarly and popular – the focus has likewise tended to be on its time in government. In many ways, this is understandable. These were the years in which the party was put to the test of office. It is natural for scholars and commentators to ask how successful it was in achieving its goals, how competent it was in governing the country, to what extent it succeeded in its aim of changing society, whether it remained true to its principles and beliefs when

1

tested in the crucible of government. But such questions are themselves dependent upon, and are only intelligible in terms of, other questions. How did the party determine its goals? How did it prepare for the task of governance? In what way did it seek to change society? How did it determine its principles and beliefs and how have these changed? Such questions can only be answered by turning instead to the time the party spent in opposition, during which, relieved of the task of governance, it had the leisure to engage in self-examination, institutional preparation and policy formation. These are vitally important tasks without which the party's time in government would be inexplicable.

In recent years, there has been some recognition of the importance of opposition as a subject of political study. In 2010, a Centre for Opposition Studies was established, now based at the University of Bolton. One of the co-founders, Nigel Fletcher, has edited *How to be in Opposition: Life in the Political Shadows* (2011).[2] There have also been volumes studying the Conservative Party in opposition – *Recovering Power: The Conservatives in Opposition since 1867* (2005) – and the party leaders in opposition – *Leaders of the Opposition: From Churchill to Cameron* (2012).[3] All of this is to be welcomed, but it is striking that so little attention has so far been paid to the Labour Party in opposition. Where the Labour Party has been considered, this has tended to focus on the particular individuals who served as Leaders of the Opposition, rather than the experience of the party more generally. Such neglect is surprising for at least two reasons. First, because of the sheer number of years that the party has spent in opposition. In the 100 years since it first became the official party of opposition, it has spent only about a third of those years in government. The party is therefore much more used to being in opposition than in government, which makes an examination of its time in opposition all the more pertinent. This also, of course, raises the further question of why the party has spent so much of its time in opposition. Is this because it has squandered much of its time in opposition or more because of its failures in government? Again, this is a question that cannot be answered by an examination of the party's time in government alone.

Secondly, an examination of its years spent in opposition is particularly relevant for the Labour Party which understands itself to be a party of 'change', in contrast to the Conservative Party which, in principle at least, ultimately seeks to 'conserve'. The change that has been sought has been primarily to the economic system of capitalism, which is why the Labour Party has historically defined itself as a 'socialist' party. But the party has had to answer the fundamental question of what form this change should take. In the early years, this entailed the party asking whether it should seek to dismantle capitalism or to reform it. As we shall see, the 1930s were decisive years in which the party ultimately decided to reform capitalism. But this raised further questions over the nature and extent of this reform, prompting arguments that raged throughout Labour's time in opposition in the 1950s and, again, in the 1980s. In the 1990s, the party decided less to reform capitalism than to administer it more fairly, later expressing considerable dissatisfaction with this minimalist approach in the 2010s. These were vitally important decisions in the evolution of what the party meant by 'change' and they were all effected during periods of soul-searching in opposition. It would not be an exaggeration to say that its time spent in opposition has served to define the party. This, in turn, has determined the party's agenda at the times it has entered into government. And yet, the party's experience of opposition has not been accorded the attention it deserves. In the chapters that follow, we seek to rectify this neglect.

In the 100 years or so covered by this book, the country, society, politics and the Labour Party have changed enormously. Sensitivity to this has necessitated a chronological approach, and each chapter in what follows is devoted to a particular period of time that the party spent in opposition. But equally, one of the aims of this book is to think across and between these periods, to draw comparisons and to analyse thematically across the broad sweep of the century during which Labour has been one of the two major parties. In order to do this, we have adopted a common set of criteria by which Labour's time in opposition may be judged. Again, sensitivity to the differences between these periods has led us to apply these criteria in a malleable rather than a rigid way, thus allowing us to work with a common standard of assessment while avoiding undue distortion.

In a very broad sense, we may say that the duties of a party in opposition are of two main kinds – those that look outward and those that look inward. In terms of Britain's parliamentary system of government, the most important – and outward-looking – role of the main opposition party is to hold the government of the day to account. The Official Opposition in Parliament is meant to scrutinise, question and criticise government legislation. The existence of the opposition in Parliament is to ensure that there is a tangible body of critical opinion to which the government of the day is answerable. An effective opposition does not, of course, indiscriminately oppose everything the government does. Rather, it has to measure the government's legislative proposals against its own standards, policies and principles and demonstrate the ways in which such legislation is wanting. How to measure the effectiveness of an opposition in this respect is a difficult question. An opposition is at its most effective when it is able to force a government to change course or even bring a government down. There are some examples of an opposition being able to do both of those things. For instance, the Labour opposition in 1935 was able to persuade the government to change its plans for the provision of unemployment benefit, and in 1990 it helped to ensure a change of policy on the poll tax. In the late 1930s, it helped to secure the end of the policy of appeasement. It made a direct contribution to the fall of Neville Chamberlain as prime minister in 1940 and an indirect contribution to the deposing of Margaret Thatcher in 1990. But the very fact that an opposition is in a minority in Parliament means that the opportunities for forcing such radical government concessions are rare. Furthermore, it is usually able to achieve them only by harnessing wider public opinion or by exploiting discontent within the government party itself. More frequently, the success of an opposition in holding a government to account will be measured by the extent to which an opposition is able to persuade the wider electorate that they are a government in waiting who would be more effective than the current incumbents.

This, indeed, is the second of our outward-looking criteria. As much as looking at the government benches facing them in the House of Commons, an effective opposition must communicate successfully to the wider population outside Parliament itself, upon which it depends for its transformation from opposition to government. The nature of this task has changed considerably over the century covered by this book. In the 1920s, the challenge was to persuade voters to trust an untried and untested party with the reins of government. When they were tried and tested, the results were not encouraging. After the Second World War, and Labour's decisive electoral victory, the voting habits of the electorate settled down into remarkably stable patterns and political identities became markedly tribal. Election results were determined by one or more of three things: Labour supporters staying at home and failing to vote; a change of vote on behalf of the small number of 'floating' or undecided voters; and the electoral fortunes of the Liberal Party. In the case of the first two groups, the Labour opposition had to pursue quite distinct tactics to persuade them to vote Labour. The Liberal vote could produce unexpected outcomes. It grew considerably between 1951 and 1964, but the increase tended to come from disaffected Conservative voters, thus allowing Labour to win in 1964, albeit with a smaller vote than in the previous three elections, which it had lost.

After 1979, the nature of the electorate changed considerably. For various societal and cultural reasons, it became much less tribal and entrenched. There was an increasing level of political disengagement, party membership numbers fell, political disillusionment grew and the turnout at elections was smaller. Political ideology waned and public relations, image, social media and 'spin' became increasingly important. This meant that the task of appealing to the electorate changed considerably from what it had been fifty years before. The Labour Party became adept at mastering this art in the late 1990s and into the new millennium, and it was rewarded with a sustained period in government. But after 2010, there emerged a new political re-enchantment; a younger generation of voters was politically engaged but found the established political parties to be wanting. The Labour Party was able to appeal to this new constituency of the electorate by decisively renouncing its 'neo-liberal' and image-obsessed recent past and adopting a new and more radical set of policies and leaders. The party increased its vote considerably, especially in 2017, but the resistant government vote increased even more, thus making victory elusive. In recent years, the party has shed its radicalism and has been leading in the polls for some time, although whether there is a causal connection between these two things is less clear. As in some previous periods covered by this book, Labour's recent poll lead may have more to do with an increasing disillusionment with the Conservative government than with a groundswell of popular support for the Labour opposition.

But however much media presentation, advertising and public relations may have been important tools in cultivating the support of the electorate, these can ultimately be no substitute for the formation of a clear and coherent policy offering. This is the first of our inward-looking criteria by which we assess Labour's respective periods of opposition. A party's time out of office provides an invaluable opportunity for it to reassess, take stock and reformulate its policy agenda in response to changing political and societal circumstances. As we shall see, different periods of opposition have been of varying degrees of significance in this respect. For instance, the 1930s were of decisive importance in terms of the party's policy formation. Its previous period in office had not been a success, and this was in large part because it had failed to do detailed and specific policy planning in its previous periods in opposition. It now undertook extensive policy planning which created an ample agenda for Labour's period in government in 1945–51. In contrast, Labour's period in opposition from 1951 to 1964 witnessed much policy debate, but little policy innovation. It essentially committed itself to the consolidation and enhancement of the policy agenda it had set itself in the 1930s. By the 1990s, such an agenda was unequivocally repudiated when the party essentially made peace with the country's free-market reforms of the 1980s, and sought instead to advocate policies of social justice that would work within rather than dismantle those reforms. All of these decisions were to determine the nature and achievements of successive Labour governments, but it is impossible to understand them fully without an appreciation of how these policies were formed during periods of opposition.

There is, however, another important sense in which opposition parties must look inwards during periods out of office. At the party conference of 1960, the young MP Roy Jenkins declaimed, 'we exist to change society. We are not likely to be very successful if we are horrified at any suggestion of changing ourselves.'[4] A period in opposition is indeed an ideal opportunity for a party to change itself – its infrastructure, processes, electoral machine, constitution. As much as a party's policies, its own organisational structures have to be reassessed, updated and adapted to changing circumstances. Although, on the surface, they can appear to be unexciting exercises in bureaucratic reform, they can nevertheless have far-reaching consequences with the capacity both to galvanise and to demoralise party members. Many Labour Party reforms have been advanced under the banner of 'democratisation', such as that of

1937, which gave local parties the right to elect directly their own representatives to the National Executive Committee (NEC). The watchword of 'democratisation' was also much heard during the ascendancy of the left in the 1980s, when it came to focus particularly on the method used to elect the party leader.

This was itself an indication of the increased importance of the role of the leader. In the earlier years, the leader of the parliamentary party had been an important source of authority, but one alongside others such as the NEC, the Shadow Cabinet, conference, the parliamentary party and the trade unions. But as time went on, the leadership succeeded in wresting more and more power from these various bodies. There was therefore increasingly more at stake in the election of the party leader. As a result of a process of 'democratisation', the electorate for the party leadership evolved from being the parliamentary party, through a series of electoral colleges to being the membership of the party as a whole. This last reform resulted in a more dramatic change in the political complexion of the leadership than had been seen for decades, perhaps ever, when Jeremy Corbyn was elected leader in 2015. This was a graphic illustration of the fact that internal party reform was by no means simply a matter of bureaucratic proceduralism.

The final criterion by which we assess the Labour Party's periods in opposition is simultaneously both outward- and inward-looking, namely, its relationship with the trade unions. This must be regarded as both an outward- and an inward-looking criterion because of the trade unions' uniquely ambivalent relationship with the Labour Party. On the one hand, the trade unions are an integral part not only of the Labour movement, but of the Labour Party itself. Indeed, the party was created as a result of the combining of the trade unions with the Independent Labour Party in Parliament, as well as with the various socialist organisations outside. But at the same time, the trade unions have never been subsumed by the Labour Party, and have been concerned to protect their own independent interests and existence. This semi-detached relationship has also well-suited the party itself. It has relied on the trade unions for support, personnel and finances. But it has always been careful to preserve its own independence and to avoid impressions that it is 'controlled' by the unions. Consequently, the party's handling of its relationship with the trade unions has been a delicate matter, and has occasionally been fraught with controversy. The relationship has been rendered more complicated still by the political complexion of the trade unions in relation to the wider party. In the earlier years, the unions were firmly allied to the 'right-wing' of the party and were seen as a constant stumbling block to the left. Their concern was with securing a better deal for their membership in the here and now under the current conditions of capitalism; they were impatient with the socialist idealism of those on the left of the party. But in later years, as the party aligned itself more with free-market values, both the unions and the party became increasingly alienated from each other, and the unions now found themselves considerably to the left of the party itself. Although, during these years, relations with the unions were weakened, they were never entirely repudiated. How to manage their relationship has been a tricky question for both party and unions to negotiate. The party's times in opposition have given the necessary pauses to reconsider the nature of the relationship.

The purpose of this book is to refocus attention away from the Labour Party's periods in government to its periods in opposition. The party's *raison d'être*, of course, is to be in government, and so any time spent in opposition is, by definition, a falling short. But in a democratic system, such opposition periods are inevitable. Further than this, we want to argue that such periods are not only inevitable but also indispensable. A party constantly in government would have no time to take stock, reassess its priorities and policies, revitalise its organisational structures and prepare itself anew for a period of government. We also want to claim that a party's time in opposition is not to be judged solely by the speed with which it gets re-elected into government. There are a range of criteria by which a Labour opposition is to be assessed – as have been enumerated above – which may well have far-reaching ramifications beyond the simple question of how quickly the party returns to power. As we shall see, some periods of opposition have been more significant than others. Some have determined the course not only of the next Labour government but of several more to come. In others, the opposition members seem to do little more than 'kick their heels and wait, and watch the others have a go'. But either way, Labour governments cannot be fully understood without a proper understanding of their corresponding time spent as Labour oppositions.

1

In Pursuit of an 'Insane Miracle' (1922–1929)

'Not even on the wildest night of Armistice Week' had a crowd in central London been so boisterous.[1] On 17 November 1922, Piccadilly Circus was teeming with so many people that all motor traffic was blocked. The throng was mesmerised. Looming over them was an electronic sign affixed to a building on Shaftesbury Avenue. Intermittently, the name of a parliamentary constituency would appear and reveal the winner of the seat in that week's general election. The crowd would erupt in cheers, regardless of the victor, in response to this entirely new phenomenon.[2] 'The excellence of the electrical device – its swiftness of working – rather left the crowd breathless', reported an exhilarated *Manchester Guardian* journalist.[3]

The following day, the dust had settled. With 308 MPs needed for a majority, the Conservatives had won a comfortable 344 seats. Conversely, the situation looked desperate for the Liberal Party, historically the Conservatives' main rivals for power. Split between supporters of two charismatic figures claiming party leadership – Herbert Henry Asquith and David Lloyd George – the Liberals suffered their worst result to that point. Taken together, just 115 Liberal MPs were elected.

For the first time, the Labour Party secured second place – both in votes and seats. Nearly 30 per cent of the electorate had supported Labour, 8 percentage points shy of the Conservatives, returning 142 Labour MPs, a net gain of eighty-five. 'The Labour Party is to claim the full privileges of his Majesty's Opposition', announced *The Evening Standard*. The newspaper reported that John Robert Clynes, a diminutive working-class Lancashire MP and chairman of the Parliamentary Labour Party (PLP), was to become the first Labour Leader of the Opposition.[4]

At the state opening of Parliament on 21 November, Clynes walked alongside the prime minister Bonar Law in Black Rod's procession to the House of Lords.[5] Yet, that evening, Clynes was deposed by his own

MPs. It is the only instance in the history of the Labour Party in which an incumbent has been defeated in a leadership challenge. Ramsay MacDonald was elected sixty-one to fifty-five, with twenty-five MPs not voting. MacDonald's narrow victory was delivered by the party's left-wing, in part in recognition of his opposition to the Great War. It was a manoeuvre that they would seriously come to regret in the years to follow.

With the Conservatives holding a comfortable majority, no one expected an election in just thirteen months' time. Even more so, no one expected that the next election would sweep Labour into power. Yet, on 22 January 1924, Ramsay MacDonald was invited by King George V to form a government and become the first Labour prime minister. MacDonald, who had helped to found the Labour Representation Committee in 1900, called the formation of the first Labour government just twenty-four years later 'an insane miracle'.[6]

The minority Labour government lasted just over nine months and left an unspectacular legislative record. Yet, its mere existence quashed doubts over whether the Labour Party was fit to rule the United Kingdom and answered whether Labour was prepared to operate within the framework of the British constitution. To the labour movement, however, the disappointing realities of government encouraged some to seek alternative means of achieving working-class goals, culminating in the General Strike of 1926.

The Labour Party had two central challenges in the 1920s. The first was to persuade socialists and the wider labour movement that it could achieve their aims through parliamentary democracy. The temptation of direct action manifested itself in political strikes, grassroots collaborations with Communists, and disruptive stunts by Labour MPs in the House of Commons. By the end of the decade much of the labour movement had set these impulses aside, however, having been chastened by the failure of the General Strike.

The second challenge was to persuade the country that Labour was fit to govern. It was in the 1920s that the Labour Party first demonstrated that it was the only clear alternative to Conservative governments. To do this, the party rejected notions of a progressive alliance with the Liberals and made majority government its overriding goal. Labour also made clear its commitment to the constitution, winning respect from unlikely corners, not least the king himself.[7]

Organisationally, the 1920s were a triumphant decade for the Labour Party. Key decisions were made about Labour's internal structures, its electoral machinery, its ties with the trade unions, and its relationship to the revolutionary left. These choices set the tone for the party's development for a century. The Labour Party today still lives with the legacy bequeathed by those years of opposition from 1922 to 1929. Herbert Morrison, first elected a Labour MP in 1923, reflected nearly forty years later that the 'twenties, had we known it, was [sic] a shaping time for the Labour Party of the future'.[8]

Where the Labour Party in the 1920s fell short was in its policy development, especially domestic policy. Too much time was spent on organisational questions at party conferences. Efforts to create a joint policy research department with the unions ended in failure. The Labour leadership, especially Ramsay MacDonald and the (Shadow) Chancellor Philip Snowden, were essentially locked in an orthodox understanding of economics which fell well short of the grand, romantic visions they espoused for a socialist society. In addition, union leadership was far from visionary. The unions were defensive of their own bargaining autonomy, blocking party members' proposals for a national minimum wage and women's demands for family allowances. As time wore on, the Labour left grew increasingly critical of this myopia, whereas MacDonald became more hostile to suggestions of moving leftward.

At the May 1929 general election, the hard work in building the party machine and Labour's careful allocation of resources paid off. On 37 per cent of the vote, Labour won 47 per cent of seats and formed a minority government once again. Yet, the party's failure to develop a rigorous policy programme resulted in yet another lacklustre legislative record. MacDonald's, by then, caustic relationship with Labour MPs and the wider labour movement presaged his departure from the Labour Party entirely in 1931, described by Clement Attlee as 'the biggest betrayal in British political history'.[9]

Strengthening the Party Machine: Implementing the Blueprint for Success

The blueprint of Labour's organisational success in the 1920s was its 1918 constitution, written by the socialist LSE academic Sidney Webb.

The document rationalised the bureaucratic operation of the Labour Party, creating a clear structure of policy-making, electioneering and governance, as well as articulating Labour's core ideological commitments. David Howell writes that 'the Labour Party's 1918 Constitution was the organizational expression of a party committed to an ambitious electoral strategy'.[10]

Until this point, there had been no concept of individual Labour Party membership. The party had been founded as a federation of socialist organisations and trade unions in 1900. Supporters 'joined' the party through the transitive property – by being a member of an affiliated socialist society, such as the Fabian Society or the Independent Labour Party (ILP), or through membership of an affiliated trade union. While the affiliation system brought individuals into the Labour Party who might otherwise not have joined, it was a barrier to those who simply wanted to support the party as such.

After 1918, individuals were entitled to join Divisional Labour Parties (DLPs), and women could also join the party through the Labour women's sections. These innovations encouraged the formation of local Labour parties. Before the First World War, just a quarter of constituencies had a local organisation, but by the mid-1920s practically every constituency did.[11] Divisional Labour Parties became vital for electioneering – at parliamentary and local levels – and for internal party democracy, such as the selection of conference delegates. They were a home not just for political debate and discussion but for a whole variety of social activities and even social services. In London, Labour-supporting lawyers established a legal advice bureau which assisted party members on rents, housing, pensions and poor relief. Social activities included Labour amateur dramatic clubs, choirs, orchestras, informal sports teams and cycling clubs.[12] Ramsay MacDonald, however, regarded the DLPs as too parochial and believed local committees chose 'men who are quite useless in the House of Commons' as parliamentary candidates.[13]

The 1918 constitution cemented the principle of the supremacy of the annual party conference. It declared: 'It shall be the duty of the Party Conference to decide ... what specific proposals of legislative, financial, or administrative reform shall receive the general support of the party.' Equally, it held that no policy proposal 'shall be made definitely part of the General Programme of the Party unless it has been adopted by the Conference'.

In between party conferences, Labour was to be run by a National Executive Committee, comprising representatives from the affiliated unions, socialist societies, the Parliamentary Labour Party, women's sections and DLPs. Underscoring its importance, the NEC attracted some of the party's top talent. Chief among these was Arthur Henderson, 'the architect of the party modernization'.[14] In the 1920s, the NEC established several standing sub-committees on areas that would be vital for the party's development: 1) organisation and elections, 2) policy and programme, 3) literature, research and publicity, and 4) finance and general purposes. It created the position of National Agent to oversee the party's election capabilities. In addition, the NEC created a 'star speakers' rota, ensuring that leading figures of the party toured the country, enthusing local Labour parties and raising the party's profile. The institutional structure set out by the 1918 constitution meant that by the time Labour secured its shock victory in the November 1923 election, the party had, in the words of organisational heavyweight Herbert Morrison, 'a nationwide political organization covering all but a tiny handful of the constituencies'.[15]

Local government was an important base for Labour's parliamentary success. Morrison wrote in 1918, 'until Labour has shown its capacity in the field of municipal statesmanship it is questionable whether the electorate will be anxious to send our candidates to Westminster'.[16] In addition to demonstrating Labour's capacity to govern, local government provided a training ground for some of the leading Labour figures of the generation of MPs first elected in the 1920s. Labour frontbenchers Clement Attlee, John Wheatley, Manny Shinwell, Herbert Morrison and Sidney Webb had all served in local government prior to their election to Parliament.

Morrison observed in 1921: 'A machine without high principles is a machine of no real value. And high principles without an efficient machine constitute but a voice crying in the wilderness. We have to make an efficient machine for a high moral purpose.'[17] It is, therefore, understandable why the 1918 constitution set out not just details about the technical organisation of the party machinery but also the ideological basis of the party in bold, visionary (if vague) terms. It committed the party explicitly to socialist objectives in its famous Clause IV:

> To secure for the producers by hand or by brain the full fruits of their industry and the most equitable distribution thereof that may be possible upon the basis of the common ownership of the means of production and the best obtainable system of popular administration and control of each industry or service.

As with all constitutions, the written word is only as meaningful as the actual practices and norms of politics around it. Labour's constitutional order was shaped by the party's electoral advances in the 1920s. For example, the 1918 constitution contained the principle of the sovereignty of the party conference, yet this ideal collided with the demands of electoral strategy, party management and leadership. To illustrate, in 1928 the Labour conference voted to establish a commission that would investigate the feasibility of a national minimum wage. Ramsay MacDonald simply shrugged his shoulders and indicated that he would ignore the commission's recommendations, whatever they found.

Another example was the invention of the party leader. Before 1922, it is not strictly accurate to say that the Labour Party had a leader at all. The 1918 constitution makes no mention of the position. Since 1906, Labour MPs had elected a chairman, but this position was effectively passed around by MPs and was mostly administrative. This helps to explain why Labour failed to take up the mantle of Official Opposition in 1918 even though after that election it became the largest opposition party to take its seats.[18] Alastair Reid and Henry Pelling write, 'MacDonald was a leader in a sense that none of his predecessors in the party chairmanship (including himself before the war) had been.'[19] For the first time, the position became known as 'chairman and leader' to indicate that the holder was also Leader of the Opposition and a potential prime minister.[20] A strong party leader, however, ran in tension with the constitution's organisational structure. MacDonald grumbled that he was being suffocated by party bureaucracy, writing in 1928: 'It is very easy to make the position of the leader of the Labour Party – with all its committees and sub-committees – perfectly impossible, and that is what is happening at present.'[21]

One of the biggest organisational challenges for Labour in the 1920s was deciding its relationship with the far left. Some local Labour parties, especially in London and South Wales, had expressed sympathies with the Communist experiment in Russia. Upon its founding in 1920, the British Communist Party sought affiliation to the Labour Party. The initial request was rejected by the NEC, but in 1921 an NEC sub-committee was formed to consider the matter in more detail. They concluded that affiliation was out of the question on constitutional grounds. Arthur Henderson, who served on the committee, explained: 'Parliamentary democracy is the method by which we hope to secure our object ... You repudiate the view that the social revolution can come through Parliamentary democracy and I say again that by the repudiation of that view there is a difference which is fundamental.'[22] At the 1922 Labour conference, the question of Communist Party affiliation was considered and rejected. The General Secretary of the Miners' Federation, Frank Hodges, called British Communists 'the intellectual slaves of Moscow ... taking the judgement of middle-class Russia – the residue of the old regime – not even the judgement of the plain Russian people, but the dictates and decrees of the same type of intellectual whom they despised in this country'.[23]

Although the Communist Party could not affiliate, individuals were still allowed to be members of both parties. One, Shapurji Saklatvala, even stood as a joint Communist and Labour candidate in Battersea North. Winning the seat in 1922, he became the first Labour MP of Asian heritage.[24] In 1925, the Labour conference banned dual Labour and Communist individual membership, but Communists could still attend Labour conference as union delegates. It wasn't until 1928 that Labour conference finally closed this loophole, bringing an end to the participation of Communists within the Labour Party at any level.

Not all local Labour parties were enthused by this decision. Bethnal Green Labour Party had surreptitiously stood on a joint slate with the Communists in the 1925 local elections, leading to their suspension. The local council defiantly named a new housing estate 'the Lenin Estate' in 'recognition of the great work he had done on behalf of the workers of the world'.[25] In the summer of 1927 alone, the NEC suspended twenty-three local Labour parties, including fifteen in London, for Communist infiltration.[26]

Outside of the formal apparatus of the party, the 1920s saw the blossoming of a left-wing media environment which tried to provide alternative perspectives to the right-leaning broadsheets. The main voice of the Labour movement was the *Daily Herald*, restored as a daily in 1919. From 1922, it fell under the financial control of the Labour Party and Trades Union Congress (TUC), which held a 49 per cent stake. Its editorship transferred from the rebellious George Lansbury to the more pliant Hamilton Fyfe. The Transport and General Workers' Union (TGWU) leader Ernest Bevin even called the *Herald* 'my newspaper'.[27] Bevin believed strongly that Labour needed a daily newspaper that could compete with the *Mail* and the *Express*, and in this decade its reach increased enormously. By 1929, its circulation was 300,000, climbing to 1 million by 1933. The *Herald* was the first daily newspaper in the world to reach a circulation of 2 million.[28]

There were also weekly publications, usually aimed at more intellectual audiences. These included the *New Statesman* and the ILP's *New Leader*. The circulation of the latter peaked at 70,000 in the mid-1920s. The *New Leader* attracted high-quality articles from H.G. Wells to E.M. Forster to George Bernard Shaw, as well as attractive drawings and wood cuts. Unlike the *Herald*, the *New Leader* regarded itself as the purveyor of Labour's socialist conscience and regularly attacked the leadership for philosophical deviations. Eight months into his first ministry, the Labour prime minister bristled: 'As to the *New Leader* frankly I have lost all interest in it. It is not the kind of paper that does any good to anybody. It has neither weight nor place and its egotistical aloofness would kill any movement.'[29]

Assessing the Record of the Previous Labour Government (1924): A Study in Disappointment

On 18 January 1924, four days before King George V invited Ramsay MacDonald to form the first Labour government, Winston Churchill wrote to *The Times* to warn the country of impending catastrophe. In apocalyptic terms, he raged, 'The enthronement in office of a Socialist Government will be a serious national misfortune such as has usually befallen great states only on the morrow of defeat in war.'[30] Unlike the apoplectic Churchill, Conservative MP Neville Chamberlain speculated that Labour would be 'too weak to do much harm, but not too weak to get discredited'.[31]

The first Labour government lasted from January until November 1924. Labour came to power when the Conservatives, who had lost their majority in the November 1923 election, lost a vote of confidence in January 1924. Rather than call another election, the king decided to ask his Loyal Opposition to form a government. Even though it held just under a third of the seats in Parliament, Labour had ruled out any idea of a coalition with the Liberals and chose to govern as a minority instead.

In hindsight, Labour's decision to govern alone was probably the right one. It helped to establish Labour as the alternative to a Conservative government and blocked the Liberals' access to power. Labour's problem was that it entered government with few ideas of what it wanted to do. So accustomed had Labour been to opposing the other two parties, that it lacked a coherent domestic policy agenda. Attlee explained that this was partly because Labour had not expected an election in 1923, let alone to be the victor. So, the party programme, except in foreign affairs, had not had time to develop as it might have in a four- or five-year Parliament.[32] There is some plausibility in this argument.

The new prime minister Ramsay MacDonald showed his interest to be in foreign affairs, deciding to appoint himself as his own Foreign Secretary. In this role, MacDonald made a couple of significant achievements, chief among these was getting the French to agree to the Americans' Dawes Plan, which resolved the question of outstanding German war reparations. The Labour government also formally recognised the Soviet Union for the first time, in spite of King George V warning MacDonald at their first meeting that he 'hoped I would do nothing to compel him to shake hands with the murderers of his relatives'.[33]

For many in the labour movement, the 1924 government was a bitter disappointment. Labour MP Oswald Mosley wrote acerbically to MacDonald: 'No abiding mark, except possibly in the foreign sphere, will have been left by the first Labour Government with power. In this eventuality, the cause of Labour might be retarded for a generation.'[34] In the view of some in the trade union movement, the Labour government had been actively hostile to their interests. The first week of the Labour government saw a nine-day strike by train drivers in the ASLEF union. The 'big 4' railway companies had tried to force through reduced pay and longer hours. Much to the irritation of the striking train drivers, the Labour government declined to intervene on their behalf. ASLEF's leader John Bromley was furious. 'If the success of the Labour Party and of a Labour Government can only be built on such serious losses in wages and conditions, I am not sure that the workers will very much welcome a Labour government', he warned.[35]

Sharing frustrations over government inaction, the Labour left blamed the Labour government for lacking a clear political vision of how to bring about socialism. After Labour's defeat in the October 1924 election, left-wing Labour MPs tried to remove MacDonald from the leadership. James Maxton of Glasgow and Richard Wallhead of Merthyr proposed George Lansbury as a challenger, but Lansbury declined their nomination.[36] MacDonald was saved, but he interpreted the challenge as treachery. He fumed in his diary: 'The Left Wing were out for my blood, and had not the sense to restrain itself.'[37]

However, it was the left of the party that had delivered Labour's one major domestic policy achievement in government. The Housing Act 1924, known more widely as the Wheatley Housing Act after the minister responsible, substantially increased central government subsidies to local councils to build social housing. It led to the construction of half a million new council homes and was the first housing bill to require that the new homes were equipped with an indoor bathroom.[38] John Wheatley was that Cabinet's 'only one out-and-out left-winger',[39] as a scion of 'Red Clydeside' and the Independent Labour Party (ILP).

Upon re-entering opposition, the ILP became the bastion of left-wing critique of the 1924 Labour government. The ILP had been founded by Keir Hardie in 1893 with the aim of electing socialists to Parliament. With little money and no trade union support, the ILP could not survive on its own. Consequently, it teamed up with other socialist groups and trade unions to form the Labour Representation Committee in 1900, considered to be the founding moment of the Labour Party. After 1900, the ILP maintained its distinct identity as an affiliated socialist society within the Labour Party and was generally seen as the high-minded socialist counterbalance to the hardnosed political caution of the trade unions.

The ILP burnished itself as the keeper of the flame of true socialism throughout the 1920s. It was a 'cave of Adullam for socialists', a hideout for those awaiting the New Jerusalem.[40] MacDonald became increasingly irritated by their harping criticism. Things came to a head at the

1925 ILP conference, the first after the fall of the Labour government. MacDonald, rather condescendingly, told delegates that governing the country was 'quite different from getting resolutions passed at ILP conference'. In response, Campbell Stephen, a Glaswegian MP and ILP stalwart, charged that there was no evidence 'sufficient to differentiate [MacDonald's Government] from Mr Baldwin's Government today'. An ILP delegate recorded MacDonald's reaction:

> The knuckles of his hands gripping the edge of the table were white with the unconscious pressure he was exerting as he listened to the insulting words. His face was red and his eyes alight with the fury that he was with difficulty repressing ... [MacDonald] spat into my face with a hoarse whisper, 'That damned little swine – Campbell Stephen.'[41]

It was the last ILP conference MacDonald would ever attend. In 1926, he swore, 'I can speak at no Conference promoted to popularise absolutely meaningless phrases and to mislead the whole of our Socialist movement.'[42] In 1927, the ILP retaliated by refusing, for the first time, to nominate MacDonald to be Treasurer of the Labour Party, a position he had held since 1912. In 1930, he resigned his membership entirely.

Forming a Clear Policy Agenda: Workers' Wages, Birth Control, and the King

The 1920s were not a decade of significant policy development in the Labour Party. Much of the business that occupied the NEC and party conference was administrative in nature, such as questions about the party's relationship to Communists. Many of Labour's leading figures from both the left and right lacked a clear sense of how socialism ought to be brought about. Trade unionists maintained a sectional focus on improving workers' wages and conditions, with little interest in wider questions of economic and social organisation. Many of Labour's supposed 'intellectuals' also had relatively undeveloped ideas about socialist economics.

For many of them, like George Lansbury, socialism was oppositional. It manifested itself in reaction against a capitalist enemy. In the London Borough of Poplar, Lansbury had helped lead a revolt in 1921 by local councillors against local government legislation which required the council to tax their poor residents at much higher rates to bring in the same amount of revenue as richer boroughs. Thirty of Poplar's councillors, including Lansbury, were sent to prison for setting an illegal budget. The 'Poplar Rates Rebellion' won mass acclaim amongst London's poor, with thousands turning out on the streets to support their councillors. But, for critics, 'Poplarism' was essentially gesture politics that presented socialism only in a series of glorious defeats. Lansbury's biographer John Shepherd writes that 'MacDonald disliked and even loathed "the John Bull of Poplar" [Lansbury].'[43]

For MacDonald and his finance chief Philip Snowden, socialism was essentially an ethical phenomenon. While they believed capitalism was evil and a socialist society was a vital imperative, they tended to view socialism as one might a religious faith: as a question of men's and women's hearts. Therefore, socialism would come about through conversion rather than through central planning. Labour's most important figures of the 1920s had surprisingly little to say on the practical shape of a socialist economic agenda, retreating to the liberal orthodoxies of the day, with mild policy prescriptions such as cutting consumption taxes or lowering tariffs as ways of alleviating the condition of the poor.

Recognising its deficient policy detail, the Labour NEC believed that the party needed effective, dispassionate and detailed research support. Labour was fortunate to have been founded partly by a socialist think tank *avant la lettre*, the Fabian Society, which produced numerous tracts on policy ideas, based on empirical research. Popular topics in the 1920s included a capital levy, local government organisation, housing, education and the League of Nations.[44] As part of Labour's organisational reforms in 1918, the Fabian Society Research Department was reconstructed as the Labour Research Department. Two years later, under Arthur Henderson's guidance, it was merged with the TUC's equivalent body to create the Joint Research Department. Its secretary, Arthur Greenwood, was described as 'one of the rising Labour stars of the twenties', but by 1925 the enterprise had collapsed.[45]

One of the relatively few concrete economic policy ideas debated by the Labour Party in the 1920s was the proposal for a national minimum wage, advocated chiefly by the ILP. However, MacDonald asserted that a minimum wage was such an unrealistic policy idea that it would ruin

Labour's credibility in the eyes of the electorate. 'Socialism is not going to come by the legal declaration of a minimum nominal wage', he warned. 'Such a method is to swamp us in untold industrial difficulties and to foredoom our great first Socialist offensive to disastrous defeat. It will be our Verdun.'[46]

Trade union leaders opposed the minimum wage on the grounds that it undermined their bargaining position and autonomy. Additionally, Ernest Bevin claimed that the supporters of a minimum wage, many of whom were from the professional classes, failed to understand 'the psychology of the workers' who liked the idea that they had secured their wage through their own efforts rather than government regulation.[47] A union delegate, who also happened to be a Communist Party member, told the 1927 Labour conference that the proposal for a minimum wage was 'utopian nonsense'. According to the delegate, the capitalist system needed to be brought down first before there could be talk of anything as fanciful as minimum wages.[48]

Another key challenge for Labour in the 1920s was how to respond to the new electorate of female voters. As a question of policy, Labour disappointed on two key issues at the forefront of the women's movement: birth control and family allowances. The male-dominated trade unions objected to family allowances because they threatened collective bargaining agreements. Unions believed that their ability to argue for a 'family wage' would be severely curtailed if mothers received state benefits, holding down wages for all.[49] Feminists like Eleanor Rathbone argued that family allowances strengthened the labour movement because they made the cost of going on strike less severe, but these arguments were to no effect.[50]

Different dynamics were at play in the birth control debate. In 1924, Labour women's conference supported a motion calling for public funds to disseminate information about birth control. This caused some worry among the male party leadership, who were mindful of the party's support among working-class Catholics.[51] At the same time, party operatives recognised the need not to alienate the new women voters. The NEC devised a 'compromise' in which the party would be neither for nor against birth control but leave it to individual MPs to decide, a classic policy fudge that is possible in opposition but much harder to maintain in government. By a majority of 771,000, delegates at the 1925 Labour conference endorsed the NEC's statement that 'the subject of birth control is in its nature not one which should be made a party political issue, but should remain another upon which members of the party should be free to hold and promote their individual convictions'.[52] These two controversies give weight to Keith Laybourn's conclusion: 'There was little evidence throughout the 1920s that the Labour Party had taken women's issues on board.'[53] Martin Pugh goes further in concluding that at this time 'women were largely treated as hewers of wood and drawers of water for the party'.[54]

One of the questions that Labour could not avoid answering concerned its stance on constitutional matters, especially the monarchy. Labour's rejection of republicanism is perhaps the one significant policy legacy of the 1920s. The public mood was 'intensely monarchical', and Labour MPs were no exception.[55] Ramsay MacDonald had argued in his book on socialism that the removal of the monarch had little relevance to the establishment of a socialist order. He wrote: 'Kings can be removed and a republic established by revolutions, but in establishing Socialism we change organic relationships, not superficial forms of government.'[56]

Some Labour MPs were, in the view of one contemporary observer, 'more royalist than the King'.[57] The railway union leader and Labour MP Jimmy Thomas was said to be the sort of man 'to appear at a dinner in trousers and a coat made out of a Union Jack and shout for Empire'.[58] Thomas wrote fulsomely about his 'cherished memories of the Royal House' in his autobiography.[59] Even left-wing Labour MPs found themselves caught under the royalist spell. When the 'bowler-hatted revolutionary' John Wheatley went to see the king upon becoming Minister of Health, he spontaneously fell to both knees, grabbed the king's hand and kissed it.[60] George V recorded in his diary: 'He is an extreme Socialist & comes from Glasgow. I had a very interesting conversation with him.'[61]

At the 1923 Labour conference, the North Kensington Labour Party submitted a motion 'that the hereditary principle in the British Constitution be abolished'. The motion attracted the attention of the international press, with the *Chicago Tribune* excitedly reporting on 'the touchy question of labor [sic] and the throne'.[62] MacDonald was keen to defeat the motion, and in order to do so he enlisted the unlikely assistance of George Lansbury. The fiery left-winger acknowledged why instinctively a socialist might feel uncomfortable with a hereditary head of state. Lansbury's socialism came from his Christian belief in the basic equality of all God's creation. He told the delegates that he had met the Royal Family, and 'they are just ordinary common clay like anybody else'.[63] Yet, Lansbury begged his comrades to reject the motion. He reminded them that it was capitalism, not the king, that fuelled poverty and inequality in Britain. Labour should not 'fool about with a question of no vital importance'.[64] The motion was defeated overwhelmingly.

The Labour Party's rejection of republicanism in the 1920s was vital for its establishment as a legitimate party of government within the British constitutional system. While viewed by some as a 'selling out' of Labour's radicalism, many in the party came to realise that monarchy was no inhibitor of a radical socialist programme. The Fabian socialists Beatrice and Sidney Webb argued that in their vision of a socialist Britain, the 'national organisation herein proposed does not involve the abolition of the ancient institution of an hereditary monarch'. The Webbs saw value in a symbolic, non-partisan head of state and that Britain's monarchy 'may certainly be accepted in the Socialist commonwealth'.[65] This positioning served Labour well when the Conservative minority government of Stanley Baldwin collapsed in January 1924. The king made the historic decision to send for Labour to form a government, knowing he had little to fear on this question.[66]

Holding the Conservative Government to Account: Bark but No Bite

After the 1922 election, the new MP for Stepney, Clement Attlee, wrote excitedly to his brother Rob about the new Parliamentary Labour Party: 'We are very pleased with the results, which have given us a fine fighting force. We shall have the best intellects of the party in the House now.'[67] The party's leader was less impressed. MacDonald's diaries are full of scathing assessments of his parliamentary comrades: 'the vain and empty-headed Neil MacLean', 'the asinine Geordie Buchanan', 'the raucous-voiced George Lansbury'.[68] Attlee, in turn, criticised MacDonald's lack of magnanimity: 'He had no idea of treating his colleagues properly. He used to recall to me the contempt that he had for his colleagues. I thought it was quite wrong.'[69] Herbert Morrison agreed that MacDonald possessed a 'remote and defensive attitude to those around him which in the end left him with virtually no friends'.[70] Even Philip Snowden, who remained an ally to the end, warned him, 'You seem to be protected by some impenetrable barrier. I called it aloofness.'[71]

In truth, the PLP was a mixed bag. It contained a collection of 'drunks and ascetics, workaholics and idlers, careerists and diligent advocates of constituency interests'.[72] Serious divisions emerged over the methods by which Labour should hold the Conservative governments of Bonar Law (1922–23) and Stanley Baldwin (1923–24, 1924–29) to account. For most Labour MPs, their new status as Official Opposition required them to behave constructively. Labour would try to place pressure on the government but in order to win concessions, minimising the scale of the damage from Conservative legislation. Preston MP Tom Shaw summarised, 'the duty of us as an Opposition was to get as much as possible for our people'.[73]

Other Labour MPs, however, held out little hope that the Conservatives could be reasoned with. For them, Parliament was an unparalleled public platform to put the ideological case for socialism to the wider world – or at least for it to be recorded in the annals of *Hansard*. These 'obstreperous' MPs made long, impassioned speeches in the House of Commons that denounced the evils of a capitalist system and spoke boldly of the New Jerusalem to come.[74] Given that the force of sheer argument seemed unlikely to move Conservative and Liberal MPs closer to socialism, the more restrained members of the PLP grew irritated with their loquacious comrades. Shaw criticised them for 'talking night and day about things that do not matter'.[75] Labour MP for Penistone, Rennie Smith, complained, 'I have little sympathy with this sort of fighting. 3 or 4 speeches are enough to do all that requires ... There is something pathetic if not mad in so many men behaving like parrots and even wasting nights as well as days in the process.'[76]

For the Leader of the Opposition, these antics were deeply embarrassing. In his diary, MacDonald seethed: 'Some members do no work but much talking and wish to turn the floor of House into a sort of national street corner soap box.'[77] Harris writes that MacDonald 'winced, fumed, and inwardly disavowed' his left-wing colleagues as they 'ranted revolution and roared out personal insults across the floor of the House'.[78] During a debate over cuts to milk provision for Scottish children, the left-wing Glaswegian MP James Maxton called a Conservative MP a 'murderer'. Maxton was suspended from the House, followed by three more Labour MPs who repeated the charge.[79]

In previous decades, Irish Nationalist MPs had hampered the day-to-day business of the House of Commons to force the Irish Question to the fore. Some Labour MPs believed that they could follow a similar path by disrupting the proceedings of the House and attempting to prevent MPs voting on legislation which they despised. George Lansbury vowed in November 1925, 'I intend on every possible occasion to obstruct, hold up, and in every way hinder the progress of business.'[80] In April 1926, on the eve of the General Strike, thirteen Labour MPs, including Lansbury, blocked the voting lobbies, preventing the tellers from reading the Aye results for the Economy (Miscellaneous Provisions) Act. The Serjeant at Arms was forced to remove them, and they were suspended from the sitting by the Speaker.[81]

In June, similar tactics were tried in relation to the Miners' Eight Hour Bill. On this occasion, the Labour MPs were publicly disowned by MacDonald. Sidney Webb wrote to his wife Beatrice, 'MacDonald is very much annoyed and vexed at the turbulence of the backbenchers.'[82] He was joined by other MPs, like Arthur Ponsonby, who worried that these antics risked scuppering the respect given to Labour by the Speaker in its new role as Official Opposition. Ponsonby wrote: 'We are gradually alienating the sympathy of the Speaker who hitherto has given every possible consideration to all of us.'[83]

Over time, however, Labour MPs became domesticated. In reference to Maxton and the other left-wing MPs from Glasgow, Herbert Morrison reflected that the 'so-called "Wild Men of the Clyde" came in time to be strong advocates of correct procedure and thereby gained the respect and love in the House which can soar far above party differences'.[84] H.N. Brailsford, the prominent socialist journalist, warned his fellow left-wing colleagues in 1923 that a politics of direct action could lead down the slippery slope to fascism:

> Now, it may be true that a scene, followed by agitation, wins support among masses whom we reach slowly, if at all, in other ways. But there are the gravest dangers to this course; such scenes would soon pall if they became frequent.

To keep up the stimulus, you must increase the dose. From scenes you must soon move onto violence, and transfer your activities to the streets. To that, one answer would be the parallel growth of a fascist movement, and the ruin of any hope of fundamental change by democratic means.[85]

In the House of Lords, things were more sedate. In a chamber dominated by Conservatives and Liberals, MacDonald was compelled to create several new peerages, as well as to recruit from the few existing hereditary peers who were amenable to socialism. They formed a doddery assortment. Arthur Ponsonby's diary gives a rather succinct description: 'Arnold [a former Liberal MP] excellent and indispensable. [Lord Sankey] so far silent. [The 9th Earl] De La Warr useful and charming. Sidney Webb very clear but not always on the right line. [The 2nd Earl] Russell very able but quite undependable. Thomson, not really Labour, pleasant but unreliable.'[86]

Managing Relationships with the Trade Unions: The General Strike and Its Aftermath

In spite of Labour's growth in parliamentary stature throughout the decade, David Howell writes, 'the sense of the Labour Party as a wing of the labour movement remained central to its organizational culture'.[87] During this period, the unions and the PLP overlapped heavily. Many Labour MPs were sponsored by unions, meaning that they owed their selection (and continued position) as Labour candidates to unions' patronage. In the 1924 election, forty out of Labour's 151 MPs (26.5 per cent) were sponsored by just one union: the Miners' Federation of Great Britain.

Trade union MPs tended to be more right-leaning than those who had come through the ILP or the Divisional Labour Parties. There was a running suspicion from the middle-class left of the party that some union-sponsored MPs might not even believe in socialism. In a Commons debate, the Liberal MP Sir Alfred Mond claimed that some Labour MPs 'are no more believers in Socialism than I am, and I invite them to think twice or three times before they commit themselves to a policy which is as fatal to the best interests of the class which they represent'.[88]

With more than a hint of class snobbery, it was presumed that many trade unionists were incapable of grasping the full nuances of parliamentary tactics or political strategy. They were sometimes viewed as lazy, particularly due to the impression that a seat in the House of Commons became 'a convenient place of retirement for redundant officials'.[89] Beatrice Webb complained in her diaries of the 'dull-headed miners' and called one union-sponsored MP 'a notorious old slacker'.[90]

The bitterness went both ways. Ernest Bevin told the Oxford don G.D.H. Cole, 'The difference between the intellectuals and the trade unions is this: You have no responsibility[. Y]ou can fly off at a tangent as the wind takes you.'[91] Bevin lumped MacDonald, a former teacher, in this category, describing him as a 'man who has never had industrial responsibility in his life' and who was attempting 'in a most subtle manner to destroy the power of the unions; presumably he thinks this will help him politically; but he is wrong'.[92]

Throughout the decade, monthly meetings were held between the NEC, PLP and the TUC's General Council, known collectively as the Joint Council of Labour. Yet, in spite of these close organisational links, major ruptures still occurred. In 1924, when Labour was in office, London dockers and tram workers in the TGWU went on strike. As Bevin later recalled, MacDonald 'rushed down to Windsor' to approve emergency powers to break the strike. The strike was then called off. Bevin never forgave MacDonald for this betrayal. At the 1925 Labour conference, Bevin moved a motion that would ban a future Labour government from forming unless it had an outright majority of seats in the House of Commons. The motion failed, but it indicated an exasperation in the unions about the benefits of a parliamentary strategy for their members.

The culmination of this dissatisfaction emerged in the General Strike of 1926. To provide some background: in April 1925 the Conservative Chancellor Winston Churchill returned Britain to the gold standard; as John Maynard Keynes predicted in *The Economic Consequences of Mr Churchill*, the move would prove to be economically disastrous, seriously overvaluing the pound and leading to a British exports crisis. At the same time, thanks to the Dawes Plan which MacDonald had helped negotiate the previous year, France had withdrawn its troops from the Ruhr, enabling Germany to boost its domestic coal production. The consequence was the plummeting of the value of British coal. The owners of the mines reacted to this squeeze on their profits by seeking to reduce workers' pay and increase their hours to maintain productivity. Initially, the British government stepped in, agreeing in July 1925 to subsidise miners' wages, but the agreement expired at the end of April 1926.

The unions threatened a general strike if the miners' salaries were not maintained. This was probably a bluff designed to get Stanley Baldwin to pressure the mine owners, but the prime minister called the bluff. The socialist journalist Raymond Postgate described the TUC's shock: 'It is like asking for an elephant or a dragon, not expecting to receive it, and lo, here it is walking up the garden path.'[93] The scale of adherence to the General Strike amazed both government and unions alike. Not one of the 3,300 London General Omnibus's vehicles operated. Just forty out of 14,000 London dockers showed up for work. There was just one train operating between London and the North each day.[94] In all, 2 million workers went on strike and a further million were locked out by their employers. However, the TUC could see no resolution. They blinked first, offering the Conservatives almost complete, unconditional surrender, failing even to secure assurances that trade unionists would not be sacked for having taking action. Bevin rued, 'the best way to describe today … is that we have committed suicide'.[95] Over the next eighteen months, the unions lost 500,000 members. The following year, in retribution for the General Strike, the Baldwin government passed the Trade Disputes and Trade Union Act 1927, which changed the way members paid towards their union levy, resulting in unions losing a third of their income. It was not repealed until the Attlee government nearly twenty years later.

The General Strike was a mixed blessing for the Labour Party. Many Labour MPs felt cross-pressured because they sympathised with the miners' plight but were worried about the constitutional implications of a strike that was perceived as aiming to bring down an elected government.[96] Bevin was furious at MacDonald's failure to rally to the strikers' cause. In the aftermath of the General Strike, he initially refused to be seen in public with MacDonald, telling Arthur Henderson, 'I am not prepared to go on a platform in support of the leader whom I regard as having been wantonly guilty of stabbing us in the back at the moment when we had the whole forces of capital unleashed against us.'[97]

On the other hand, the unions were chastised by their failure, causing them to return to the Labour Party as their main vehicle for positive change. After the disappointment of the 1924 Labour government, there had been a growing sense of disenchantment in the labour movement. Some trade unionists questioned whether Labour governments would materially improve the lot of the working class, emboldening some to think strikes could do a better job. The miserable experience of the General Strike brought many trade unionists back into the parliamentary fold. At the 1928 TUC conference in Swansea, Bevin asked: 'Is the strike the only way to fight? Cannot we fight by discussion as well as by starvation? Cannot we fight by intelligence?'[98]

Building the Party's Relationship with the Electorate: Women and Workers First

The 1920s were electorally speaking a fruitful decade for Labour, especially when one considers its fortunes in the previous two decades. Labour unequivocally cemented its position as the second-largest party in Britain, relegating the Liberals to a permanent third-party status. Part of this was thanks to important structural changes in the eligible electorate. The 1920s are the first decade in which Britain can be meaningfully described as a full democracy, and Labour was the main beneficiary of this transformation of British politics.

The Representation of the People Act 1918 had given all men the right to vote for the first time. The legislation nearly doubled the male electorate, enfranchising over 5 million working-class men who had previously been excluded due to property requirements. In the 1920s, about 80 per cent of the British electorate was working class, an enticing prospect for a party established to represent working-class interests.[99] Yet, Labour never won more than 37 per cent of the vote in this decade, implying a substantial working-class vote for other parties, or disengagement. Historian Martin Pugh emphasises the obdurate conservativism of a sizeable proportion of the working class, especially outside of industries with an organised labour force, which immured them from socialist appeals.[100]

The 1918 Act also granted suffrage to property-holding women over the age of thirty, with equal suffrage to arrive finally through further legislation in 1928. All parties were suddenly faced with the imperative to address women's issues. Organisationally, Labour responded well. Its 1918 constitution encouraged women's membership through women's sections, women's representation on the National Executive Committee, and a stand-alone annual women's conference. In 1922, over 100,000 women were members of the party's 600 women's sections.[101] By 1927, there were 300,000 women members and 1,728 of these sections.[102] On the other hand, as has been shown, Labour did a poor job of including women's policy demands into its policy programme.

Nevertheless, there is some evidence that young women were drawn to Labour over the Conservatives. The Representation of the People Act 1928 fully abolished the previous property and age barriers that stopped working-class women and women under thirty from voting. The legislation expanded the electorate by about 5 million, leading to an increase in the total votes for all parties at the 1929 election. With women comprising a majority of the electorate for the first time, Labour benefited from this growth far more than the Conservatives. Labour's number of votes between 1924 and 1929 increased by over a third, whereas the Conservatives grew by just 10 per cent of their previous figure (see Figure 1.1).

There were four general elections in the 1920s, and at each, Labour won more votes than the previous. When examined in retrospect, Labour's electoral advances were not inevitable but attributable to its efficient organisation. The party maximised its electoral resources by taking advantage of the first-past-the-post electoral system to boost the number of Labour seats in as efficient a manner as possible. This meant that at the start of the decade, Labour tended to concentrate its efforts on a smaller number of constituencies where they had existing capacity and natural support, such as mining areas or amongst unionised urban labourers.

In 1922, Labour won just 23 per cent of the seats in Parliament overall, but had a better than one in three success rate in the seats where it actually stood candidates (see Table 1.1). In that election, Labour won eighty-five of its seats with over 50 per cent of the vote, and Labour MPs were elected unopposed in a further four. Labour's number of votes increased at each election in the 1920s, but this is partly flattered by the fact that the party stood more candidates at each successive election.

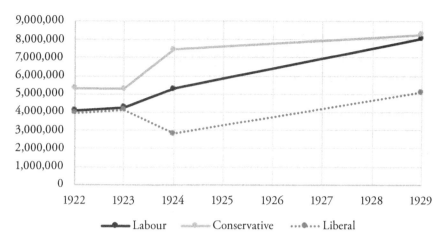

Figure 1.1 Number of votes cast for Labour, Conservatives and Liberals, 1922–1929
Note: The 1922 Liberal vote is calculated by combining the votes for Liberals and National Liberals.
Source: Mortimore and Blick, 2018

Table 1.1 Growth of Labour candidates in the 1920s

	Constituencies with a Labour candidate	Share of these seats won by Labour	Share of all seats won by Labour
1922	67.3%	34.3%	23.1%
1923	69.4%	44.7%	31.1%
1924	83.6%	29.4%	24.6%
1929	92.5%	50.4%	46.7%

Source: Mortimore and Blick, 2018

The most significant increase was between the 1923 and 1924 elections, when the number of Labour candidates jumped from 427 to 514. This helps to explain why Labour's vote increased in spite of its unspectacular record in government and an eve-of-poll controversy surrounding a (faked) letter purportedly from the head of the Communist International claiming a Labour government would hasten a Bolshevik revolution.[103]

A vital organisational decision made by the Labour Party in the 1920s was not to cooperate with the Liberals. In the very early years of Labour's existence, the party had conducted deals with the Liberals to help secure power. These sometimes took the form of agreements to stand one candidate from each party in a two-member constituency. The Representation of the People Act 1918 substantially diminished the number of multi-member constituencies, and its successor act in 1948 abolished them entirely.

After the 1918 election, the Liberal leader David Lloyd George had formed a coalition with the Conservatives, which lasted until just before the 1922 election. This peacetime Liberal–Conservative cooperation was anathema to many in the Labour Party and sullied the Liberal Party's image in the eyes of the left. Having begun life as a Liberal, George Lansbury found himself totally disgusted with the Liberal Party of the 1920s. He wrote in 1923 that 'We of the British Labour Movement will, as ever, keep ourselves clear of that unholy thing which now masquerades as Liberalism.'[104] Lansbury went so far as to say he would rather die without ever seeing a Labour government than 'see any arrangement, open or secret, with the [Liberal] party'.[105]

Labour also rejected Liberal overtures for proportional representation. Herbert Morrison made his second-ever speech in Parliament opposing a Liberal motion to change the electoral system. He wryly noted that it was only once the Liberals began to lose elections that they had become full converts to an alternative system.[106] The 1926 Labour conference voted down a motion to support proportional representation. Egerton Wake, the National Agent of the Labour Party responsible for organising Labour's campaigns, asserted that 'Proportional representation was an attempt to load the dice against Labour.'[107]

For most in the Labour movement, there was little sadness over the demise of the Liberals. They were not a group of fellow-travellers. Socialism and Liberalism were two totally different ideologies. As Clement Attlee explained in 1923: '[A liberal's] conception of society and its ends is different from ours. Our gods are not his gods.' For liberals, the nineteenth century was a century of progress, but for socialists it was a disaster. The Industrial Revolution was the 'first act of the tragedy' which transformed 'an order of society in which each person has a definite status in the community to a system where the vast mass of the population are proletarians, wage-slaves with no right or position in industry'.[108] It is striking that Labour's ambition from this early stage was to win a majority in Parliament. Indeed, as early as 1919, when Labour occupied just 8 per cent of the seats in Parliament, Ramsay MacDonald wrote in the *Socialist Review* that Labour had 'its eye upon a Parliamentary majority won by retaining the confidence of all sorts and conditions of opinion'.[109]

The elections of the 1920s transformed the social composition of Labour's parliamentary representation. In the first two decades of the twentieth century, the Parliamentary Labour Party had been overwhelmingly composed of working-class MPs sponsored by the different affiliated trade unions. The PLP of the 1918–22 Parliament was particularly dominated by these union-sponsored MPs because they had been loyal to the war effort in the First World War, whereas many of the party's intellectuals had opposed the war and were punished by the electorate at the fiercely patriotic 1918 election.

By 1922, most of the anti-war MPs had been forgiven and returned, and their numbers were augmented by the arrival of a cadre of university-educated, middle-class MPs, including Clement Attlee, Labour's first Oxford graduate.[110] A growing number of Labour MPs were, like Attlee, privately educated. Some were even aristocrats. Labour MP Sir Oswald Mosley (a baronet, educated at Winchester) was said to 'stink of money and insincerity' by Hugh Dalton, who himself was the son of George V's tutor and educated at Eton and King's College, Cambridge.[111] Mosley's wife, Lady Cynthia, became a Labour MP, puzzling the German journalist Egon Wertheimer when she was proudly introduced at a socialist rally as 'Lord Curzon's daughter' (the Viceroy of India) and addressed her fellow comrades 'in heavy costly furs'.[112] The Sheffield MP Arthur Ponsonby was born in Windsor Castle to Queen Victoria's private secretary, and attended Eton and Balliol College, Oxford. The Newcastle MP Sir Charles Trevelyan was a baronet like Oswald Mosley. He and Lady Cynthia spent the 1927 Labour conference at Blackpool Pleasure Beach, where 'we went down breathless water shoots and frightful toboggans. It was great fun.'[113]

These colourful characters illustrate that for a century the PLP has contained its fair share of middle-class MPs who came to the Labour Party through socialist conviction rather than their own personal material circumstances. The PLP was by no means a mirror image of the overwhelmingly working-class Labour electorate. However, it seems that working-class voters rarely had a problem electing middle-class Labour MPs as long as they were true to their socialist convictions. Where tensions did arise was with union leaders, who were regularly exasperated by the sense that these well-to-do socialists were detached from the realities of the working world and, therefore, made demands that were excessive and unrealistic.

Conclusion

The 1920s could be said to be one of Labour's most important decades because the party became the Official Opposition for the first time and, subsequently, unlocked the door to Number 10. Labour firmly established itself as the alternative party of government to the Conservatives. In the century that has followed, Labour has never relinquished this position. Infrastructurally, the 1920s were a fruitful decade, thanks to the seeds planted by the party's 1918 constitution. Local party organisation blossomed, and roots were put down across the country in local government and trade union organisation. Partly due to the expanding franchise in fertile territory, Labour grew its total number of votes at each election. Some weeds were allowed to grow when Communists began to infiltrate local parties and union branches, but they were successfully trimmed back. Policy development, however, was insufficiently nurtured, and this showed when Labour entered government in both 1924 and 1929, producing an inadequate yield.

Already, we can see in the 1920s many of the conflicts that will arise time and again in this book: the leader versus the party's democratic structures, cautious trade unions versus idealistic socialists, the threat of far-left infiltration, and problems of discipline. The fact that these struggles reoccur suggests that they are in part structural, an inescapable element of a party founded by a coalition of different interests and acting simultaneously as a vehicle for both ethical socialist idealism and material working-class advancement. What can be said for Labour in the 1920s is that, despite these obstacles, it met its two great challenges of the decade: to convince trade unionists and the left of the parliamentary path to socialism and to persuade the country of its responsibility as a viable party of government and Loyal Opposition. If not an 'insane miracle', then certainly a considerable feat.

2

A Battle Over Peace (1931–1940)

The Labour Party's period of opposition from 1931 to 1940 neither began with an electoral defeat nor ended with an electoral victory. Rather, it started with a minority of the outgoing Labour administration entering into a National government and ended with senior members of the party entering a wartime government and a War Cabinet. Although superficially similar, these two events were in reality very different. Both were occasioned by national crises – the breakdown of the economy in the case of the former and the outbreak of war in the case of the latter. But the first did not have the wide support of the party and was followed by recrimination and bitterness, while the second was approved by both the NEC and the party conference and was reflective of a common mind and unity of purpose.

These two bookend events are also indicative of the wider national and international climate of crisis in the 1930s. The decade was inaugurated by a world economic slump that was to have devastating effects on people around the world. It ended with the outbreak of a war that was to engulf the world for almost six years. This, in turn, was accompanied by a climate of crisis within the Labour Party itself. For one thing, the party had to decide how to respond to external crises that were evolving at bewildering speed. For another, the party itself had been plunged into an internal crisis by the traumatic nature of the ending of the previous period of Labour government and by the deep and bitter split caused by its demise. It was also a decade in which Labour Party policy had to undergo significant evolution. As we shall see, the party responded to the collapse of the previous Labour government by making a pronounced leftward turn; pacifism, which had long held sway in sections of the left of the Labour Party, was once again dominant. By the end of the decade, the senior members of the party entered into a wartime government. The mutation took some years to effect, but it enacted a decisive and transformative shift. In policy, it was felt that the vague aspirations which had held sway among the leadership of the party for some time had been shown to be wanting and deemed a failure. Something far more specific was needed in policy terms, as was a practical plan of action that would implement such decisive change.

Thus, although the decade of the 1930s was spent by the Labour Party in opposition, essentially on the sidelines of power, the decade provided the party with an invaluable period in which to regroup after an event of internal trauma, reconsider its policy approach from first principles, and adapt itself to warfare conditions in which it was ultimately to play a full and central part. The policies, principles and formulae of action that were hammered out and adopted in the 1930s were to have long-lasting effects. They equipped the party with a plan of action when it eventually formed a majority government in 1945, and were to constitute the parameters within which Labour thought and action developed for some considerable time beyond this. The party's period in opposition in the 1930s is therefore a vitally important one for an understanding of the party's subsequent development, not only in opposition but also in government, and for some decades to come. But it is impossible to understand developments in this period without an appreciation of the extent to which the party was reacting to the legacy of the previous Labour government.

The Record of the Last Labour Government: Collapse and Betrayal

The Labour Party took office in government for a second time following the general election of May 1929 with, as before, Ramsay MacDonald as prime minister and Philip Snowden as Chancellor of the Exchequer. For the first time, the party had won the largest number of seats in the House of Commons and had achieved its largest poll to date. On the other hand, it had polled slightly fewer votes than the Conservatives, and its parliamentary seats fell short of a majority. More significantly and more ominously, the election had taken place against the background of a worrying rise in unemployment, which was to bedevil the government throughout its period in office. At first, having taken office, the unemployment figures improved, which gave grounds for cautious optimism. But this turned out to be short-lived. The American stock market crash of October 1929 had worldwide repercussions, and in Britain the unemployment figures reached levels not previously seen.

At first, the Labour government seemed to be making a positive mark. As in the previous Labour administration of 1924, MacDonald played a key role in foreign affairs. He made a triumphant visit to the United States (the first by a British prime minister) in October 1929, and succeeded in negotiating a settlement to the naval rivalry that had plagued relations between Britain and the United States since 1918. At home, there were some modest moves towards the provision of social services, particularly in housing, due to the efforts of Arthur Greenwood as Minister of Health. But as the economic situation worsened and the unemployment figures moved inexorably upwards, members of the government found themselves at a loss as to how to respond.

In letters, diaries and memoranda, MacDonald repeatedly said that he was 'baffled', that the figures were 'baffling', and that the unemployment situation continues to 'baffle' us.[1] The word was appropriate and revealing. No government, of any party, had previously had to face such a challenge, and the traditional economic remedies proved to be ineffective and woefully inadequate. To onlookers, both within the Labour Party and outside it, the government seemed to be complacent and lacking in drive and vision. The reality was more complicated. Members of the government were fully aware of the scale and urgency of the problem but could not agree on how to address it. Various possibilities – public works and a road building programme, import tariffs, devaluation – were advocated by some and rejected by others. Out of frustration with this stagnation, Sir Oswald Mosley, Chancellor of the Duchy of Lancaster, put forward his 'Mosley memorandum', a Cabinet paper which advocated 'vigorous premature Keynesianism'.[2] It was a bold and ambitious attempt to escape from the orthodox financial straitjacket by means of expansion through public spending. It was too bold, however, for Snowden's stringent fiscal orthodoxy, and so this too was rejected. One by one, the Cabinet had blocked off all their possible escape routes, either because Snowden vetoed them or because they were unable to agree. As a result, 'it seemed to many that the country was slithering towards a crisis with which a weak and divided minority Government could not deal'.[3]

Having ruled out all the alternatives, there was nothing left for the Cabinet to do but economise. This was going to be unpalatable to the party and, particularly pertinently, to Labour MPs. Perhaps with this in mind, Snowden agreed to an independent committee of enquiry into public expenditure policies, chaired by Sir George May. Not for the last time, a government was effectively dodging a politically difficult decision by 'outsourcing' it to an independent committee. The fact that it was independent (with Labour occupying less than a third of its membership) meant that its recommendations were almost bound to be unpalatable to socialists and trade unionists. The resulting report predicted a budget deficit of £120 million, and said that economic collapse could only be averted by cuts of £96 million, of which £66 million should come from cuts in unemployment benefit. The question now was whether the recommendations of the report should be accepted. It was not a question that could be considered at leisure. The report had proclaimed to the world the parlous state of the British economy, and foreign sterling holders responded accordingly; the economy suffered an accelerating loss of gold that, unstemmed, it was said, could lead to disaster.

The task before the Cabinet was now to give effect to the main contours of the May Committee's recommendations. It had demanded £96 million of economies, while Snowden's economy committee had recommended £78 million of cuts and the Cabinet had only firmly agreed to £56 million. The only way to get from £56 million to £78 million was to enact a 10 per cent cut in unemployment benefit, on which the Cabinet was divided. The opposition parties, the Bank of England, foreign sterling holders and potential foreign lenders were all of the view that £56 million was nowhere near enough. At first, the Cabinet had decided to stick with that figure, but it soon became clear that this would not be sufficient to secure loans from New York and Paris necessary to prop up sterling; without these credits, sterling would crash. The Cabinet was therefore asked to consider again an additional £20 million of cuts deriving from a 10 per cent cut in unemployment benefit. This proposal was finally approved by a majority of the Cabinet, but the minority made it clear that they would resign rather than accept the cuts. The government could not sustain resignations on this scale, so this in effect meant the end of the second Labour government.

At this point, it seems that MacDonald's settled view was that he would resign along with the government and support the proposed unemployment cut from the back benches.[4] There has been much speculation as to what happened in the following twenty-four hours to induce him to change his mind and agree to lead a National government including three (later four) of his Labour colleagues, alongside Conservative and Liberal members.[5] But whatever the reasons, it seems that both the 'remainers' and the 'resigners' expected the split to be short term (lasting only for weeks or at most months). Arthur Henderson, who later succeeded MacDonald as leader, assured others that the split 'was only an interlude in the life of the Party' and compared it to MacDonald's earlier temporary estrangement over the war in 1914.[6] But a series of both accidental and more deliberate missteps on both sides in the ensuing days ensured that the split became permanent, and attitudes to it increasingly bitter. On the first day of the party conference in Scarborough in September 1931, the National government ministers were expelled.

These traumatic events cast their shadow over Labour's entire period in opposition in the 1930s – and beyond. The envisaged short-term and temporary status of the National government was decisively cast aside when MacDonald requested a dissolution and a general election, in which 'National' Labour and Liberal made an agreement to protect each other's candidates with a view to a continuation of the National government. But if the effects of these seismic events on the Labour Party in the 1930s were beyond doubt, how did the wider electorate respond in the two general elections of that decade?

Rebuilding Labour's Relationship with the Electorate

Just as the two bookends of Labour's period of opposition from 1931 to 1940 were highly unusual, not to say unique, so too the general elections of those years, certainly the election of 1931, hardly took place in conventional circumstances. When the electorate was, in effect, asked to endorse the new 'National' government, the Labour Party was placed in an unenviable position. It had to defend the record of the previous government, while also attacking the very people who had led that government and their policies. Furthermore, they had hardly had time to develop a convincing policy alternative. The outcome, unsurprisingly, was a disaster: 'the 1931 election was the greatest landslide of British democratic history, producing the most unbalanced Parliament since the Great Reform Act. Labour had been reduced from 288 seats in 1929 to 52. Only nine other members would not support the new Government ... The new House would contain 554 Government supporters.'[7]

That the election result was a disaster for the Labour Party is undoubted. Subsequent discussion has for the most part revolved around two questions. First, just how bad was this bad result? And second, how is the scale of the defeat to be explained? With regard to the first question, some have suggested that, given the unique circumstances in which Labour was forced to fight the election, the result was not quite as disastrous as might initially be thought. For one thing, the number of parliamentary seats gives a misleading sense of the scale of the defeat because of the first-past-the-post electoral system. Although the number of Labour seats dropped from 288 in 1929 to fifty-two in 1931, the drop in Labour's total vote was much smaller – from 8,048,968 (37.1 per cent of the vote) in 1929 to 6,339,306 (30.6 per cent of the vote) in 1931. According to one calculation, under proportional representation 'Labour would have won only 225 seats in 1929, instead of 288, and 168 in 1931, instead of fifty-two. The electoral system worked strongly in favour of Labour in 1929, and drastically against it in 1931.'[8] When set in the context of the economic slump, the vast surges in unemployment, the apparent failure of the Labour government to deal with it, and its ignominious demise, it is perhaps more surprising that the Labour vote held up as well as it did. It seems to justify Pimlott's comment that 'the 1931 vote, though a severe setback, did not indicate a disintegration of support'.[9]

As for the explanation for the defeat, there has tended to be a difference of emphasis on the part of those more partisan and closer to events and those more disinterested and distant from them. Labour members and supporters in 1931 tended to portray themselves as victims of external forces – including but not restricted to the relentlessly hostile media coverage, which was seen as a manifestation of an anti-Labour conspiracy. More recently, however, historians such as Andrew Thorpe in *The British General Election of 1931* (1991) have rejected such 'conspiracy theory' analyses.[10] Although conditions may well have been unfavourable, the explanation for the defeat was actually much simpler. He says that it was, at base, a national repudiation of a government which had shown itself incapable of dealing with an economic crisis and the ever-increasing unemployment to which it gave rise. Pimlott concurs with such an analysis when he succinctly says that 'the most plausible explanation is that Labour had manifestly failed to deal with unemployment'.[11] If that was the case, then the late Labour government had either been economically and administratively incompetent or it had been following the wrong policies. In the aftermath of the election, the party determined that the latter had been the case, and, as we shall see below, set about developing resolute policies for immediate implementation.

By the time of the next general election in November 1935, the 'National' government was only nominally so, especially now that Ramsay MacDonald had been succeeded as prime minister by Conservative leader Stanley Baldwin. Because of this, the clarion call of the 'Nation' was much less potent, and voting habits reverted to more traditional patterns. This was especially evident from Labour's own poll, which seemed to revert to the level of its previous high point in 1929. In that year, the party had polled 8,389,512 votes; in 1935 it achieved 8,325,491. Its share of the vote too was very close to that of 1929, when it achieved 37.1 per cent; in 1935 it was 37.9 per cent. But in 1935 the party was again a victim of the electoral system. In 1929, it had 288 seats in the House of Commons, whereas in 1935, on a similar vote, it had only 154 seats.

Although Labour's vote had recovered to 1929 levels, this was nowhere near enough to make it the largest party in the House of Commons, as it had been in 1929. This was partly, as just noted, an effect of the electoral system, but that was by no means the only nor the most important factor. More significant still was the movement of the Liberal vote, which plummeted from 5,308,510 (23.4 per cent) in 1929 to 1,422,116 (6.4 per cent) in 1935. It seems that many of these erstwhile Liberal voters transferred their adherence to the Conservative Party, which polled 11,810,158 (53.7 per cent) compared to 8,656,473 (38.2 per cent) in 1929. Indeed, it appears that much of this transference had already occurred in 1931, when the Conservative vote was very close to what it was in 1935. What was of decisive importance, then, was the marked decline in the Liberal vote in the 1930s, and the transference of

Liberal votes to the Conservatives, making the latter a much more formidable electoral enemy than they had been hitherto. Thus, although it was a considerable achievement for Labour to have won back the votes it lost in 1931, returning to its 1929 electoral highpoint was nowhere near enough if it was to mount an effective challenge to the now much more entrenched Conservative hegemony. It seems that it had little chance of doing this in 1935.

In his post-election analysis of the results, Harold Laski considered some of the reasons for this. He said that the sitting government went into the campaign with several advantages. The election was called at a time of national crisis (the Italian invasion of Abyssinia) which, he said, tends to favour the status quo; there were considerably improved economic conditions, with the country reaping the benefits of the adoption of import tariffs, together with a fall in unemployment and an increase in house building; it also had the advantage of the popular political personality of the Conservative leader and prime minister, Stanley Baldwin. These were all factors about which the Labour opposition could do nothing. On the other hand, there were factors which the Labour opposition now urgently had to remedy. It still had not shaken off the obloquy arising from its handling of the earlier financial crisis: 'the nation had a shock in 1931; and it has not yet sufficiently recovered from the experience to be willing to trust Labour with authority'.[12] Another factor was that the Labour Party seemed too divided, and there was a lack of clarity about its actual policies.

Addressing this point, Laski said that 'the party has to make up its mind whether it wishes to be a socialist party or a social reform party ... This is, no doubt, the fundamental issue before the Labour Party. It is not easy to say what decision it will make.'[13] There was no doubt about Laski's own answer to this question. He said that the party must take the 'longer and more difficult' path of a 'frontal attack' on capitalism: 'It means taking over the control of the levers of power at once so that their direction is not left in the hands of those who seek, at all costs, to prevent the coming of socialism.'[14] And there can be no doubt that Laski spoke for many – though by no means all – in the Labour Party in the wake of the 1931 defeat. Many blamed that defeat on the path of 'gradualism', and for them the whole crisis had vividly shown that such a path would inevitably be crushed by the juggernaut of capitalism. In the wake of that defeat, therefore, the party's most important and immediate task was to reconsider its whole policy offering.

Forming a Resolute and Detailed Policy Programme

While some in the party agreed with Laski that the crisis of 1931 was a failure of gradualism, by no means everyone did. For others, it was not so much that the gradualist approach was to blame but, rather, that it had failed to be buttressed by concrete plans of action and detailed blueprints for delivery. Instead, it had been wreathed in vague aspirations and pious slogans which had proved hopelessly inadequate in the face of harsh economic realities. The task, therefore, was not so much to develop a policy of a full-frontal attack on capitalism, but to provide the detailed and informed policy planning which alone could make a success of the gradualist approach. As Labour began the process, therefore, of forming policy from the ground up, a fault line emerged between those who sought the development of a full-scale socialist *alternative* to capitalism, and others who set about developing policy for a socialist *reform* of capitalism.

Both camps had their own means of promoting their respective causes. Herbert Morrison and Hugh Dalton utilised the NEC Policy Committee to develop 'new plans for industry and finance in the 1930s', while Ernest Bevin was instrumental in the Economic Committee of the TUC, and the two bodies worked closely together. Furthermore, Hugh Gaitskell and Douglas Jay were closely involved with the XYZ Club, which had been set up by junior bankers in the City who were sympathetic to Labour, but who had been shocked by the previous Labour government's ignorance of the financial market and lack of contact with major players in the City. Together, these groups were instrumental in the formation of a reformist economic policy. Meanwhile, on the other side of the divide, G.D.H. Cole had been instrumental in founding the Society for Socialist Inquiry and Propaganda (SSIP) and the New Fabian Research Bureau (NFRB), and 'both of these bodies initially included dominating elements of left-wing intellectuals'.[15] They too were concerned with developing the detailed policy prescriptions which were felt to have been sorely lacking in the last Labour government.

Ultimately, however, it was the 'reformers' who prevailed over the left, as was made clear by the policy document 'Socialism and Peace', which was adopted by the party conference at Southport in 1934, and formed the basis upon which the party fought the general election of 1935. Elizabeth Durbin has summarised the main provisions of the document as follows:

> The new programme called for the central planning of key industries, to include the immediate nationalization of the banking system, transport, coal and power, water supply, iron and steel and land and the drastic reorganization of electricity, gas, agriculture, shipping, shipbuilding, engineering, textiles, chemicals and insurance. Plans were also promised to extend social services, to provide medical care, to clear slums, to raise the school-leaving age, to abolish the means test and to give adequate maintenance to the unemployed. Finally, to deal with unemployment and not to be outdone by the Liberals, extensive plans were proposed to build roads, bridges, harbours, houses, schools and hospitals, to electrify the railways, to re-equip nationalized industries, to drain land and to plant trees, all to be financed by government loans.[16]

It was an ambitious programme and, by later standards, seemingly left-wing. But by the standards of the 1930s, it represented a defeat for the left. They fought back and, at the Southport conference, Labour MP Sir Stafford Cripps and the Socialist League tabled seventy-five amendments to the document, although the Standing Orders Committee reduced these to twelve, all of which were defeated.[17] There were several issues on which the left were defeated, including their proposals for direct ministerial control of nationalised industries or, alternatively, workers' control in the manner of guild socialism. They were also defeated in their proposal not to pay compensation to owners and shareholders of industries that were nationalised.[18]

Beyond these objections to particularities in the emerging party policy programme, others on the left objected more generally to the overall strategy of superimposing measures of socialisation on what would ultimately still be a capitalist economy. G.D.H. Cole, for instance, in his book *Principles of Economic Planning* (1935), set out a model for a fully planned national economy extending to the controlled distribution of incomes as well as the coordinated organisation of production. He was particularly critical of the kind of 'half way house' that had been adopted by the Labour Party at its Southport conference in 1934. He said that a socialist economy would have to advance to the point 'at which the entire system of distributing incomes, as well as the control of industrial and agricultural production, would be brought under public auspices'.[19] Needless to say, a fully comprehensive national economic plan of this kind has never been attempted in Britain, neither has it ever been adopted as Labour Party policy.

Why did the left so comprehensively lose the arguments on policy debates in the 1930s? Ben Pimlott has said that 'it was not inevitable that the Labour Left should play little part in the process of detailed policy-making', especially 'at a time when many people in the Labour Party were rethinking their ideas, and were especially prepared to consider left-wing solutions'.[20] In his influential book *Labour and the Left in the 1930s* (1977), he argued that the left essentially squandered their opportunities for making a decisive difference to party policy because they were distracted by other pursuits and activities. The left-leaning policy bodies the SSIP and the NFRB moved in different directions. The SSIP evolved to become the Socialist League and soon left detailed policy research behind. The NFRB evolved into a body for economists and researchers 'who found Dalton and Morrison more constructive as leaders than Cripps'.[21] Meanwhile Cripps himself and the Socialist League got distracted by symbolic campaigns and moral crusades that gained a high profile but made little contribution to the detailed policy planning that others saw was so badly needed in the wake of the 1931 defeat. The net result was the victory of gradualism and Keynesian revisionism, as articulated in Douglas Jay's *The Socialist Case* (1937), adorned with a foreword by Clement Attlee. This approach set the parameters for Labour policy not only in the 1930s, but for many decades afterwards. There was much more continuity than development between the policy document 'Socialism and Peace' (1934) and its successors 'The Immediate Programme' (1937) and 'Let Us Face the Future' (1945). As Pimlott concludes, 'embryonic "Gaitskellites" established a tradition of reformist economic management which Labour's 1945 document *Let Us Face the Future* plainly reflects, and which soon became the basis of post-war British socialism'.[22]

In the 1930s, however, the international situation was such that the formation of foreign policy became as important as developing domestic policy. After the 1935 election, which was itself held in the shadow of a threatened Italian invasion of Abyssinia, it seemed that one international crisis rapidly followed another. In this new volatile context, it was far from clear that the Labour Party had international and defence policies that were sufficiently equipped to deal with the new threats, not least the prospect of war. In the early 1930s, pacifism loomed large in the Labour Party. By the middle of the decade, however, many could see that this was clearly inadequate. At the party conference of October 1935, the National Executive drew up a policy of collective security under the auspices of the League of Nations. The corollary of such a policy, of course, was that this might entail the use of force. The new policy was opposed by the pacifists, led by George Lansbury, now party leader, and also by another group led by Sir Stafford Cripps, who would only endorse the use of force if it were undertaken by an alliance of socialist countries. Both groups were easily defeated, and the new policy was adopted. An immediate result was the resignation of Lansbury as leader, to be succeeded by his deputy, Clement Attlee. But it also signalled to the world an unequivocal renunciation of pacifism as Labour Party policy.

This was more of a staging post than a settlement, however. By adopting a policy of collective security, the party had accepted, in principle, the possibility of armed resistance. After 1935, as month succeeded month, this possibility looked less like a principle and more like an impending reality. And yet, the Labour opposition continued to vote against the government's defence estimates. This placed the party in an illogical position, as it called for the government to stand by collective security and resist armed aggression, and yet refused to vote for the armaments that would allow it to do so. Furthermore, it opened the party to the charge that, had they been in government, their policies would not have allowed them to develop an alternative to the appeasement they were soon to criticise so bitterly.[23] Hugh Dalton, the party's foreign affairs spokesman, was acutely aware of the bind and sought to escape it. He had attempted – and failed – to persuade the PLP to abstain on the defence estimates (rather than vote against) in July 1936. But after a year of hard canvassing, Dalton managed to reverse this decision in 1937 (in spite of opposition from Attlee, Greenwood and Morrison), and the PLP duly abstained on the estimates. Dalton took advantage of this momentum to produce a pro-rearmament statement, 'International Policy and Defence', which was endorsed by the TUC and by the party conference in October 1937. This was a decisive moment: 'With the help of the unions, Dalton had moved Labour's official defence policy away from the pacifism of 1933 to an uncompromising opposition to appeasement and firm support for rearmament.'[24]

It is difficult to think of another period in Labour's opposition years when its policies – both domestic and international – developed in such significant ways and with such enormous consequences. In foreign policy, Labour had gradually abandoned pacifism and embraced collective security and support for rearmament. This paved the way for it not only to hold the government to account for its failing policy of appeasement (as we shall see below), but also ultimately to enter the wartime coalition of 1940. In domestic policy, Labour had to decide what strategic approach to take in the wake of the crisis of 1931. In steering a path between left-wing demands for a full-frontal attack on capitalism on the one hand and the old vague and aspirational gradualism on the other, the party formulated a specific and detailed policy programme that was simultaneously both resolute and gradualist and that would take it into government in 1945.

Redefining the Party's Relationship with Members and the Unions

If the 1931 crisis had engendered a full-scale reassessment of its policy formation, it was also a catalyst for the party to reconsider its very structures and organisation. It had, of course, not been created as a political party *ex nihilo*, but had started life as a somewhat uneasy coalition of different interests and pre-existing bodies, which was to be a source of continuing tensions. The party structures reflected this, with numerous bodies and loci of power, and with the relationship between them being malleable rather than rigid. Who actually controlled the party and its policy was not clearly defined, and much depended on the contingencies of who was successful in jockeying for power. During the 1920s, the parliamentary leaders had succeeded in gradually gaining control of both party and policy, and this had been vividly displayed in the 1931 crisis. Many felt that the parliamentary leaders had become dangerously isolated and detached from the larger body of MPs, the trade unions and the wider party at large. There were therefore various attempts to bring the leadership under control and to make it more answerable to these various groups.

This mood was very clearly reflected in many of the resolutions that were proposed and carried at the party conference in Hastings in October 1933 which, among other things, called for Labour government policy to be determined by the party's annual conference. The Executive accepted such resolutions with reluctance, doubtless aware that they were of questionable constitutional propriety. In time, they were quietly dropped, and there was no question of the 1945 government acting in accordance with them. But more important than their longevity is their indication of a pronounced mood in the party which was to produce much more long-lasting changes to the party's organisational structures.

The trade unions were among the first to stake a claim for a more defined role in the party's policy-making. Their dominant leaders were Ernest Bevin and Walter Citrine, and they had been stung by the confrontational meeting they had had with leading members of the government at the moment of crisis in the dying days of the 1929–31 government, when their alternative policies had been rejected and they themselves had been rebuffed. They were determined that they should never be placed in such a position again, and looked for ways of tying the party and TUC more intimately together. They were, in fact, pushing at an open door, for the party was equally eager to collectivise decision-making and exercise some control over the leadership. The TUC made the initial overtures. They invited the party to nominate two members of its NEC to attend the meetings of the TUC Economic Committee. In late 1931, it was agreed to change and revitalise the functions of the National Joint Council (NJC). This had been founded in 1921 as a consultative body which brought together the TUC, the parliamentary party and the NEC with each section being equally represented. It had never had a central role, however, and had withered on the vine in the ensuing decade.

Already, in 1930, an attempt had been made to revive it, and its membership had been changed. Under these revisions, the parliamentary party and the NEC would each send three members to sit on the council (the chairman and two others) while the General Council of the TUC would send its chairman and six others. Each would also send a secretary as additional members.²⁵ As a result, not only was the TUC now the largest group (as opposed to the previous parity in representation), but it also had a built-in majority. This became even more significant when, in 1932, a TUC memorandum on the NJC's functions was largely accepted by the party conference, giving the body a significantly enhanced role. Its new status and functions were reflected by a new name: it became known as the National Council of Labour (NCL) from 1934.

How significant was this body and how much power did it give to the unions? Alan Bullock has said that 'during the course of the 1930s, the National Council became the most authoritative body in the Labour movement in formulating policy, especially on foreign affairs', and Henry Pelling went so far as to say that the Labour Party in the 1930s was 'the General Council's party' and was under 'TUC ... tutelage'.²⁶ Jerry Brookshire, however, has argued that such descriptions are 'incorrect or misleading' and he thinks Pimlott 'more astute' when he says that 'the main function of the National Joint Council was to give weight to party pronouncements by demonstrating that the Movement spoke with a united voice. It was never out of step with the majority view on the NEC.'²⁷ It seems fair to say, then, that the changes in composition and function of the NJC/NCL certainly gave added weight to the voice of the unions, but without going so far as allowing them to dominate the NEC or the parliamentary party.

But the unions were not the only ones demanding a greater voice in the national affairs of the party. Individual members and constituency parties had seen their numbers growing but without any real increase in their influence. The increasing weight being given to the voice of the trade unions in this period only made their plight more acute. Matters were exacerbated by the fact that the unions had historically been on the right of the party, while individual members tended to be on the left. In the ten years since individual membership of the party had been made possible by the reforms of 1918 (as we saw in the last chapter), membership had slowly risen to 215,000 and by 1936, that number had more than doubled to 431,000. This rapidly growing constituency had no effective way of making its voice heard. Divisional Labour Parties (DLPs) had virtually no power, other than the right to select parliamentary candidates. The Constituency and Central Labour Parties section of the NEC contained five members nominated by local parties but they were elected by party conference, which meant that even these members were in the control of the trade union bloc vote.[28]

Discontent had been brewing through the early 1930s, but after the general election of 1935 the feelings of resentment burst into the open and were given organised shape through the leadership of Ben Greene, who had been a parliamentary candidate in 1931, but who otherwise had no place in the national party hierarchy. He organised an Association of Labour Parties, but their efforts were repeatedly rebuffed by the NEC, which regarded the campaign and Greene himself with suspicion. At the 1936 conference in Edinburgh, the constituency parties' demands were once again rejected outright, provoking a strong response from the DLP delegates at the conference. Two hundred of them (out of 280) attended a meeting at which it was agreed to set up a Provisional Committee of Constituency Labour Parties in order to 'bring these parties into consultation with one another, so that proposals may be put forward unitedly of such remedies as will lead to the Labour Party constitution becoming a great democratic instrument'.[29] Greene himself became secretary of the committee, while Sir Stafford Cripps agreed to become chairman. Among other members were names that would later become well known, such as Aneurin Bevan and Sara Barker.

At this point, a stalemate might have been reached, giving rise to years of festering bitterness. Crucially, however, the incoming party chairman, Hugh Dalton, turned out to be an unexpected convert to the DLPs' cause.[30] After holding extensive discussions at area conferences with local representatives and individual interviews with Greene, Dalton devised a plan that would meet the local parties' main demands. He first obtained the agreement of the organisation sub-committee, and then – despite considerable opposition – also won over the NEC. But final approval had to be given by the party conference in Bournemouth in October 1937, and here trade union votes would be decisive. After considerable lobbying and some last-minute negotiations with the unions conducted by Dalton himself, the opposition was overcome. The outcome was that the constituencies' section of the NEC would be directly elected by the local parties themselves and the section increased from five seats to seven. At first, the changes seemed to make little difference to the membership and political complexion of the NEC. But in time, the left of the party was able to make use of the new rules for their own ends.[31] For instance, it allowed for the Bevanite sweep of the NEC at the Morecambe conference in 1952 (in which Dalton lost his own seat), and also later gave a platform for the rising Bennite left after 1979.

The 1930s therefore witnessed considerable party reform, as both the trade unions and the local parties sought to amplify their voices in party governance in relation to the leadership. At the time, the unions seemed to have achieved the greater success, while the local parties, although scoring a symbolic victory, seemed to have secured relatively little in practice. But in the longer term, these fortunes were reversed. The role of the National Council of Labour became less significant after the party entered the wartime coalition of 1940, and effectively fizzled out altogether after Labour formed a majority government in 1945.[32] In contrast, the new rules for the election of the constituencies' section of the NEC were not only long-lived, but provided an increasingly important platform for the left of the party to challenge the leadership, which it used with considerable effectiveness at recurring periods in the subsequent decades.

Holding the Government to Account: The Approach of War

The manner in which the Labour opposition held the government to account before 1935 differed markedly in both form and content to its approach after 1935. Before 1935, the opposition was small in number, facing an overwhelmingly large government side, and its focus was on domestic policies, particularly unemployment. After 1935, the opposition was of a more respectable size, and found itself increasingly having to hold the government's foreign policy to account, not least its policy of appeasement.

After the 1931 election, the opposition witnessed the strange spectacle of the government abandoning many elements of financial orthodoxy that the previous government, and particularly Snowden, had defended to the hilt.[33] Slowly the new measures began to take effect; the financial crisis was negotiated, and unemployment gradually began to come down. But for the Labour opposition, this was all too little and too late. In Parliament, it relentlessly pressed the point that the fall in unemployment was too slow and was not shared equally by the whole country. Attlee charged that the government had produced no policy for dealing with the unemployed, even as they had been reduced to penury by the benefit cuts and had been insulted by the means test. The Unemployment Assistance Board – introduced in 1934 but denounced by Attlee as a 'centralized Poor Law' – was meant to supersede the local public assistance committees. It preserved the principle of the means test, and matters were made worse when it was revealed that the level of the new national payments would, in some areas, be lower than the previous local payments. The news provoked another series of 'Hunger Marches' and the opposition took up the cause in Parliament. The government conceded, promising that payments made by the new board would not be lower than the previous local benefits.[34] It was a rare example of an opposition, buttressed by wide public support, being able to secure a government concession.

After the general election of 1935, Attlee was confirmed as parliamentary leader following periods as acting leader (while Lansbury was ill) and 'caretaker' leader (after Lansbury resigned). His place as deputy was taken by Arthur Greenwood, and these two shared much of the burden of holding the government in Parliament to account as attention turned increasingly to foreign affairs and an ever more perilous international situation. In the ensuing years, as the government's policy of appeasement became ever more ineffective and self-defeating, it fell to the Labour opposition to point out the obvious. This would have been difficult to do effectively, however, had the party still had an equivocal policy in relation to rearmament. Fortunately, albeit in the nick of time, it had unequivocally committed itself to a policy of rearmament by October 1937, as we saw above, largely due to the efforts of Hugh Dalton and Ernest Bevin.

By this time, the international situation had already deteriorated rapidly. In March 1936, Germany had invaded the demilitarised Rhineland, thereby contravening both the Treaty of Versailles and the more recent Locarno Treaties, while being met by inaction from both France and Britain. That summer saw the outbreak of civil war in Spain, an affair on which the Labour opposition was curiously non-committal until dragged, seemingly reluctantly, into adopting a policy of more explicit, if still equivocal, support for the republicans.[35] International tensions were ratcheted up still further when, in March 1938, Hitler invaded Austria. The party's policy on rearmament having been settled some five months before, it was now in a better position to take a more determined line. Anthony Eden had resigned as Foreign Secretary in protest at the government's appeasement policy in the previous month, and the Labour opposition was able to build on this momentum to press its case for resistance. In the House of Commons, Attlee, in what Bevan described as 'the speech of his life', said that having listened carefully to Neville Chamberlain's speech, he 'could not discern anything in it in the nature of a policy which made for peace … I found the Prime Minister stating very strongly the principle that the rule of force should give way to the rule of law, but in actual fact he yields to force all the time.'[36] The government's sins of omission through its inaction over Austria were compounded when it signed a treaty with Mussolini's fascist regime in Italy, which the opposition attacked and voted against in the House of Commons in April.

With fascism now rearing its head all over Europe, there were calls from the left in Britain for a 'united front' of left-wing parties against fascism. The Communist Party first began pressing for coordinated action in 1933. The Labour Party's NEC consistently rejected such overtures, with many trade unionists regarding the Communists with as much hostility as they did the fascists. After 1935, the Communists had to settle for cooperation with the ILP and the Socialist League. The party responded by disaffiliating the League and declaring that membership of it was incompatible with party membership. Eventually, the League dissolved itself in 1937, rather than face expulsion from the party. But agitation for a 'unity campaign' did not disappear.

Meanwhile, Hitler turned his attention to Czechoslovakia. With a German invasion feared to be imminent, Chamberlain flew to Berchtesgaden in September 1938, where Hitler demanded the right of self-determination for the Sudeten Germans. Chamberlain seized on this as a basis for negotiation and, having consulted with the French, urged the Czechs to accept the German demands, which they eventually did. The Labour opposition continued to argue for resistance, both in public and in private, at this time proposing that a joint stand should be made, along with France and Russia. Chamberlain received two Labour delegations – the first on 15 September from the National Council of Labour, consisting of Citrine, Morrison and Dalton, and the second from the parliamentary leadership, Attlee and Greenwood, on 21 September. Chamberlain said that France was demoralised and unreliable, partly because they were sceptical that Russia would take any action, and partly because they were themselves divided on resistance. He also said that Britain was still unprepared in some essential armaments.[37] This made an impression on Dalton, who wondered briefly whether resistance was feasible. But he was reassured by confidential discussions with Sir Robert Vansittart, Permanent Under-Secretary at the Foreign Office, and thereafter neither he nor the Labour opposition wavered.[38]

Hitler now demanded an immediate occupation of the Czech areas to be ceded to Germany. Czechoslovakia rejected these demands outright, and the French ordered a partial mobilisation. By 27 September, everyone believed war to be imminent. But at this point, Hitler proposed a four-power conference (along with the Italians and the French) in Munich. There was much relief that war had been averted, but when Chamberlain returned, it became clear that Britain and the other powers had essentially acceded to all of Hitler's demands, albeit in return for German guarantees of the new Czech frontiers. In the House of Commons, Attlee attacked the agreement as constituting 'one of the greatest diplomatic defeats that this country and France have ever sustained'.[39] Greenwood moved an amendment to the motion of support for government policy which, while expressing relief that war had been averted for the time being, said that the House 'cannot approve a policy which has led to the sacrifice of Czechoslovakia under threat of armed force and to the humiliation of the country and its exposure to grave dangers'.[40] The government motion was carried, though with a significant number of Conservative abstentions.

Disillusionment with Munich gave rise to renewed calls for cross-party cooperation. There had been two by-elections in 1938 – at Oxford in October and at Bridgwater in November – where 'Independent Progressive' candidates, supported by both Labour and the Liberals locally (and, with some reluctance, nationally), stood against the Conservative candidates in protest against the government's appeasement policy. Sir Stafford Cripps took advantage of this momentum to promote again the idea of a 'popular front'. In a memorandum he argued that 'Labour standing on its own was unlikely to win a majority in any election held within the next eighteen months; it was therefore necessary to join forces with other opposition groups on the basis of a programme of limited reforms, with constituency arrangement wherever possible.'[41] These other opposition groups included the Liberals, Communists and the ILP. Predictably, the NEC rejected these proposals, and when Cripps continued to agitate at grassroots level, he was expelled from the party, along with some of his supporters, including Aneurin Bevan.

On 15 March 1939, German troops occupied Prague, thus demonstrating that its Munich guarantees had been worthless. Shortly afterwards, even the Conservative government realised that its policy of appeasement was dead. Two weeks after the occupation of Prague, the government announced that it had guaranteed the independence and integrity of Poland. On behalf of the opposition, Greenwood welcomed the development, called for its extension to other states, and for it to be made effective through cooperation with the Soviet Union.[42] Indeed, calls for closer collaboration with the USSR had constituted a theme of Labour's opposition policy throughout this period, and Attlee pressed the point again several times in May, urging the government to take seriously the Soviet proposals for cooperation, which had been received in London at the end of April. But it was to no avail: 'Chamberlain's distaste for a Russian alliance was too strong, and the negotiations continued on their dilatory and ineffectual course.'[43]

With a sense almost of inevitability, Hitler invaded Poland on 1 September 1939. Attlee had been ill since the spring, and it fell to Greenwood to guide the Labour opposition through this moment of crisis. When, in the House of Commons, Chamberlain delivered a hesitant and equivocal response to the invasion, Greenwood resolutely articulated the outrage of members on all sides of the House. Many saw this intervention as being decisive in stiffening the government's resolve, and a declaration of war was made on 3 September. On the previous day, a joint meeting of the NEC and the executive of the parliamentary party agreed that the party should support resistance to Germany's invasion of Poland and rule out joining Neville Chamberlain's National government: 'These decisions, with the adoption of an electoral truce three days later, defined the position of "constructive opposition". The party would hold itself free to criticize the war effort, while supporting the war.'[44]

This position of 'constructive opposition' had been adopted for a number of reasons. For one thing, there was no appetite in the party to enter into coalition, largely because of the deep antipathy towards Chamberlain. But it was also seen as the 'most appropriate and politically advantageous role it could adopt in wartime'. Among other benefits, it would allow the party to articulate 'a distinctively socialist view of the war effort and war aims'. At the same time, it allowed for official contacts between Labour frontbenchers and particular government ministers and departments.[45] But, as time went on, 'constructive opposition' came to be seen as a 'temporary, but ultimately unsatisfactory compromise'.[46] It offered the party no real chance of influencing the conduct of the war, while simultaneously muzzling it as a serious political force.

Matters came to a head, however, with the British evacuation from Norway in May 1940. There were calls for Chamberlain's resignation and Attlee secured a debate on the conduct of the war. In it he said: 'Norway comes as the culmination of many other discontents. People are saying that those mainly responsible for the conduct of affairs are men who have had an almost uninterrupted career of failure ... They see everywhere a failure of grip, a failure of drive, not only in defence and foreign policy but in industry.'[47] When the debate was taken to a vote, 200 voted against the government, including forty Conservatives, leaving the government with a majority of just eighty-one.

It was clear that a 'drastic reconstruction of the government' was needed, Attlee, Greenwood and Dalton said the next day in a public statement. On 9 May, Attlee and Greenwood met with Chamberlain, Churchill and Halifax. Chamberlain presented them with two questions: would the party serve in a government led by him and would it serve under another prime minister? Attlee said that he could not reply conclusively until he had consulted his Executive. The next day, Attlee and Greenwood travelled to Bournemouth, where the party conference was about to meet, in order to consult the NEC. A unanimous decision was quickly reached that Labour should join a new government, but only under a leader other than Chamberlain. When Chamberlain heard the news, he immediately resigned, and Churchill was appointed prime minister. Attlee and Greenwood joined a five-member War Cabinet, and Bevin, Alexander, Morrison and Dalton were appointed to the wider Cabinet.

This development was momentous for many reasons. From the perspective of the opposition Labour Party, it had accomplished two unprecedented things; it had not only succeeded in toppling a sitting prime minister, but it had also entered a National government with the blessing of the NEC and the party conference. In fact, the two things were mutually implicated, as Bevin made clear in his response to Attlee: 'In view of the fact that you helped to bring the other fellow down, if the Party did not take its share of responsibility, they would say we were [not] great citizens, but cowards.'[48] In many ways, it was the culmination of the previous three years of the opposition's holding the government to account for its policy of appeasement.

Conclusion

Stephen Brooke has said that 'the 1930s had been a barren decade for Labour', and, from the perspective of its proximity to government, this is undoubtedly true.[49] The party had started the decade with a disastrous government crisis, a debilitating party split and a devastating wipe-out at the polls. It ended the decade without having come near to returning to power, with seats in the House of Commons that still fell far short of a majority, and with some less than encouraging opinion polls. But viewed from another perspective, the 1930s, far from being barren, may be viewed as perhaps the most fruitful and significant period of opposition in the Labour Party's history.

The party had learned the lessons from its brief periods in government in the 1920s and early 1930s. It was not enough to implement short-term amelioration measures while being sustained by long-term hopes and aspirations. The party needed to develop a detailed programme for immediate implementation on entering into office. It adopted a gradualist, Keynesian, state-administered restructuring of capitalism in a socialist direction. It was gradualist in the sense that it did not entail an immediate and comprehensive dismantling of the capitalist economy. But it was not dilatory (which had been the fatal flaw of the previous Labour governments) because it entailed an immediate and radical series of measures for fundamentally changing the shape and character of the capitalist economy. This decision determined the policies and political complexion of the Labour Party for decades to come. It is difficult to think of another period in opposition that had such long-term implications in terms of policy, at least until the 1990s.

If, in domestic policy, the party had learned lessons from the past, in foreign policy it very quickly had to learn lessons from the present. In response to the increasingly menacing international situation from 1933 onwards, the party adapted its policies to embrace collective security and rearmament, which gave credibility to its attempts to hold the government to account over its failing appeasement policy. This ultimately paved the way for the party to enter the wartime coalition government in a way that was consistent with the recent direction of its policy development.

In matters of party infrastructure, party members were finally given a means of contributing to party governance and policy formation by the decision to allow local constituency parties to elect an increased number of representatives directly to the NEC. A means had thereby been created for local party members to challenge the dominance of the trade unions and promote a more left-leaning agenda. This was to have considerable ramifications for the party in the decades to come.

Finally, the decision to enter the wartime coalition indicated once again that the party had learned lessons from 1931. For the decision was taken not by the leadership alone, but by the NEC, and was later endorsed by the party conference as a whole. This was, however, not only an act of supreme self-sacrifice in the national interest; it was also an act that would bring the party some political advantage. As Greenwood said at the 1940 conference at Bournemouth, 'it would wean Labour from its opposition-mindedness. He added that accepting responsibility of power would also bring Labour the political credibility it had sought since 1931: "When we have played our part fully, we shall have won in this country an even greater respect than we have today. We shall have greater power than we have today."'[50] Participation in the wartime government was not only an act of honour but also had the political advantage of demonstrating that Labour was both a competent and a patriotic party of government, which could be trusted with safeguarding the national interest. This is likely to have been a major consideration for the hitherto non-Labour voters who voted for the party in 1945.

In short, the period of opposition covered by this chapter stands as a particularly striking example of the argument made by this book as a whole; namely, that some periods of opposition have been as important, formative and significant in the long term for the Labour Party as its periods in government. For many, the 1945–51 government stands as the high-water mark of the Labour Party's historical achievements. But that government would have been inconceivable without the party's self-reformation in the 1930s.

3

In Opposition to the Wartime Government (1940–1945)

It is often assumed that the Labour Party as such entered into a wartime coalition government in 1940 and remained in it until 1945. But this is not strictly true, neither from the perspective of the Labour Party nor from that of the Westminster parliamentary system. It has been said that Churchill's wartime government 'was not founded on a coalition of Parties: it was a Government of National Union, and the Parties upon whose support it depended were in a curious way at once its friends and its critics. This at least was true of the Labour Party, which continued to occupy the Opposition benches in the House, though its Opposition functions were much restricted.'[1]

From the point of view of the Labour Party, the importance of maintaining a separate parliamentary existence independent of the government was vital for keeping alive the spirit of political controversy. Although such controversy had been considerably modified by wartime conditions (which was given expression by the electoral truce agreed by the parties for the duration of the war), it was nonetheless important that the momentum for the realisation of party ideals and objectives was not lost; an electoral truce did not mean a political truce, as was specifically stated by the party's conference report of 1940. Equally, from the point of view of the parliamentary system it was necessary that the government of the day be answerable to an official parliamentary opposition, led by a Leader of the Opposition who would speak on its behalf. For both party and Parliament, therefore, it was necessary that the Labour opposition maintain its independent existence, even though the party's most senior members had entered the government.

This unusual situation created peculiar challenges. The opposition had to hold to account a government which included senior members of its own party. Furthermore, it had to hold to account a government which it had itself created, and which continued to exist only at its own pleasure.

The wartime parliamentary opposition therefore found itself having both to challenge and to support the government, and determining when and in what measure to do each was by no means an easy task. It inevitably led to moments of tension and conflict both between the government and opposition and also between the opposition's backbenches and its frontbench.

But first, a new opposition infrastructure had to be established. With most of the senior members of the Labour opposition swept up into government, there were considerable gaps to be filled. The parliamentary party elected an Administrative Committee, which would both occupy the opposition frontbench and also serve as an executive for the parliamentary party. This was described by Jim Griffiths as the 'second eleven', although Labour ministers were also members until 1943.[2] Attlee remained formally chairman of the parliamentary party, but he temporarily abdicated this position and its duties, and an acting chairman and Leader of the Opposition was elected in his place. Initially, this was Hastings (H.B.) Lees-Smith, the most senior Labour MP who had not entered the government. Lees-Smith had played a key role at various points in the party's recent history: he was instrumental in persuading the parliamentary party to stop voting against the defence estimates, had been appointed as the party's official liaison officer with the Secretary of State for War on the outbreak of war in 1939, and was centrally involved in the decision to divide the House which precipitated Chamberlain's downfall in 1940. He was therefore a considerable figure but not, perhaps, a natural leader. He acted as Leader of the Opposition with 'quiet competence' and his contemporary Chuter Ede said that his grip on PLP meetings 'was not very firm' though he managed to avoid 'catastrophe'.[3] In the winter of 1941, he died of influenza, and Frederick Pethick-Lawrence (later Secretary of State for India in Attlee's 1945 government) was elected in his place. His tenure, however, was very short-lived because only a month or so later, Churchill dropped Arthur Greenwood from the government. The party therefore welcomed its Deputy Leader back to the opposition benches and he immediately assumed the post of acting leader and Leader of the Opposition. In Greenwood, the opposition finally had a leader of weight and seniority, with the advantage of being a former member of the government. He was also widely popular across the parliamentary party, a sentiment that was reinforced by a sense that he had been 'brutally treated' by Churchill.[4]

With this frontbench and leadership infrastructure in place, the party 'maintained its separate existence and to some extent its independent voice and freedom of action for Parliamentary purposes during the war years'.[5] We have already mentioned the importance of this for the parliamentary task of holding the government to account and for ensuring that party politics was not merely put into cold storage for the duration of the war. But there was also another vital function to fulfil. When the Labour Party decided to support the government of national union and to allow its senior members to be appointed to government posts, it was on the understanding that this would be not merely for the immediate task of winning the war but would also allow Labour ministers to implement measures that were in accord with Labour Party policy. In other words, it was expected that the party's entering into government would open up the possibility for significant measures of socialisation in domestic policy. A full realisation of such measures would admittedly have to wait until such time as there was a majority Labour government, but in the meantime it was hoped that participation in government would at least allow for some preliminary progress. Inevitably, many of these hopes – such as that the railways or the coal mines would be nationalised – were dashed and, when this happened, the Labour opposition was there to take its own leaders to task. This could be uncomfortable for both sides, and it was never entirely clear whether these leaders were culpable or whether they were themselves victims. Had the Labour ministers been lacking in drive and force, or had their drive and force been defeated by the entrenched Conservative majority? The nature of government meant that the answer to this question remained opaque, and the Labour opposition often had to tread warily in voicing its criticisms. Backbenchers were sometimes less inclined to be circumspect and the opposition frontbench had to rein them in out of consideration for the Labour ministers facing them, not to mention party unity. The subtleties of these manoeuvres were quite different from the tactics customarily employed by parliamentary oppositions.

One example of these tensions related to a decision by the government in July 1942 to raise the scale rate of old age pensions by 2s 6d. The PLP Administrative Committee thought this to be insufficient, urged that the raise be doubled, and decided to move an amendment rejecting the government measures as inadequate in the absence of any specific measures to be introduced in the next session. Ernest Bevin responded for the government by saying that this was an interim measure pending the publication of the Beveridge Report, and gave an equivocal assurance that further aspects would be dealt with in the next session. Greenwood attempted to conciliate between the Labour ministers in front of him and the Labour backbenches behind him, and agreed to withdraw the amendment on the basis of Bevin's assurance. But he was repudiated by the backbenchers who engaged in angry exchanges with Bevin, and who insisted on pressing the amendment to a division. Sixty-three members voted against the government, forty-nine of them Labour MPs, the largest adverse vote against the government since it was formed in 1940.[6] It was but one example of the difficulties faced by a Labour Party that was both in government and in opposition at the same time.

A more serious rebellion occurred over the government's response to the Beveridge Report in December 1942. The report had been commissioned by Greenwood in his previous incarnation as the government minister responsible for post-war reconstruction. It was intended to provide a body of non-partisan and technical recommendations for a unified and integrated state system of social security. On its publication, it had been widely discussed and warmly received by the public at large. The response of the government was more equivocal: 'the Conservatives wanted caution; Labour demanded commitment'.[7] The compromise reached was expressed in the minutes of the relevant meeting of the War Cabinet in February 1943: 'the Government should not be committed to introducing legislation for the reform of the social services during the war; but equally, there should be no negative commitment debarring the Government from introducing such legislation during the lifetime of the present Parliament'.[8] Inevitably, such an ambivalent formula was capable of being given a more cautious and negative gloss as well as a more committed and positive one. In the debate on the report in the House of Commons on 16–18 February 1943, it was unfortunate for the Labour Party that the government spokesmen Sir John Anderson and Sir Kingsley Wood tended towards the former rendition. This provoked Labour backbenchers into a hostile response. Although Herbert Morrison wound up the debate for government, accentuating the positive, even he failed to retrieve the situation. Jim Griffiths moved an amendment expressing dissatisfaction with the government's policy over Beveridge and urging a reconsideration. Even the opposition frontbench, including Greenwood, was stung into supporting the amendment. The result was even worse for the government than the pensions vote had been in the previous year, with 119 votes cast against the government. Of these, ninety-seven were cast by Labour members, which was virtually all of the PLP outside the government. This was a cause of some embarrassment to Labour ministers inside the government, with Attlee observing that their position 'was very adversely affected by Parliamentary situations such as that of the previous week'.[9]

As well as holding the government to account, the party also had the task of formulating policy for a prospective government. With the party's divided state – part in government and part in opposition – the process of policy formation essentially travelled along two parallel but closely proximate tracks. Labour's participation in the wartime government had been on the understanding that the government would make adequate preparations for a qualitatively different post-war settlement. From the outset, therefore, there was a War Cabinet Committee on Reconstruction Problems, chaired by Greenwood, which, we have seen, was instrumental in commissioning the Beveridge Report. But neither Greenwood nor his successor William Jowitt were able to make much headway with post-war planning inside the government until the publication of the Beveridge Report brought things to a head. At this point, Attlee, Bevin and Morrison began to agitate within the War Cabinet for a more determined approach to reconstruction. When they were met with resistance from Churchill and Sir Kingsley Wood, they had to warn 'that the Coalition might be threatened. There was, after all, no point in Labour members staying in the Coalition if they could not partially fulfil the promise made in May 1940.'[10] Finally, in November 1943, Churchill established a Ministry of Reconstruction under the leadership of Lord Woolton, which gave new impetus to post-war planning. There was agreement on the objectives of a social security system and a national health service, and the Education Act of 1944 (in which Chuter Ede was centrally involved) and Family Allowances Act of 1945 were tangible steps forward, even if they fell short of the Labour ideal. In the economic sphere, there was also a White Paper on full employment and the Distribution of Industry Act of 1945. The latter was a significant achievement in post-war development area policy, and Hugh Dalton boasted that 'I got away with a good deal more Socialism in the Act than I ever expected'.[11] Nonetheless, advances in the economic sphere were limited because, as Stephen Brooke points out, there was much less consensus in the coalition on economic reconstruction than on social reform.[12]

Meanwhile, the Labour Party outside government was well aware that the formation of a post-war policy agenda was an urgent priority. In July 1941, the party established a new Central Committee on Problems of Post-war Reconstruction – chaired by Manny Shinwell and with Harold Laski as secretary – which coordinated a number of more specialised sub-committees. Laski was commissioned to draft a general statement of post-war reconstruction policy and produced 'The Old World and the New Society', which was approved by the NEC in February 1942. It insisted that 'the anarchy of private competition must give way to ordered planning under national control'. Thus, the party urged that 'the nation must own and operate the essential instruments of production; their power over our lives is too great for them to be left in private hands … common ownership will alone secure that priority of national over private need which assures the community the power over its economic future'.[13] This was very much a reiteration of the policy lines that had been laid down during Labour's time in opposition in the 1930s, as we saw in the last chapter. The document dealt with general principles rather than particular details; as Brooke notes, it served 'as a rhetorical framework on which to hang more specific policy'.[14] Such policy detail was delegated to the relevant sub-committees: on education, health and social security as well as on economics.

How significant was this process of policy formation during the war? The evidence is somewhat mixed. This is partly because of the substantial progress in policy formation that had already been made in the 1930s, which meant that the party was hardly starting from a *tabula rasa*. As we noted in the last chapter, there was considerable continuity between the policy document 'The Immediate Programme' (1937) and the post-war manifesto 'Let Us Face the Future' (1945). Nonetheless, the experience of war had sharpened the party's sense of what was possible and the means of achieving it. The war had seen socialist tools of 'planning' and 'controls' being put to effective use, to an extent not previously seen, even if they were not directed towards explicitly socialist goals. This experience emboldened the party's policy planners with a sense of what might be possible. In his survey of the party's policy formation during the war in education, health and social security, Brooke detects a radicalising, rather than a toning-down, of the party's policy agenda. In health, for instance, he says that 'the radical element in Labour's health policy had … been strengthened by the war, rather than diluted'.[15] Although health may stand as the most obvious example, such radical strengthening may be detected in other areas too. If Labour's policy planners were emboldened by the wartime experience of seeing their tools of 'planning' and 'controls' in action, many of their social services policies were fleshed out in practical detail by the Beveridge Report of 1942. Although, of course, ostensibly a non-partisan document, it usefully provided a means by which the party's social security policies might be brought to fruition, and also filled in many actuarial details lacking in the party's own policy documents.[16]

Indeed, a lack of detail with regard to policy execution was perhaps one area in which the party's policy planning during the war fell short. From his vantage point as chair of the Central Committee on Post-war Reconstruction, Manny Shinwell could see that this was one of its failings. He later said that the transport sub-committee, to take just one example, 'considered public ownership but no detailed plans were framed because the various unions involved had to be consulted. The differences were evident: some wanted State ownership; some followed Morrison's idea of a public corporation. General lines of policy were debated but how the changes should be effected was hardly touched.'[17] Indeed, Shinwell himself was to suffer from such lack of detailed blueprints for the execution of policies when, as Minister of Fuel and Power in 1945, he found himself responsible for nationalising the coal mines. As he conceded to the party conference in 1946: 'we recognise our limitations and our shortcomings in the field of preparation'.[18] But the absence of such preparations did not in any way impede the implementation of policy; the coal mines were duly nationalised in the year that Shinwell made his confession to the party conference.

If the party's approach to policy formation during the war was not as detailed as it might have been, it was also not as diffuse as it had often been in the past. Crucially, the lack of detailed prescriptions in certain respects was not allowed to blunt the thrust of Labour's ambitions, nor did it compromise the execution of those ambitions when the party actually gained power. As we have seen, the experience of war had, if anything, radicalised the party's policy agenda, as expressed by the 'Let Us Face the Future' manifesto (1945). When the latter was endorsed by the electorate and the party entered into majority government, Labour implemented the extensive commitments of that manifesto with what Samuel Beer called a 'record of programmatic integrity': the nationalisation of the Bank of England (1946), Cable and Wireless (1946), coal (1946), civil aviation (1946), electricity (1947), inland transport (1948), gas (1948) and iron and steel (1949).[19] The Second World War, and Labour's participation in the wartime government, might potentially have compromised the momentum of the party's policy ambitions as developed in the 1930s; in reality, however, it seems only to have enhanced it.

4

'Fight, Fight and Fight Again' (1951–1964)

When Labour went into opposition following the general election of October 1951, it was notable for a number of reasons. For one thing, it was a very narrow defeat, not least because the party had actually won the popular vote, and few at the time can have expected that Labour's period of opposition would be very prolonged. But more significantly, it was the first time the Labour Party had experienced opposition following an extended period as a majority government, during which it had fulfilled a great many of its most prominent objectives. It now had to determine how to position itself, given that so much of its programme and agenda had been implemented (and given how much of it looked set to be accepted or tolerated by the incoming Conservative government).

This conundrum was to dominate the Labour Party's deliberations and conflicts throughout this period of opposition. It was encapsulated by the question splashed around liberally on headlines and editorial titles throughout this period: 'consolidate or advance?'[1] Had the Labour Party essentially fulfilled its reforming mission, such that its future role was to consolidate, preserve and protect the far-reaching changes to the economy and society it had implemented in 1945–51? Or should these reforms be conceived merely as the foundation for a much greater socialist revolution that was still to come? Inevitably, this question deeply divided the party. Although the question of how 'socialism' is to be defined was and is deeply contentious, for the left of the Labour Party in the 1950s, that question was answered by Clause IV of the party's constitution which, as we have seen, committed the party to the 'common ownership of the means of production, distribution and exchange'. Although Clause IV didn't specify the form that 'common ownership' should take, in practice it was understood in terms of nationalisation. In turn, this meant that socialism itself came to be identified – almost equated – with the nationalisation of all major industries. For others in the party, there seemed little point in further extensive nationalisation beyond that which had been achieved in 1945–51. There was a risk of alienating the wider electorate beyond the party, there was a danger of encroaching too much on the long-cherished British commitment to individual liberty, and in any case further nationalisation seemed irrelevant to the pursuit of the overriding socialist goal of equality.

This divide is worth formulating at the outset because it constituted the ever-present backdrop against which all of the party's activities and deliberations between 1951 and 1964 were played out. As a result, this period of opposition, under three markedly different party leaders (Clement Attlee, 1951–55; Hugh Gaitskell, 1955–63; Harold Wilson, 1963–64), was highly fractious. It might be tempting to conclude that this period was so long and sustained precisely because of the divided and fissiparous nature of the alternative government that was being offered to the electorate. As we shall see, however, such a conclusion would be too simplistic. But insofar as internal divisions plagued the Labour Party in opposition between 1951 and 1964, this could be attributed to differences over how the legacy of the previous Labour government was to be carried forward.

The Previous Labour Government: Mission Accomplished?

As we saw in the last chapter, the Labour Party in the 1930s had to determine in what way it would seek to implement socialism on entering into government. The party had effectively resolved on a 'mixed' economy which would leave the broad structures of a free-market capitalist economy intact, while superimposing upon it significant measures such as the nationalisation of major industries, the inauguration of a fully comprehensive 'welfare state', the flagship of which was a free National Health Service, and a system of progressive taxation, which would serve not only to fund these nationalisation and welfare measures, but would also reduce inequalities of income and quality of life. Within the parameters of the objectives the party had set itself, the record of that government was remarkably successful. Despite facing a severely challenging economic situation, the government had refused to compromise on its commitments to socialistic reform and had carried through an astonishing number of legislative measures in a remarkably short period of time.

Furthermore, these measures had in turn produced visible and tangible outcomes in terms of reducing poverty and inequality. This was confirmed by a study published in October 1951, *Poverty and the Welfare State*, written by B. Seebohm Rowntree and G.R. Lavers and based on a survey undertaken in the previous year in York.[2] It found that, whereas in 1936 one-third of the city's working-class population had been in poverty, in 1950 it was just one-fortieth. In an accompanying newspaper article, Lavers wrote: 'By far the greatest part of the improvement since 1936 has been due to the welfare legislation introduced since 1945 ... To a great extent, poverty has been overcome by the Welfare State.'[3] In his survey of the general election of 1951, David Butler noted that this report 'was eagerly seized on by the Labour Party as impartial and irrefutable evidence of their general thesis about the benefits of their rule, and it was often quoted by their speakers, particularly in answer to hecklers'.[4]

But this very success created problems. The Labour Party's political opponents showed no sign of wanting to challenge or undo most of these very considerable accomplishments. The Conservative Party made no commitments to dismantle the welfare state or (with the exception of steel) to privatise the nationalised industries, neither did they signal a more confrontational relationship with the trade unions. The way was therefore open for electors to vote Conservative without putting in jeopardy the popular accomplishments of the previous Labour government. Furthermore, insofar as the Labour government was associated in people's minds with the lingering post-war system of rationing, queues and restrictions, there was perhaps a sense that in voting Conservative, people could have the 'best of both worlds': the maintenance of the welfare state, but without the stifling bureaucracy of a socialist government. So successful had the Labour government been that it seemed to have inaugurated a new national consensus; but amid this new consensus, Labour's electoral advantage – as the promoter, initiator and defender of the welfare state – was now compromised. Furthermore, the previous government's very success in welfare reform raised the question of its future political role and mission: 'the very fact of a widespread perception that poverty was a thing of the past implied that a central part of Labour's historic mission had been completed'.[5]

The question of Labour's future policy agenda therefore became an urgent one. For the left of the party, it was an easy question to answer. For them, Labour's historic mission was far from having been completed. They cast the achievements of the previous Labour government not as a great accomplishment but merely as the necessary preliminary laying of the foundations. Much had been done, but there was still much to do. Too much of the economy remained in private hands, and further nationalisation was seen as a political imperative. More was still to be done in the extension of the free provision of social services. Inequality and poverty had been reduced but not eradicated. Even the already nationalised industries had not moved sufficiently in the direction of democratisation and workers' participation in management. Aneurin Bevan developed an eloquent defence of these principles and policies in his book *In Place of Fear* (1952), and, although some expressed disappointment with the quality of the book's content, both the author and the book became rallying symbols for the left of the party.

The question of Labour's future policy agenda was a trickier one for those on the right of the party. The principle of 'consolidation' hardly translated into an inspiring clarion call. The challenge was, however, confronted head on by the young party intellectual, Tony Crosland, who in an essay entitled 'The Transition from Capitalism' in the *New Fabian Essays* (1952), and then at greater length in what became the landmark *The Future of Socialism* (1956), developed his own answer to this conundrum. For Crosland, specifically economic measures, such as nationalisation, taxation and the extension of free social services, had probably delivered as much as they could without transitioning to a fully-planned Soviet-style economy. And yet the socialist ideal of equality, of a classless egalitarianism, was still far from being achieved. To address this, Crosland looked away from economic measures to cultural and political ones, such as policies to reduce inequalities of wealth (as opposed to income), to move to a fully classless and egalitarian education system, and to implement democracy and participation in the workplace. Crosland also, therefore, wanted to recast the achievement of the previous Labour government as a 'laying of the foundations'. But rather than advocating more of the same, Labour now had to use qualitatively different tools – cultural rather than narrowly economic – to advance to the next stage of socialist achievement.

The publication of Bevan's and Crosland's books clearly demarcated the internal party differences and drew up the battle lines. But the divisions periodically exploded into open and public warfare, such as at the party's annual conferences, particularly those held in Morecambe in 1952 and in Scarborough in 1960. Labour's previous successful period of government had bequeathed to the party two problematic inheritances in opposition: first, a lack of a sense of direction arising out of that very success; and second, a deep and bitter internal division as to how to address this lack of direction. This combination of an uncertain direction and bitter division was not an auspicious one for a party seeking to move from opposition into government. These factors in themselves might seem sufficient to explain the party's thirteen years in opposition, as the electorate turned away from a party divided over its direction. But would such a conclusion be borne out by an examination of Labour's relationship with the electorate during this period? An analysis of the electoral statistics suggests that other factors were in play and were perhaps more significant.

Labour and the Electorate: Reluctant Supporters?

As the Labour Party moved from defeat in 1951 to victory in 1964, we find some surprising electoral data.[6] In October 1951, Labour won 48.8 per cent of the popular vote; in October 1964, it won 44.1 per cent. In other words, as the party moved from defeat to victory, we see Labour's vote actually going *down* in this period in absolute terms in each election. Its share of the vote gradually decreased throughout this period, before recovering slightly in 1964. In other words, when Labour won in 1964, it did so with fewer votes and with a smaller share of the vote than when it had lost in 1951. As far as other variables are concerned, turnout remained relatively stable, ranging from a high of 82.6 per cent in 1951 to a low (albeit still relatively strong) of 76.8 per cent in 1955. Other factors affecting the distribution of seats in the House of Commons include the performance of the Liberal Party, the major third party throughout this period, and the distribution of Labour's support, that is to say, the extent to which it was concentrated in particular areas or was more widely dispersed.

As far as the Liberal Party was concerned, its performance was in inverse proportion to that of the Labour Party during this period, with its share of the vote increasing from 2.5 per cent in 1951 to 11.2 per cent in 1964. Variations in the Liberal vote played a decisive role both in Labour losing the election in 1951 and in its win in 1964. In 1951, the average swing from Labour to Conservative was 1.1 per cent, but, as David Butler pointed out, the 'swing tended to be greater in those constituencies where the Liberals fought in 1950 but not in 1951'.[7] There were fewer Liberal candidates in 1951, such that Liberal voters either abstained or voted for one of the two major parties. Where they did the latter, it seems that a great number of them voted Conservative. Butler estimates that they divided about six-to-four in favour of the Conservatives, which would be sufficient to account for eight of the twenty-one seats which the Conservatives won from Labour. On a seven-to-three assumption, it would account for eighteen of the twenty-one seat changes.[8] If this is so, it would support the contention that, although Labour lost the election, there is little evidence that voters were converted *from* Labour convictions.[9] It therefore seems unlikely that in 1951 voters were put off by a sense that Labour had 'run out of steam' or by party divisions and infighting.

The general election of 1955, which Labour fought under the continuing leadership of Clement Attlee, was an unusual one. Witness after witness – of all political parties – described it as quiet, lacking in interest or enthusiasm, apathetic, with an absence of any great or clear issue.[10] A few weeks before the election, Dick Crossman noted in his diary on 3 May that the Conservatives' 'best way to win is to have a quiet election and a low poll'.[11] This was effectively what they got. The turnout, at 76.8 per cent, was considerably lower than in 1951 (though still relatively strong, especially compared with pre-war levels). This low turnout was reflected in the fact that both the Conservative and the Labour votes decreased, although the latter decreased considerably more than the former. This led some to suggest that Labour's poor performance was produced not so much by vote switches from Labour to Conservative as by Labour voters abstaining. This theory was propagated, for example, by Harold Wilson.[12] Such an interpretation has been questioned by David Butler, however, who pointed out that 'if this was indeed the case, then the greater the drop in turnout, the greater should the swing to the Conservatives have been. But in practice there was not much sign of this. The extent of the swing seems to have been relatively little correlated to the fall in turnout. It appears that abstention was relatively partisan.'[13] The primary explanation for Labour's poor performance was likely to have been, as Hugh Gaitskell suggested, the general satisfaction with the rising level of prosperity and a disinclination for any significant change, and only secondarily because of an inefficient electoral machine and an insufficiently attractive policy offering.[14] The party could certainly improve its electoral machine and reconsider its policy offering (which it did, as we shall see below), but the ultimate reason for its defeat in 1955 was thought by many to lie in external factors beyond its control.

If Gaitskell's analysis was right, Labour's prospects at the next election, which turned out to be in 1959, appeared to be brighter. The prosperity that had been so appreciated in 1955 seemed to have slowed considerably between 1955 and 1958, and the Gallup opinion poll showed Labour well ahead with an exceptional 12 point lead in the summer of 1957; it fell back after the London bus strike in the summer of 1958, but recovered and held until early 1959.[15] Furthermore, the party had given considerable attention to its organisational infrastructure and policy offering (as we shall see below) and had adopted a much more professional approach to presentation and public relations, especially on television. When the election was called in September 1959, Labour therefore had every reason for optimism.

These hopes, however, were soon to be dashed, and key to this change in the party's fortunes was once again a return of a sense of prosperity in the year before the election: 'After three years of stagnation the index of production once more began to rise … By 1959 there was a general atmosphere of well-being, for which the government did not hesitate to take credit.'[16] Much was made, on all sides, of the error Gaitskell made in denying that Labour would increase income tax, which sat ill at ease with the party's spending commitments. Gaitskell insisted the increased spending would be met by increased productivity, but the incongruous nature of the commitment left a bad impression. Whether this incident was of decisive importance is doubtful; the polls had in any case already begun to move against Labour, after a brief narrowing of the gap. When polls closed, a Conservative majority of 100 was predicted, which turned out to be accurate. The Conservative vote increased, although their share of the vote was slightly down at 49.4 per cent. Labour's vote decreased, as did its share of the vote to 43.8 per cent.

This was a bitter blow to the Labour Party, and particularly to its leader Hugh Gaitskell. It was difficult to avoid the conclusion that while the party's electoral campaigns since 1951 had been getting ever better, its vote was getting ever worse. This led to some considerable soul-searching both within and beyond the party. Some began to suspect that the 1950s had witnessed deep-seated demographic shifts in the electorate that were unfavourable to the Labour Party. A survey conducted by Mark Abrams suggested that the party's class appeal was being undermined because the working class itself had 'emerged from its earlier unhappy plight' and many of the young were crossing into the middle class: 'the ethos of class solidarity is beginning to crumble in the face of the new fluidity of our society, the new opportunities for advancement through individual effort'. Furthermore, 'the experience of public ownership has been insufficiently successful or inspiring to arouse a desire for more. On the contrary, the majority of people seem positively to dislike the idea of further experiments in this direction.'[17]

The general election result and findings such as these stung Gaitskell into a much more confrontational style of leadership as he sought to reform the party's image and policies accordingly. The most high-profile of these reforms was his ill-judged attempt to drop Clause IV from the party's constitution. Not only did this reignite the internal party warfare that had been successfully contained in the late 1950s, it also resulted in a defeat for Gaitskell himself, as he finally had to accept the inevitable and withdraw his attempts to strike Clause IV down. Furthermore, as we shall see below, there were no significant changes to the party's policy offering. A great deal of acrimony had been unleashed and party divisions exposed to no obvious advantage.

Nonetheless, the next general election, in October 1964, produced the elusive and much longed-for swing towards Labour – a very small one, but enough to secure a Labour victory. Curiously, however, in 1964, by which time the party had a new leader in Harold Wilson, it achieved this victory with fewer votes than in 1959, and with only a small increase in its share of the vote. Again, in 1964, as in 1951, the role of the Liberal Party and its voters was a decisive one, albeit this time producing the opposite outcome.[18] The Conservative share of the vote fell considerably, from 49.4 per cent in 1959 to 43.4 per cent in 1964, and a great many of these Conservative defectors voted instead for the *Liberal* Party. But even so, this was of indirect benefit to Labour, because defections on this scale were sufficient to undermine Conservative majorities in particular constituencies, thereby producing Labour victories in those seats. To take just two examples – Bury and Radcliffe in Lancashire, and Carlisle – the fall in the Conservative vote almost exactly corresponded to the increase in the Liberal vote (in both seats, there had been no Liberal candidate in 1959). There were enough instances of this trend to make a decisive difference to Labour's overall result in 1964, even without a significant increase in its vote share.

It seems that the general election of 1964 was not so much won by Labour as lost by the Conservatives, whose performance and image in the early years of the 1960s left much to be desired. As we have seen, there was some uncertainty as to whether Labour's electoral plight in the 1950s was primarily due to a failure of its own supporters to vote. But whatever the answer to this question, there was an increasing sense that the party's electoral machine and infrastructure was in need of urgent attention.

The Party's Electoral Infrastructure: Wilson to the Rescue

Already, before the 1955 election, dissatisfaction with the party's organisation and its structural leadership had been expressed. This had been directed primarily at Morgan Phillips, the General Secretary, and Len Williams, the National Agent, although admittedly, such discontent had been voiced predominantly by the left of the party. In the wake of the 1955 election defeat, the press had predicted Phillips' dismissal.[19] Instead, Harold Wilson stepped in to propose to the National Executive a committee to study the party structure and organisation, and to report to conference. In spite of some resistance from the right (who were suspicious of Wilson's intentions), the Executive agreed, and appointed Wilson himself along with Jack Cooper, Peggy Herbison and Arthur Skeffington to the committee. Wilson was elected chairman and the report, when published, became informally known as 'The Wilson Report'.

From July to September 1955, Wilson convened some 145 meetings all over the country in what has been described as 'the most systematic study of local organization ever conducted in the Labour Party'.[20] The findings revealed an infrastructure in a parlous state. Reflecting on the report some thirty years later, Wilson recalled that:

> Some of the safest seats had some of the smallest individual memberships, majorities of well over 20,000 with membership of 300 or 400. There was reason to think, not only that some of the recorded members had long been dead and buried, but that the returns were inflated in other ways. The reason, I knew, was that in safe Labour seats new, and possibly active, members were resented.[21]

This situation generated additional negative side-effects. Safe seats had failed to give support to neighbouring marginals, and the proportion of voters canvassed was wildly erratic, ranging from nil in four constituencies to 90 per cent or more in others. In some constituencies at the previous election, the only party workers consisted of the candidate and the agent. Individual membership had declined by 17 per cent in the two years since it had peaked at a million in 1952–53.

The Wilson Report made forty-one recommendations. In his discussion of it, R.T. McKenzie identified four which he considered to be of 'outstanding importance'.[22] First, the report recommended the setting up of a sub-committee to supervise the organisational work of the party, comprising both NEC members and party officials, which would take over much of the work hitherto performed by the General Secretary. McKenzie noted that this sub-committee would take on a role somewhat similar to that of the Party Chairman in the Conservative Party. Second, it proposed the establishment of a National Agency Service, which would recruit, train and deploy a number of new party agents, paid out of party funds, and concentrated in marginal seats. Third, it recommended a new basis for calculating local party contributions to national funds. In light of Wilson's comments above, it is clear that many safe seats had moribund parties with small memberships, which therefore made a minimal financial contribution to the national party. In future, contributions would be made on the basis of either the size of the local party membership or the size of the Labour vote in the constituency, whichever yielded the bigger return. Fourth, the report recommended ending the practice whereby prospective parliamentary candidates were expected to make financial contributions to constituency party finances.[23] In addition to these four, Pimlott identifies another recommendation that was particularly pertinent for the party's future electoral success, namely, that less time should be wasted on converting non-supporters, and more time spent on bringing to the polling booth those who were already converted. Clearly, canvassing was thought to be critical to Labour success, and the party machine, especially at the local level, had to be reoriented in recognition of this.

The Wilson Report was comprehensive and wide-ranging. But how significant was it and did it go far enough? McKenzie, who had recently published his study *British Political Parties* (1955), was well placed to compare the recommendations of the review with similar recent attempts at reform in the Conservative Party, especially after their defeat in 1945. First, he makes the point that the remit of the Wilson Committee was restricted to the party's electoral machinery, whereas the Maxwell-Fyfe Committee, set up by the Conservatives in 1948, had a much wider remit, extending to party finance, the constitution of the National Union (the party in the country) and its relationship to the parliamentary party. For McKenzie, this restriction was a missed opportunity for Labour, not least because inconsistencies and lack of clarity regarding the relationship of the wider party, and particularly its conference, to Labour governments had contributed to the demoralisation of party workers which was portrayed in the Wilson Report.[24] Furthermore, in each of the four key recommendations identified by McKenzie, he compared the situation with that in the Conservative Party. In each case, he argued, the recommendations of the Wilson Report would allow the Labour Party to go some way towards catching up with the Conservatives, but without going far enough to bring them to parity.[25] H.J. Hanham made a similar point when he said that: 'There is as yet no Labour Lord Woolton [Conservative Party Chairman] to impart that sense of common purpose in organization, which the Labour Party so badly needs, and which alone could enable the Wilson report to achieve for the Labour Party what the Maxwell-Fyfe report of 1948–49 did for the Conservatives.'[26]

But even if McKenzie and Hanham were right that the Wilson Committee's remit was too restrictive and its recommendations too timid, to what extent was it effectively implemented? Even the answer to this more constrained question is mixed. As Pimlott points out, changes were certainly made, the organisation sub-committee did indeed become a permanent body, the provision of agents was enhanced, and the financing of marginal constituencies improved considerably. But 'the agency service remained underpaid and poorly trained, and there was no radical transformation in the running of the Party, which remained as shambolic as ever at the time of the next election in 1959'.[27] And even though the number of full-time agents had been increased, the party still had only half as many as the Conservatives.[28] The glacial pace of reform is also indicated by the fact that the much criticised Morgan Phillips remained as General Secretary until he was struck down by illness in 1960, at which point he was replaced by the equally criticised National Agent, Len Williams, until he, in turn, was enticed away to become Governor-General of Mauritius in 1968. Furthermore, as Pimlott notes, after Wilson himself became party leader in 1963, he made no further attempt to modernise party organisation.[29] Thus, although Labour undoubtedly made some significant progress in revitalising the party organisation and electoral infrastructure, it nonetheless fell far short of what was actually needed.

Relations with the Trade Unions: Wooing Frank Cousins

In the dying days of the Labour government of 1950–51, there seemed to be a crisis of leadership and an emerging vacuum. Attlee apart, most of the other front-rank figures were in eclipse, either suffering from ill health or manifestly past their peak. In stark contrast, the trade unions and their leaders held a position of 'consolidated strength' within the Labour movement: 'full employment, high trade union membership, and the important role they had played in the wartime and postwar economy had made [them] ... the predominant power group within the Labour Movement'.[30] The key leaders were Arthur Deakin of the Transport and General Workers, Will Lawther of the Miners and Tom Williamson of the Municipal Workers. These three were augmented by Sam Watson, leader of the Durham miners and a member of the National Executive.

Politically, all four of these leaders were on the right-wing of the party. Some, like Watson, wore his political ideology lightly; he formed a close relationship with Attlee and, unusually, was friendly both with Bevan on the left and Gaitskell on the right. In contrast, Deakin was unashamedly partisan. After Labour went into opposition in 1951, he emerged as the self-appointed hammer of the Bevanites in general and of Bevan himself in particular, even at one point going so far as to agitate for Bevan's expulsion from the party. Indeed, he clashed with left-wingers not only in the party but also in his own union, where his policy of using union bargaining power with restraint in the post-war years had led to skirmishes with the left who wanted the union to take a more confrontational approach. In the unofficial Liverpool dock strike of February 1951, this enmity reached new heights, with the strikers accusing Deakin of 'selling out' and Deakin denouncing the strike leaders as 'saboteurs'. As this suggests, the conflictual fault lines were less between the party and the unions and more between the union leadership and some of its rank and file (and also between the union leadership and the party left-wing). Indeed, the party leadership often took refuge in the union block votes at party conferences to protect them from the left-wing demands of local party delegates. It was thus less a case of the party seeking to 'manage' its relations with the unions, and more of the party leadership relying on union leadership to 'manage' its relations with the party.

In May 1955, shortly before he was due to retire, Deakin died suddenly while addressing a May Day rally in Leicester. He was succeeded by Jock Tiffin, who himself became seriously ill and died just six months after succeeding Deakin. When he, in turn, was replaced by Frank Cousins, this represented a significant sea change. Cousins broke the mould of recent trade union leadership in that he was unequivocally on the left of the party and was willing to use his newfound position of power to promote the causes in which he believed, many of them lying outside the traditional domain of trade union politics. Cousins's succession to the leadership of the TGWU coincided with Gaitskell's succession to the leadership of the party, thus creating the unusual spectacle of a left-wing union leadership and a right-wing parliamentary leadership. Perhaps inevitably, these two determined and contrasting characters were set on a collision course.

Initially, Cousins kept his peace in the interests of party unity. But by 1958, he was ready to break out into the open, saying that 'I have never believed that the most important thing in our lives is to elect a Labour Government. The most important thing is to elect a Labour Government that is determined to carry out Socialist policy.'[31] Cousins engaged in some initial skirmishes before the general election of 1959; the TGWU conference held in July, three months before the election, unanimously rejected the party policy document 'Industry and Society', calling for full-scale nationalisation policies instead. But the real challenge came afterwards.

Cousins was a passionate advocate of nuclear disarmament. The party policy in 1959 had been one of multilateral disarmament that was finely balanced between anti-nuclear ideals and *realpolitik*. The party would seek to end the nuclear arms race, would end nuclear tests, and advocated a disarmament treaty and a 'non-nuclear club' of nations, which Britain would join. On the other hand, it would defend Britain's military alliances, and would remain in a nuclear-armed NATO as long as Russia had the bomb. With the election over, Cousins saw his chance to challenge this policy. Indeed, wider public opinion was turning his way as there was an increasing public anxiety about nuclear weapons in general. The Campaign for Nuclear Disarmament (CND) became more widely subscribed and support for unilateralism grew, not only in the trade unions but also within the party itself. The ultimate clash came at the Scarborough conference in 1960, where Cousins sought to defeat the official multilateralist defence policy.

More was at stake in this battle than the issue of defence alone. For one thing, it exposed the inconsistency of the party's understanding of the relationship between conference and a potential Labour government. As we have seen, R.T. McKenzie had criticised the Wilson Report for failing to grasp this nettle, which seemed to imply that conference would determine government policy, and that a Labour Cabinet would ultimately be answerable to conference. (As we saw in the last chapter, a conference resolution to this effect had been passed in 1933, but was quietly ignored after 1945.) The illogicality of this position could also be quietly ignored so long as the trade union leadership used their block votes at conference to support the party leadership. But when the two diverged, the question of the relationship between conference (with its trade union block votes) and the Labour leadership once again took on a new urgency. The conference clash culminated with Gaitskell delivering a tense and provocative speech in which he rejected Cousins's unilateralist demands and said that he and others would 'fight, fight and fight again' to save the party they loved. The result, however, was a defeat for the party leadership. It was reversed at the party conference the following year, after some minor concessions to the left, but the whole episode gave a damaging impression of the trade union leadership being at loggerheads with the party leadership.

When Wilson became leader in 1963, he was determined to avoid any such showdowns. Indeed, he had challenged Gaitskell for the leadership in 1960 under the banner of 'unity'. Furthermore, he was acutely aware, as noted above, that Labour's lead in the polls had fallen back in the wake of the failed London bus strike in the summer of 1958. This was something he was determined not to see repeated: 'in the run-up to the election, a disruptive series of strikes was the one thing, above all, that he wished to avoid. In addition, he wanted to demonstrate – by the cordiality of the Party-union relationship before the poll – how well a Labour government would manage its industrial relations.'[32] To this end, Wilson was determined to secure the support and cooperation of Cousins; he was at least better placed to achieve this than was Gaitskell, given that Wilson and Cousins came from the same wing of the party and had a better personal relationship. His chosen means of doing so was to ensure Cousins's participation in a future Labour government. The precedent was Cousins's predecessor as TGWU General Secretary Ernest Bevin's membership of the Labour Cabinet from 1945 to 1951; the pretext was a need for left-wing support in what was predominantly a right-wing Shadow Cabinet. Cousins was initially cautious when Wilson raised the idea and suggested the ministries of Labour, Trade or Transport. But, after detailed talks in the Scilly Isles in the summer of 1964, he eventually agreed.[33] The settlement seemed to pay rapid dividends: there was 'a panegyric on Harold Wilson in the TGWU *Record*, and the union gave Labour's election fund an extra £25,000. A dock dispute two weeks before polling day showed how prudent Wilson's wooing of Cousins had been: the union leader did his utmost to prevent the escalation of what might have been a politically disastrous strike.'[34] Labour thus entered the general election of 1964 enjoying more harmonious relations with the unions than it had had for some time. Following victory, the TGWU leader entered government as the new Minister of Technology.

Holding the Government to Account: Suez, the EEC and Profumo

If a central role of the opposition is to hold the government of the day to account, this was in many ways peculiarly difficult for the Labour Party in their initial period of opposition from 1951 to 1955. As we have observed, the Conservative government was careful to do nothing to upset the new post-war welfare consensus and was punctilious in cultivating good working relations with the trade unions. It was therefore difficult for the Labour opposition to gain much leverage in attacking the government on domestic policies. The *Economist*, in one of its lighter moods, invented a composite Chancellor figure, 'Mr Butskell', when the moderate Labour Chancellor, Hugh Gaitskell, was succeeded by a moderate Conservative Chancellor, Rab Butler, in October 1951. The 'Butskell' moniker gained considerable currency, especially among partisans in both parties who were suspicious of such apparent economic consensus.[35]

In contrast to domestic affairs, foreign policy provided a major issue, indeed a world crisis, around which the Labour opposition could unite and unequivocally hold the government of the day to account. This was, of course, the Anglo-French and Israeli invasion of the Suez Canal, following the Egyptian President Nasser's nationalising of the canal in July 1956.[36] At first, there was some uncertainly as to what Labour's stance would be. In August, Gaitskell (and, indeed, Bevan) made speeches condemning Nasser's unilateral action, leading some to believe (including, at first, the prime minister, Anthony Eden) that there might be a bipartisan approach to the problem. But when it became clear that the government was contemplating an attack on Egypt, without UN approval, and in defiance of the USA and the Commonwealth, Gaitskell and the party were unequivocally opposed. Labour's stance was to be the source of some controversy. There were many Conservatives who interpreted Gaitskell's August speech as indicating that he would be supportive of resolute government action against Nasser. But, they held, he then treacherously embarked upon a 'political summersault' for cynical political reasons, and under pressure from the left of the party. There is no evidence of this, however; although the tone of Gaitskell's speech was belligerent, it nonetheless contained a warning against military action attached as a coda. It was perhaps unwise that the condemnation was delivered *forte*, while the coda was rendered *piano*. But there was no change of line. Labour's condemnation of the government became louder as the extent of the government's folly became increasingly clear.

Labour's stance on Suez was principled and, in hindsight, may be thought to have been vindicated by history. But it did not bring the party any political advantage at the time: 'in the country as a whole, opinion polls demonstrated support for government policy, especially after troops had been committed, and even after the humiliating withdrawal'.[37] For those of this view, Labour and Gaitskell were guilty twice over: first, for not supporting international action that was deemed necessary to protect Britain's interests; and second, for not supporting such a policy while British troops were being actively deployed. This gave rise to charges of a lack of patriotism and, at worst, treachery, which had a lasting effect both on Labour's performance in the polls and on Gaitskell's personal reputation. Philip Williams observes that 'a Gallup poll on 14 November showed both the rallying to Eden, and Labour's loss of its six-point lead … politicians on both sides thought that three years later the memory of Suez brought more votes to the Conservatives than to Labour'.[38] The episode revealed the electoral perils for an opposition party of giving an impression of a lack of patriotism or national loyalty, especially in a time of international crisis.

Another foreign policy issue on which the opposition held the government to account was Britain's failed attempt to enter the EEC in 1962–63. On the issue itself, the Labour Party was divided. There were committed partisans on both sides of the debate, as well as a broad swathe in the middle who were either open to persuasion or content to follow the leadership. As a matter of principle, Gaitskell himself was neither for nor against entry. On the political and economic merits of the case, he considered the arguments very finely balanced. In this context, therefore, the specific conditions under which Britain might enter the EEC took on a heightened significance. If they were favourable, this would constitute a decisive reason for entry; if unfavourable, they would equally constitute a decisive reason for staying out. At first, government and opposition were fairly close. When the government launched its application to join in July 1961, it set out three conditions: protections for British agriculture; safeguards for Commonwealth interests; and provisions for the EFTA countries. To these, Labour added two further conditions: the retention of an independent foreign policy; and the protection of economic and social planning. But, 'in reality, there was little in these additions that the Government disagreed with'.[39]

When the government published its White Paper in August 1962, it was quickly apparent that it had failed to achieve its own stated conditions. It had 'accepted French plans that denied overseas association to large parts of the Commonwealth, ruled out the "Morocco Agreements" and threatened to end the Commonwealth preferences by 1970'.[40] To onlookers in the Labour Party and beyond, it appeared that Britain had been forced to make major concessions, thereby failing to meet its own previously stated conditions, without being granted anything in return. For Gaitskell, this development was decisive, and signalled the end of Labour's 'wait and see' policy; there could now be no alternative but for Labour to oppose EEC entry on the proposed terms.

Gaitskell was not alone in moving in this direction: 'Prior to conference, 39 resolutions opposed EEC entry, only three approved, and the remainder were either undecided or waited to follow the leadership line. Amongst Labour's elite, the TUC General Council remained uncommitted, the Shadow Cabinet was dominated by anti-Marketeers, and the PLP had moved firmly against entry.'[41] The NEC therefore prepared a policy statement, which declared Labour to be opposed to entry on the proposed terms, and which was to be presented for approval to conference in October 1962. To accommodate pro-Marketeers, the document left open the possibility of membership on the basis of new and better conditions at a later stage. But as is well known, Gaitskell's conference speech in support of the document went considerably beyond the document itself in the emotion and tone of its anti-EEC rhetoric, causing consternation among pro-Marketeers. The whole debate was rendered otiose, however, by President de Gaulle's veto of the British application in January 1963.

If Labour's stance on Suez brought opprobrium on the party for perceived national disloyalty and even treachery, its stance on the EEC had the opposite effect. Labour could now be portrayed as the party defending the nation state and its 'thousand years of history', as Gaitskell put it in both a broadcast and his conference speech, over against a government pursuing a policy that could turn Britain, as he also said, into a Texas or California of a United States of Europe. This brought approval not only from floating voters, but also from some anti-Market Conservatives.[42] The party's holding the government to account over EEC entry carried the additional advantage, for some onlookers, of atoning for its sins of national disloyalty over Suez.

In contrast to Suez and the EEC application, the Labour opposition's next major opportunity to hold the government to account involved 'a scandal of puzzling triviality'.[43] This was, of course, the infamous Profumo affair of 1963, widely regarded as a staging post in the collapse of the Conservative government. The issue involved the revelation that a Cabinet minister, John Profumo, had had an affair with a model, Christine Keeler. While not in itself a cause for national scandal, there was a security aspect, in that Keeler was thought also to have had a relationship with a member of the Soviet Embassy (the security aspect was later dismissed), and Profumo had made matters worse by denying the affair to the House of Commons. For the Labour opposition, now led by Harold Wilson, following Hugh Gaitskell's death, the question of how to respond was particularly tricky. On the one hand, they could maintain a dignified silence, but could thereby miss a superb opportunity to strike a killer blow against an ailing government. On the other hand, if it looked too much as though they were cynically taking political advantage of a sleazy but ultimately insignificant scandal, there was a danger it could backfire and leave the opposition with dirt on its hands.

Here, Wilson's supreme tactical political skills came to the fore. He was acutely aware of the dangers on both sides, and careful to avoid any damage to Labour's reputation, while taking advantage of the supreme political opportunity presented by the scandal. Gleaning details of the affair from his security adviser, George Wigg, Wilson was scrupulous in passing on all received information direct to the prime minister himself. Harold Macmillan had finally, in Wilson, met his match as a practitioner of the dark arts of political opportunism, and was outwitted by the encounter. He made a number of false steps and walked into several traps. He first denied the need for any enquiry, and then conceded one. When Profumo's guilt (and misleading of Parliament) was made public, Macmillan appeared to lack control over his own government. The climax came with a debate in the House of Commons on 17 June. Once again, Wilson played his cards well, with Dick Crossman recording in his diary that 'Harold made an absolutely magnificent speech … It was really annihilating, a classical prosecution speech, with weight and self-control.'[44] Although objectively a relatively minor affair, the Profumo scandal was one from which Macmillan never quite recovered his authority. Wilson had handled the affair so deftly that the Labour opposition was well-placed to benefit from the increasing disillusion with the Conservative government. It is impossible to say what part this played in Labour's winning the general election the following year. But Pimlott notes that 'the narrow margin of Labour's eventual victory … underlines the clear verdict on Wilson's handling of the Profumo affair: that it was a triumph of political opportunism'.[45]

Formation of Policy: Continuity Gives Way to Planning?

As we have seen, after three successive election defeats, many in the party argued that its policies needed to be reconsidered, changed or abandoned altogether. The conditions were ripe, it seemed, for a wholesale reorientation of Labour Party policy. But did this actually happen? A glance at the policy documents and manifestos produced between 1951 and 1964 reveals rather more continuity than radical change or even gradual evolution. Given the high-profile public debates around nuclear disarmament and Clause IV, one would perhaps have expected more radical policy change than there was. As far as nationalisation was concerned, heated though the debates were, it seems that the policy agenda had been settled in the last years of the 1950–51 Labour government and was not significantly changed thereafter. In the dying days of the last Labour government, left-wingers in Cabinet had successfully fought to prevent the nationalisation of steel from being dropped from its legislative programme.[46] This left-wing victory was preserved in the sense that the re-nationalisation of steel (one of the few industries de-nationalised by the Conservatives) was retained in the manifestos of 1955, 1959 and 1964. But there was perhaps a more significant right-wing victory in the sense that there were no further significant nationalisation measures in any of those same manifestos. In 1955, 'Fabian caution exerted itself; not whole industries but sections of chemicals and machine tools would be nationalised, and the state would start new enterprises where necessary.'[47] In 1959, while there were once again commitments to nationalise steel, road haulage and water, this was accompanied by the unequivocal statement that 'we have no other plans for further nationalisation' (although a door was left open with regard to failing industries or those 'failing the nation').

In the wake of the defeat in 1959, attempts to 'modernise' the party coalesced around the issue of nationalisation and, as we have seen, resulted in Gaitskell's unsuccessful attempt to drop Clause IV from the party constitution. But these debates centred around image, presentation, ideals and long-term goals. They had little effect on the party's short-term policy programmes, because almost everyone was agreed on the short-term need for further nationalisation of a small number of specified industries. Beyond nationalisation, 'consolidation' seems to have prevailed in the policy documents and manifestos of the 1950s and early 1960s. There was a commitment to comprehensive education as early as 1955, there were pledges to reverse cuts to the health service and welfare state, and aspirations around house building. But for the most part, one searches in vain for any major innovative policy initiatives. There was a novel policy in 1959 for the state to invest in shares in the 500 leading big corporations, the idea being not to gain control of management, but to ensure that taxpayers would share in the capital gains from these firms. This was an interesting alternative to full-scale nationalisation, but it sat alongside rather than replaced the previously stated nationalisation plans. The idea was short-lived, for it had already disappeared by the time of the 'Signposts for the Sixties' policy document of 1961.

Perhaps the most significant policy initiative during these years was one that envisaged the inauguration of a new pension scheme. Dick Crossman chaired a working group of senior parliamentary colleagues, supplemented by academics from the London School of Economics, Richard Titmuss, Brian Abel-Smith and Peter Townsend. The scheme would be mandatory, contributory, and would deliver roughly half pay on retirement. The contributions would be relatively high but would ensure that pensioners would get their share of a growing national income. This, as Crossman observed, was the original and radical aspect of the plan, as 'an attempt to make sure that the old people get their share of the rise [in national income] automatically and are not merely jerked up out of the slough by political pressure every now and then'.[48] It was also radical in its financial implications as 'it enlarges the domain of State control of finance and poaches on the preserve of the insurance companies'.[49] Furthermore, as an ambitious, detailed and sophisticated policy, it was, as Crossman also noted, an example of what the Labour opposition could do in policy formation, but very seldom did.[50] There can be little doubt that the Crossman pension plan was the outstanding example of opposition policy formation in the 1951–64 period.

This broad continuity in policy also extended to defence, in spite of manifest appearances to the contrary. As we have noted above, the battle between multilateralists and unilateralists in the party reached ferocious heights in the clash between Frank Cousins and Hugh Gaitskell at the Scarborough party conference of 1960. But we saw that the defeat for the party leadership was ultimately reversed at the party conference in the following year. It seems that a great deal of heat and light had been expended simply in order to preserve a broad multilateralist continuity in the party's defence policy.

This policy continuity – not only in defence but more generally – might itself be thought to constitute a victory for the right over the left, given that the latter were constantly agitating for more radical and ambitious policies. Furthermore, a case may also be made that each manifesto moved incrementally further to the right between 1951 and 1964. In a recent article, Michael Jacobs and Andrew Hindmoor have utilised the Manifesto Project's 'Rile Scale' to demonstrate that this was indeed the case.[51] But they also qualify this in a crucial way. They point out that the Manifesto Project utilises a whole range of criteria to determine the ideological positioning of any particular party manifesto. But they argue that if one focuses more specifically on economic policy, a different picture emerges, and we can see that the 1964 manifesto was certainly not to the right of the preceding one in 1959: 'Labour's 1964 manifesto promised to introduce "socialist planning", proposing a new Ministry of Economic Affairs and Ministry of Technology, regional planning, a detailed Charter of Rights for all employees, stricter controls over monopolies and mergers, and a national incomes policy … None of this had appeared in the 1959 manifesto, in which economic policy was limited to a few imprecise paragraphs.'[52]

This leftward tack in economic policy is consistent with Jacobs and Hindmoor's general claim that Labour's economic policy moves right and emphasises a redistributive economic strategy when the economy is performing well, but moves left and advocates structural economic reform when the economy is performing poorly.[53] As they point out, by the early 1960s the economy was faltering, the balance of payments had moved further into the red, the economy fell into recession in

1961–62, and 'the 1964 general election was dominated by arguments about the poor performance of the UK economy'.[54] After a period of prosperity in the 1950s, therefore, when Labour policies moved incrementally to the right, there followed a period of economic decline, when Labour responded with more radical economic policies to the left of the preceding ones.

But Jacobs and Hindmoor also make a further argument, which is that in periods of economic decline or crisis, public opinion itself shifts so as to make it more receptive to these more radical policies. In other words, when Labour shifts to the left in periods of economic difficulty, this shift goes with – rather than against – the grain of public opinion. In support of this, in the specific context of 1964, they follow Wilson's biographer Ben Pimlott in saying that, 'by 1964, both political consensus and public sentiment in relation to economic policy had already shifted towards Labour's platform of planning and reform'.[55] If this is right, then it could go some way towards explaining Labour's victory – and the ending of its period in opposition – in October 1964.

Conclusion

When Labour went into opposition in 1951, few can have predicted that it would remain there for the next thirteen years. Many, both inside and outside the party, and both at the time and subsequently, have asked why it lasted so long. As we have seen, Labour did not squander its time in opposition. Its record was not perfect, but there is little evidence that its minor failings (or incomplete achievements) themselves accounted for Labour's defeats. Furthermore, most of the positive accomplishments had been achieved by 1959, and Labour's conduct of its election campaign that year was regarded by many as a model of its kind. And yet still the party lost.

There was little Labour could have done better, and little it could have done to avert defeat. Contentment at a time of economic prosperity, together with demographic changes that undermined tribal loyalty to the party amongst the young, meant that external conditions had determined the outcome of the election in 1959 (even more than in 1955), and there was little Labour could have done to change this. But helpless impotence is a difficult condition to accept, and the 1959 defeat galvanised various players into action. The right saw an opportunity to abandon what it considered dated policies (not least nationalisation), the leader was shocked into adopting a much more confrontational and aggressive leadership style, and the left was stung into a rearguard defensive action. None of this helped; many of the old divisions once again came out into the open, while the major arguments resulted in continuity rather than change; Clause IV was retained in the party constitution, and the multilateralist defence policy was perpetuated.

In retrospect, the right-wing of the party was mistaken in 1959 in thinking that electoral victory lay in a continuing rightward shift to the centre ground. As we have seen, the 1964 manifesto finally reversed this shift economically and resulted in victory. But the right was correct to point out that further large-scale nationalisation was not a vote winner, as polls had repeatedly showed. The failure of the left was to equate socialism almost exclusively with nationalisation. This was partially rectified by 1964, as the party adopted a bold and ambitious approach to economic planning that was not contingent on further large-scale nationalisation. Labour narrowly won the general election of 1964, but how much of this is attributable to its policies, electioneering and positive action is debatable. The sense of economic prosperity that formed the backdrop to the elections of 1955 and 1959 had started to crumble and there was a growing disillusionment with the Conservative government. There were sufficient defections from the Conservatives to other parties, and the Labour vote held sufficiently steady, to secure a Labour victory.

What the 1951–64 period of opposition shows, as perhaps do other periods, are the *limitations* on the capacity of an opposition to determine its destiny. The wider economic and political context and events beyond its control seem much more decisive in determining election outcomes than anything that an opposition party actively *does*. But this is no excuse for a Labour opposition to relapse into somnolence. When the economic and political winds begin to blow in its favour, an opposition needs also to prove itself worthy of the confidence of a sufficient number of new voters, as well as to galvanise the enthusiasm – so as to secure the turnout – of its own supporters. All of these factors finally coincided in October 1964, thus ending Labour's thirteen years in opposition.

5

Yesterday's Men (1970–1974)

On the eve of the 1970 general election, a clear victory for the Labour Party, which had governed since 1964, was widely regarded as a foregone conclusion. All but one of the last opinion surveys conducted before polling day (18 June) suggested a Labour lead, by margins of up to 12.4 percentage points. The bookmakers had either stopped taking bets or were quoting Labour at odds which were unlikely to attract working-class punters.[1] A newspaper printed in advance of the result devoted its inquest into the election campaign to an explanation of a third consecutive Conservative defeat.[2] The opposition's fabled 'men in grey suits' were preparing themselves for an awkward encounter with their leader, Edward Heath, whose position would be untenable if the verdict of the voters proved as bleak as expected. It looked as if Labour strategists had been justified in depicting Heath and his senior colleagues as 'yesterday's men' during the campaign; evidently they had not anticipated that one combative Tory frontbencher, Margaret Thatcher, might turn out to be tomorrow's woman.

The outcome of the election confounded the pundits and the pollsters. Compared to the previous (1966) contest, Labour's share of the vote fell from 48 to 43.1 per cent, and its tally of seats from 364 to 288. A year after the election, the BBC – to Labour's considerable irritation – screened a programme which turned the 'yesterday's men' jibe against Wilson and his team, now consigned to opposition. Fortunately for the commentators who had been explaining why Labour was bound to win, it proved relatively easy to rationalise the party's defeat. After all, Labour had trailed in the polls almost continuously since the 1966 general election, in which the four-seat majority it had secured in 1964 was increased to ninety-seven. For Wilson, the main task between the elections of 1964 and 1966 had been to convince the public that Labour would achieve its stated aims if only it enjoyed a secure parliamentary position. In truth, its ambitious objectives had been thwarted at the start of its six-year stint in office by the realisation that the economic situation bequeathed by the Conservatives was even less propitious than anticipated. Having presided over an unsustainable pre-election 'boom', the outgoing Conservative Chancellor Reginald Maudling handed over to his Labour successor James Callaghan with a cheerful quip: 'Sorry, old cock, to leave it in this shape.'[3]

It was a shame for Callaghan that in those days political etiquette meant something; otherwise he could have pre-empted the Liberal Democrat coalition minister David Laws who, in 2010, publicised a similar piece of good-natured banter for political advantage. Unlike the situation in 2010, in 1964 Britain's economic problems were directly attributable to the mismanagement of the outgoing government, heavily influenced by electoral considerations. As a result, Maudling and his colleagues had landed Labour with a looming crisis over the value of the pound sterling. Refusing to contemplate a repetition of the damaging 1949 devaluation of the currency until further resistance became futile (in 1967), the Wilson governments could never hope to live up to their leader's rhetoric about economic growth propelled by the white heat of technological innovation. The alarm bell was sounded by Wilson's first conference speech as prime minister, in which he complained bitterly about the situation his government had inherited. In 1961 he had derided politicians who appealed to 'the Dunkirk spirit' to help Britain through troubled times, insisting that 'It is the long haul, not the inspired spirit, that we need.' Three years later (before an audience which included the octogenarian Attlee) he expressed the hope that the 'spirit of Dunkirk will once again carry us through to success'.[4] Presumably (unlike Attlee and Wilson himself) many delegates were too young to remember that Dunkirk was an heroic retreat.

Roy Jenkins, who succeeded Callaghan at the Treasury in the aftermath of the 1967 devaluation, considered that the economy was too precarious by 1970 to allow gimmicky vote-winning give-aways. Initially, Jenkins was praised for his responsible approach; with hindsight (especially after 1981, when he defected to the Social Democratic Party), 'it became a settled part of Labour mythology to make him the scapegoat' for the 1970 electoral defeat.[5] Even on the supposition that a more generous budget could have won the election for Labour, the party (unlike

Maudling and his colleagues back in 1964) would have been left to clear up an economic mess of its own making.

With Jenkins again to the fore in his previous guise of Home Secretary (1965–7), the Labour government had condoned (and sometimes even encouraged) liberal legislation in the social sphere. However, its response to the wave of racist sentiment which swept through Britain in the late 1960s, exemplified and fostered by Enoch Powell's 1968 'Rivers of Blood' speech, had been insufficiently robust: limited laws to combat the most egregious discriminatory practices were not enough to balance the government's capitulation to 'Powellite' fears about a potential flood of Asians after their expulsion from Kenya. Dr David Owen, a young MP who admired Jenkins, could only persuade himself to vote for the restrictive 1968 Commonwealth Immigrants Bill with 'a heavy heart', on the grounds that it would be wrong to withhold support from a Labour government even when it was doing 'dirty work'. In his speech on the Bill, Owen contradicted explicit government reassurances and acknowledged that the measure was 'undoubtedly racial in nature'.[6] The motives behind the legislation cast an ironic light on the biblical quotation which Harold Wilson had included in his 1964 conference speech: 'He hath made of one blood all nations to dwell upon the earth.'[7]

Those who evaluate a government's foreign policy performance cannot overlook its initial stated ethical intentions, and in this respect Wilson's administration was woefully wanting. It failed to prevent Rhodesia's illegal declaration of independence in November 1965, and although it won praise on the left for avoiding overt British participation in America's war in Vietnam, it continued the Conservative policy of offering 'deniable' logistical support of various kinds as well as insisting that Britain's chief global ally was right to fight. Wilson's position owed much more to fear of backbench unrest than to a principled re-evaluation of the 'special relationship' with the United States; his reported comment that 'we can't kick our creditors in the balls' was difficult to reconcile with bombastic assertions of undiminished British global significance which left overseas observers unimpressed.[8] During the Nigerian civil war of 1967–70 – itself, like the plight of the Kenyan Asians, a tragic symptom of the problems Britain had hoped to leave behind after abandoning its Imperial role – the government deployed a combination of Cold War 'logic' and undisguised economic self-interest.[9] Television coverage of the humanitarian disaster inflicted by the British-backed central government on the secessionist region of Biafra provoked considerable public disquiet and the possibility of a Cabinet revolt until Biafran resistance crumbled and ministers were able to conclude that 'the best had probably been made of what was a thoroughly bad job'.[10] Little noticed at the time, perhaps the most demeaning contrast between Wilson's depiction of Labour as a 'moral crusade' and the unpleasant realities of international affairs was the government's deportation of the inhabitants of Diego Garcia, an island in the Indian Ocean, to make way for American military facilities.[11]

In a final provocation of its most active supporters, the Labour government had sought to amend the legal framework relating to trade unions. A 1969 White Paper – entitled *In Place of Strife* in a maladroit allusion to Nye Bevan's 1952 tract *In Place of Fear* – proposed new institutional machinery to promote workplace conciliation, and that ballots should be held in advance of industrial action. At best, to those who took seriously Labour's claim to represent working people, this could only look like a technocratic solution to the 'problem' which trade unions had allegedly become. At worst, it played into the narrative of economic liberals who had argued since the late 1950s that Britain's post-war economic woes were chiefly attributable to the privileged legal status of the unions. Having embarked on a legislative course which emboldened its ideological opponents and alienated its friends, the government was forced to shelve its proposals thanks to opposition within the unions and the parliamentary party (where a prominent obstructive role was played by Callaghan, who had been moved to the Home Office after his unhappy tenure of the Treasury).

David Marquand – who, like Owen, was a 'Jenkinsite' MP at the time – later referred to 'the atmosphere of shabby expediency which hung over the Government like a pall'; for the British left, 'It was an era of lost innocence, of hopes betrayed.'[12] Although apparently not intended as such, The Who's classic song *Won't Get Fooled Again* (recorded in March 1971) stands as an epitaph for the idealism which had helped Labour back into office. While well-informed observers could attribute the 1970 defeat to unpromising economic indicators – relatively high unemployment and inflation, along with freakishly bad trade figures released in the last days of the campaign, reinforced by an astonishing television interview in which the former Governor of the Bank of

England, Lord Cromer, claimed that the situation was even worse than in 1964 – more humdrum explanations for Labour's surprising defeat were available.[13] Just four days before the election, England's football team was knocked out of the World Cup by West Germany (of all countries) thanks to a goal scored in extra time: in the game's earlier stages, England had seemed set for a comfortable victory. England might not have gone on to retain the trophy it had won in 1966, but the prospect of playing in another World Cup final would have generated a very significant 'feel-good factor' in at least one part of the United Kingdom. Although the precise electoral impact of a football match can never be ascertained, almost certainly it helps to explain a significant drop in turnout – at 72 per cent, almost four points down from 1966, and much more sharply depressed in England than in Scotland or Wales where voters were unlikely to be mortified by English misfortune. Opinion polls had already been suggesting that the majority of likely 1970 abstainers would be lukewarm Labour supporters. For English nationalists, defeat at the hands of West Germany compounded a humiliating pre-tournament incident in which England's highly respected captain Bobby Moore had been arrested on a dubious charge of stealing a bracelet in Bogotá. The Wilson government had embarked on feverish diplomatic activity to resolve what seemed an incomprehensible slur on the country's honour and prestige; the episode supplanted political news in the national press headlines for several days of the election campaign.[14]

Oblivious to the risk of a premature ejection from the World Cup, Harold Wilson had called an early poll in the hope of maximising his party's chances of securing a third consecutive term in office. He had dominated the Labour campaign, which was centrally controlled as well as being personalised to an unusual extent. In the immediate aftermath of defeat, Wilson requested and received a vote of confidence from his party's MPs. However, his leadership, and the nature of the policies pursued by the outgoing government, were bound to come under scrutiny once the dust of defeat had settled.

Holding a Hapless Government to Account

Between June 1970 and the general election of February 1974, the Conservative government acted inadvertently as Labour's most effective ally. The government's general approach (epitomised by Heath himself) was not to challenge the key pillars of the post-war 'consensus' – a mixed economy; constructive relations between government, unions and employers; a well-funded welfare state; moves towards a more egalitarian education system, etc. – but rather to reconfigure such policies, practices and institutions along lines which were more congenial to pragmatic Conservatives. Thus, for example, hardly any Tory ministers objected to nationalised industries in principle; their chief concern was to reduce the level of government largesse on behalf of private sector companies which ran into trouble. Heath's vaunted 'new style of government' would be selective in its approach to welfare, but its drive to prune the budget by targeting assistance at those in genuine need had also characterised the post-devaluation phase of the 1964–70 Labour administrations.

In its practical import, this approach suggested a government which was defining itself against its own tax-slashing, state-hating right-wing supporters (notably followers of Heath's personal enemy Enoch Powell) rather than aiming to disrupt the general tenor of post-war policy. Yet in their anxiety to keep the Powellites at bay, ministers were not averse to echoing elements of the right's vocabulary. Thus John Davies – a businessman turned politician who had been promoted to the Cabinet before acquiring the necessary skill-set – used a phrase which was misconstrued as a warning that the government would never use the nation's resources to save industrial 'lame ducks' from the consequences of their own inefficiencies. For his part, at the 1970 Conservative conference Heath promised nothing less than a 'revolution' in government (albeit one which would be both 'quiet' and gradual).

By deploying right-wing rhetoric, the newly elected government seemed to verify Labour's pre-election warnings of a wholesale ideological onslaught on the post-war settlement. This narrative had been established by Wilson four months before the 1970 election, in a speech which personified the Conservatives in the loathsome figure of 'Selsdon Man'. The latter sobriquet was inspired by a meeting of the Shadow Cabinet at the Selsdon Park Hotel near Croydon, which had attracted considerable publicity because, in the absence of concrete policy developments of any kind, shadow ministers had chosen to 'spin' the event in terms which would appeal to their 'core' right-wing supporters.[15] Whatever Wilson thought about Heath's real intentions, he was quick to turn

Tory attempts at media-management to his own advantage, warning of 'a wanton, calculated and deliberate return to greater inequality' should Selsdon Man get his prehensile hands on the British people.[16] This sally did not help Wilson to retain office in the 1970 election, but it caused considerable discomfiture for Heath, whose right-wing detractors never ceased to accuse him of betraying the wholly fabricated 'spirit of Selsdon Park'.

Whatever their private reservations, Wilson's colleagues had good reason to thank him for his attacks on the Heath government between 1970 and February 1974. Like a tired, ageing matador faced with a hornless cow, Wilson consistently bested Heath in their personal duels at Prime Minister's Questions. More importantly in those days before Parliament was televised, he was always ready to criticise the government's policies in set-piece speeches outside Westminster, without pausing to consider if, in the same circumstances, he would have taken very similar decisions. This brazen cynicism infuriated Heath, but in essentials it merely followed the opportunistic approach which the Conservatives themselves had adopted between 1964 and 1970. The Labour leader's legerdemain was on display when, after its alleged mid-term 'U-turn', Heath's government engaged earnestly with unions and employers to devise an anti-inflationary policy which would constrain both prices and incomes. Wilson worked unobtrusively to thwart any deals which would have assisted his adversary.

In fact any chances of a rapprochement between Heath and the labour movement had effectively been extinguished by the government's approach to the trade union issue which Wilson had bungled in 1969. The Conservative Industrial Relations Act (1971) was admittedly different from the ill-fated *In Place of Strife* proposals, but is best understood as a symptom of the more general 'Heathite' desire to place a Tory twist on policies which enjoyed the general approval of both frontbenches. However, having faced down Wilson and his Secretary of State for Employment and Productivity, Barbara Castle, the unions had no intention of complying with legal restrictions imposed by their Conservative enemies. Resistance to the Bill – given its second reading before the end of 1970 and passed in March 1971 – provided a sense of common purpose among members of the labour movement who might otherwise have been distracted by differing assessments of the

Wilson government's record and contrasting approaches to economic and political problems which were assuming critical proportions. As one journalist put it, unconsciously the Heath government had acted as 'the marriage broker between the political and trade union wings of the Labour movement'.[17]

While the unions led the movement's assault on the Heath government – with a string of successful strikes, particularly those conducted by the National Union of Mineworkers (NUM) – they were vulnerable to negative portrayal in the Conservative-supporting press. Having perfected his pose as a pipe-wielding custodian of the national interest, Wilson was well equipped to allay the fears of floating voters who regarded Labour's trade union allies as a source both of social division and economic malaise. Determined to serve at least two more years as prime minister, he was prepared to continue in his role as the public face of the party. Yet he lacked the aptitude, inclination or opportunity to formulate its guiding principles; these were always likely to be shaped by people who regarded the 1964–70 Labour governments as a bitter disappointment.

Policy Development and Relations with the Unions: The Advent of 'Bennism'

Scoring points against a luckless government was the easy part of Labour's task between 1970 and 1974. In order to regain office, it could not rely on the electorate merely reacting against the existing government's various mishaps – in effect, a 'come back Labour, all is forgiven' strategy. Disillusioned supporters needed evidence of fresh thinking, especially in view of ominous developments in the domestic and international contexts over the 1970–4 Parliament.

For Wilson and his remaining allies, the chief problem in these years was not a paucity of innovative ideas within the labour movement, but rather a perceived need to restrain the party's radicals for fear of alienating an electorate whose typical representative was assumed to occupy a 'centrist' position on the ideological spectrum. The leader's own views had not changed since he assumed the role in 1963; although critics underestimated his commitment to social justice, he is best understood as a technocrat whose primary concern was to maximise economic efficiency. Labour's social democrats – while differing from Wilson in important respects, deploring his political style and resenting his 1960 leadership challenge to their hero, Hugh Gaitskell (see Chapter 4) – were willing to tolerate his approach while he retained the reputation of an electoral asset. Wilson's goal of enhanced economic growth, after all, was essential to their primary ethical purpose of a well-funded welfare state, and his emphasis on 'meritocracy' was obviously compatible with their aspiration for something akin to 'equality of opportunity'.[18]

The notion that the cause of socialism could advance under the ambiguous Wilson had worn pretty thin before the 1970 general election. However, while the unimpressive record of the 1964–70 governments implied that a different approach was in order, subsequent events made life even more difficult for social democrats who believed that Wilson's licence had reached its expiry date. Robbed of the easy assurance of economic growth, and confronted with the new phenomenon of 'stagflation' – rising unemployment, combined with relatively high price inflation – leadership aspirants like Jenkins and Crosland had no convincing answers. In 1974 the latter published a new book (*Socialism Now*) whose contents demonstrated that his intellectual heyday had passed. Jenkins, who had been elected very comfortably as Deputy Leader in July 1970, proved more willing to learn lessons from Labour's defeat, evincing renewed enthusiasm for public ownership in his speeches, along with deepened concern for the problem of poverty.[19] However, while retaining strong support within the PLP and in the press, Jenkins found himself hamstrung by his agreement with the Conservative Party on one fateful issue.

To its advocates, British membership of the EEC seemed certain to boost the country's economic growth – or, in the worst case, to cushion it from any global downturn after the collapse of the post-war Bretton Woods framework in 1971. For Labour's social democrats, the prospects of prosperity trumped considerations of popular input to EEC policies – or the feeble chains of accountability attached to key Brussels decision-makers. A clear majority of grassroots Labour supporters – and a significant proportion of MPs – continued to take a different view for a variety of reasons, despite the fact that Wilson (by no means a Eurofanatic) had led a second unsuccessful British bid for EEC membership as recently as 1967. The official party line after a special conference on the subject in June 1971 was that Labour was not opposed in principle to joining the EEC, while ensuring some wriggle-room to allow it to oppose the terms of any successful membership bid under a Conservative government. No vote was taken on that occasion, but the case against joining on Tory terms was endorsed overwhelmingly at the annual conference in October. Before the end of the month, Jenkins had led sixty-nine pro-European Labour MPs into the government's lobby at the end of a six-day debate on the principle of EEC membership; twenty others abstained in defiance of a three-line whip. For John Campbell, this was 'the proudest moment of Jenkins' career'. Others were less laudatory; the deputy Chief Whip Walter Harrison was among those who resorted to the language of 'treachery', which would become over-familiar in relation to 'Europe'.[20] Jenkins was left with a choice – between making a serious attempt to seize the leadership of the party, or leaving it. To the consternation of his supporters he did neither.

While Jenkins tried to evade the horns of a dilemma, Wilson himself was comprehensively impaled by his previous tergiversations over the EEC and his knowledge that Callaghan, from the 'Eurosceptic' side, posed an even greater threat to his position than the vacillating Jenkins. He was rescued by what Callaghan himself had suggested might be 'a little rubber life-raft which we will all be glad of in a year's time' – the idea, proposed by the former Minister of Technology Anthony Wedgwood Benn and advocated in Parliament by Enoch Powell, of a referendum on EEC membership should Labour be returned to office at the next election.[21] Claiming at the time to be actuated by democratic principle rather than outright opposition to the EEC, Benn had persuaded the Shadow Cabinet by the end of March 1972. However, some of his colleagues were unwilling to board a raft which Clement Attlee had once denounced as an 'alien' contrivance; indeed, the proposal had been rebuffed by the Shadow Cabinet at its previous meeting. During the 1970 election campaign Wilson had rejected a referendum emphatically, promising that 'I'm not going to trim to win votes on a question like that.'[22] Although Wilson's pronouncements were never more than provisional, a vote at the 1971 party conference had judged Benn's vessel unseaworthy. Jenkins, who had been re-elected

Deputy Leader shortly after that conference, resigned from the position in protest at the Shadow Cabinet's *volte-face*. His example was followed by the equally Europhile Harold Lever, whose replacement as Shadow Minister for Europe was the strongly sceptical Peter Shore, fresh from a speech at a PLP meeting which Jenkins later paraphrased as 'this England set in a silver sea'.[23] Although Jenkins had pledged not to repeat his whip-defying vote on the principle of EEC membership, his followers had no such inhibitions and earned themselves additional odium within the party by ensuring that the legislation paving the way for British membership passed through the House of Commons (in July 1972, after more than 300 hours of debate).

Benn's pivotal role in the campaign for a referendum pledge is not the only reason for regarding him as the central figure in the struggle for Labour's soul between 1970 and 1974. An inexhaustible enthusiast for his adopted causes, Benn was initially regarded as more Wilsonian than Wilson in his technocratic tendencies. Even before the 1970 election, however, he had been apprised of a growing gulf between the PLP and its supporters in the constituency parties and the trade unions. In contrast to Crosland, who believed that the purpose of opposition was 'the working out of effective detailed policies', Benn prioritised an educational, consciousness-raising role – 'connecting the Party to the unions, working on future policy, encouraging people, explaining things and so on'.[24] In 1971, Benn had been captivated by the potential for a democratisation of industry, epitomised by the grassroots 'work-in' initiative at Upper Clyde Shipbuilders (UCS), a consortium which Benn himself had helped to establish in 1968 but which had hatched into one of the Heath government's 'lame ducks' just three years later. Benn's growing interest in the extra-parliamentary labour movement coincided with a change in the nature of the trade union leadership. In 1968, radical candidates (Jack Jones and Hugh Scanlon) were elected as leaders of two of Britain's most influential unions, the Transport and General Workers (TGWU) and the Amalgamated Engineers (AEU). Whether or not they retained any of their youthful revolutionary sympathies – Scanlon had been a Communist, Jones a volunteer fighter in the Spanish Civil War – in practice this new breed of leaders owed their positions to a presumed ability to improve the living standards of their members *within* the prevailing capitalist system.

If Benn's embrace of socialism in thought and practice was sudden, sincere and rapturous, his most senior colleagues within the parliamentary party acknowledged the need for a tactical and (hopefully) temporary turn to the left. The authors of the Nuffield Study of the February 1974 general election noted that: 'In contrast to the situation in 1951 and 1959, there was no embittered post-mortem' after the equally demoralising 1970 defeat.[25] In part, this was because a chastened leadership seemed willing to meet its critics more than half way. The post-election party conference was presented with a document, *Building a Socialist Britain*, which showcased the 's-word' that the leader was notorious for swerving in his speeches, as well as foreshadowing a more radical approach to policy now that the party was back in opposition. From the title onwards, the document was best understood as a statement of unapologetic repentance.

The leftward shift in Labour's posture was consolidated by a similar development within key party institutions. Formal policy-making input for the unions was established by the creation of a TUC/PLP/NEC Liaison Committee, which first met in February 1972. At best, debates within this forum exposed the different underlying degrees of commitment to a truly radical alternative platform, and a gulf in thinking between the party's elected MPs and representatives of the rest of the labour movement. While the nature of the PLP had barely been affected by the 1970 general election – ensuring that in elections to the Shadow Cabinet Jenkins proved far more popular than Benn – the balance of the NEC changed in broad accordance with developments in the nature of union leadership. The veteran left-winger Ian Mikardo, chair of the party (and thus of the NEC) for 1970–1, was succeeded by Benn himself. The latter took full advantage of the position, launching an initiative ('Participation 72') which encouraged party members to submit policy ideas, and trying to ensure that new thinking was embodied in official statements before they could be diluted by more 'mainstream' colleagues. Thanks not least to Benn, *Labour's Programme 1973*, endorsed by that year's party conference, included proposals for a dramatic extension of public ownership (even into banking and insurance), and a pledge to facilitate 'a fundamental and irreversible shift in the balance of power and wealth in favour of working people and their families'.

The renewed emphasis on nationalisation – a policy which had barely surfaced under the 1964–70 governments – was a key element in the thinking of Stuart Holland, an academic (and later MP for Vauxhall, 1979–89), who had advised Wilson on European policy. Although Holland's ideas were not elaborated at full length until the publication of *The Socialist Challenge* (1975), the outlines of what became known as the Alternative Economic Strategy (AES) were reflected in *Labour's Programme 1973*. Holland's analysis was heavily coloured by his realisation that, compared to the context of the 1945–51 Attlee governments, capitalism could only be understood from a global perspective and that multinational corporations had become key actors. Where such border-crossing concerns could not be brought directly into state ownership, a future Labour government should use its purchasing power as leverage in order to persuade them to accept planning agreements; thus, although there was no intention to abolish private enterprise, the state's supervisory role would extend to all significant economic institutions and its imperatives would permeate the private sector as a whole.[26] The AES also envisaged a far-reaching regime of import controls – i.e. protectionism – as well as restrictions on the export of capital. In effect, the strategy is best understood as an attempt to insulate a progressive Britain from the reactionary impulses of the global market.

While the AES could be hailed by the Labour left as proof that it was winning the battle between the party's middle-class intellectuals, in itself it raised intractable questions which were difficult to answer. If multinational corporations really had become so powerful, could Britain, by its unaided efforts, rein them in? Or would they simply (and painlessly, to themselves) disinvest from such a recalcitrant sector of the global marketplace? Holland's preoccupation with multinationals was shared by Benn, who had highlighted the problem in a Fabian Tract composed shortly after the 1970 election, and became chair of the influential Industrial Policy Committee in late 1972.[27] Benn's new-found fervour for meaningful democratic involvement in the workplace could, in theory, also be applied to the multinationals. In practice, however, while British-based firms might be persuaded to tolerate token worker representation in the boardroom, few capitalists would relish the prospect of being outvoted by their own employees. Even patriotic businesspeople would be tempted to invest in markets which offered more freedom (and fatter profits); the controllers of multinational companies would not even think twice. In addition, a significant expansion of state enterprise implied at least some increase in bureaucracy, a development which was seriously at odds with Benn's yearning for popular participation. While Benn and Holland broadly coincided in their diagnoses of Britain's position within a globalised economy, their remedies differed in important respects. Holland regarded membership of the EEC as a necessary bulwark against wider and less controllable transnational forces; Benn, by contrast, had renounced his own previous 'federalist' tendencies and was moving towards an antipathy to a European project which was indelibly associated with unaccountable, elitist decision-makers and pettifogging pen-pushers.

Holland's economic programme was strongly contested at the time by Crosland and other social democrats; after three subsequent decades of global neo-liberalism, one academic commentator concluded that it 'no longer appears faintly realistic'.[28] Questionable as it might have been, for Labour the AES was the only invigorating intellectual show in town between 1970 and 1974. While Wilson bided his time before setting out his own views, he expected that the fully-fledged AES-infused 1973 programme would give the Conservatives an irresistible opportunity to deflect media attention from their own glaring shortcomings, allowing them to depict a vote for Labour as an invitation to uncage 'Stalingrad Man'. Again, Heath and the Conservatives offered Wilson inadvertent and invaluable help by calling a snap election in February 1974, rather than allowing the Labour left additional time in which to cement its intellectual advantage. Although the eyebrow-raising pledge to ensure a 'fundamental and irreversible shift in the balance of power and wealth' was retained in the party's manifesto, the sections on nationalisation were characterised by general aspirational phrases rather than the specific commitment to taking twenty-five of Britain's leading firms into public ownership which the left had inserted into *Labour's Programme 1973*. Also, while that document had heralded an extension of public ownership into the financial sector, the manifesto reported that this step was merely under consideration. If Wilson returned to office, he was determined to secure sufficient time and freedom of manoeuvre to offer some reassurance to the beneficiaries of the existing imbalance of power and wealth, at home and abroad.

The Party and the Electorate

Just before Heath bowed to pressure from his closest colleagues and called the February election, Benn reflected in his diary that 'one of the great arguments of the Right is that you can't win an Election with a left-wing programme. If you have a left-wing programme and you win an Election, then the right will have lost that argument, and that will be a historic moment.'[29]

Despite Wilson's rearguard resistance, the manifesto of February 1974 was indeed sufficiently radical that a Labour victory on that basis would refute the claim that a left-wing programme was an inevitable augury of electoral defeat. However, it remained possible that Labour could prevail despite, rather than because of, its most distinctive policy commitments. Taken as a whole, the public opinion polls between 1970 and early 1974 suggested that the party's ideological trajectory had left most voters unimpressed. Although Labour was ahead most of the time, its lead dwindled markedly as the Parliament progressed and the left consolidated its advantage. Both major parties, indeed, fared poorly compared to the Liberals, whose poll rating climbed to a remarkable 29 per cent in October 1973. The general wish to confer a plague on both main parties resulted in five Liberal by-election gains during the 1970–4 Parliament, four at the predictable expense of the Conservatives but one (Rochdale in October 1972) a victory over Labour.[30] It was Labour, arguably, which suffered the most damaging by-election reversal of these years, at Lincoln in March 1973. Dick Taverne, a social democrat who had angered local activists by denouncing strikes aimed at thwarting the Industrial Relations Act – and had effectively been deselected as a Labour candidate in June 1972 thanks to his disobedience to the party whip in votes over EEC membership – triggered the Lincoln contest by resigning his seat. Adopting the 'Democratic Labour' label, Taverne was re-elected with a majority of over 13,000 compared to less than 5,000 in the 1970 general election. Taverne's feat owed much to the absence of a Liberal candidate, but far from offering comfort to Labour supporters this merely drew attention to the potential electoral appeal of a 'centrist' alliance between the party's social democrats and the Liberals.

Even without the wisdom of hindsight, the Taverne episode suggested that Labour's self-proclaimed 'moderates' would be more willing than their Conservative counterparts to abandon their party when facing intellectual eclipse, not least because defectors could count on vociferous support from the right-wing press. In September 1973 Taverne attracted considerable publicity with the launch of a Campaign for Social Democracy, which in the February 1974 general election fielded unsuccessful candidates in four seats (including Benn's Bristol South East, where the Social Democrat notched up a paltry 668 votes).

More seriously for the left, detailed opinion polling suggested that its most controversial policy – the radical extension of public ownership – found limited favour even amongst its own supporters. At the time of the February 1974 election only 20 per cent of voters expressed approval, with the proportion for Labour supporters little more than a third. Such data suggest that Labour's prospects might have been damaged if the policy had gained higher electoral salience; as it was, it did not figure among the five issues most frequently cited by survey respondents, and the lacklustre support for state ownership was registered at a time when government control over the extraction and distribution of Britain's North Sea oil reserves was widely accepted, which should have made the general principle of nationalisation more palatable.[31]

As campaigning began for the February general election, the dominant issues were the sharply rising cost of living and industrial disputes which culminated in the miners' action, whose escalation from an overtime ban to an all-out strike persuaded Heath to call a national poll. Labour's expedient of a 'social contract' – a deal between government and unions, in which the latter would moderate their pay claims in return for improved social provision and price controls – helped to persuade a majority of voters of the party's competence in the field of industrial relations (although Labour's lead on this issue, just 10 percentage points over the Conservatives, was surprisingly slender given the havoc which had prevailed almost throughout the career of Heath's government). Labour was also regarded as credible in relation to the cost of living. It fared badly in areas (such as defence and immigration) which did not feature prominently in this campaign. On the Common Market, the pledge to renegotiate Heath's terms of entry and then hold either a referendum or a further general election did not gain Labour much traction against the Conservatives, who at that time were generally accepted to be 'the party of Europe'.[32] For the voting public, Benn's 'life-raft' was less impressive than the evidence of continued quarrelling among his crew-mates.

The February 1974 Election Campaign

Although Wilson hoped to play a less prominent role in this contest he could not avoid being cast by the media as Labour's chief electioneer. His tactical approach was clearly stated in his foreword to the party's manifesto, *Let Us Work Together – Labour's Way Out of the Crisis*. Lambasting the Conservatives for gross incompetence (and worse), Wilson promised that Labour would provide 'a Government of all the people'. Amidst the crisis of the post-war consensus, a Labour leader purloined the language of One Nation which previously had benefited the Conservatives. In Labour's final election broadcast, Wilson accused the Heath government of creating and fomenting social divisions which only his party could heal. By sharp contrast, shortly before the election, the former Viscount Stansgate (now sporting the populist *nom de guerre* of 'Tony Benn') had told Denis Healey that 'it is the class war and we have got to face it'.[33] Elements of the media (and not just the antediluvian right-wing press) had certainly declared war on Benn. As early as October 1972 a *Sunday Express* cartoon depicted him in Nazi uniform, following a BBC broadcast which alluded to him as 'the most hated man in Britain'.[34]

On the Conservative side, Benn's renegade role was rivalled by Enoch Powell, who followed up an announcement that he would not stand in the election with a declaration (timed to inflict maximum damage on Heath) that he had already cast a postal vote – for Labour. His sole stated reason for doing so was Labour's stance on the Common Market; apparently he considered the differences between the major parties on other issues to be secondary concerns. Since the swing against the Conservatives in this election was most pronounced in Powell's West Midlands heartlands, Benn's little rubber life-raft had turned into a torpedo which helped to hole the Tories below the waterline. On its own, however, Powell's self-dramatising intervention was not decisive. The ill fortune (much of its own making) which had dogged the Heath government throughout its career persisted up to its embittered end. In particular, William Campbell Adamson, the Director of the employers' organisation the Confederation of British Industry (CBI), and thus a key antagonist for the workers in any 'class war', played Lord Cromer in reverse by delivering a speech in which he expressed a clear preference for Labour's approach to industrial relations. The Pay Board, a quango which the government itself had established, ruled that the NUM did indeed have a strong case for a significant pay rise. With friends like these, the Heath government stood in no need of enemies to put an end to its sufferings, amidst the chaos of a three-day working week and the prospect of petrol rationing.

Despite their manifold miseries, the Conservatives were comfortably ahead in the last polls before the votes were cast on 28 February 1974. Unlike in 1970, on this occasion the pollsters correctly predicted the more popular side. But the Conservative advantage in terms of vote share was wafer-thin – a lead of less than 250,000. Translated into seats by the electoral system, this became a deficit of four compared to Labour (297 to 301). The ill-rewarded victors of the February 1974 general election were the Liberals, who attracted more than 6 million votes (19.3 per cent of the poll) but secured only fourteen seats. The upsurge in Liberal support owed much to the sharp increase in their roster of candidates – 517, compared to 332 in 1970 – but on this occasion there were far more reasons for Liberals to stand for election.

Once the outcome was known, Heath exercised his constitutional right to stay in Downing Street, struggling in vain to cobble together a series of deals with other parties which would have allowed him to continue in office. However, although there was no clear winner in February 1974, it was obvious even to Cabinet members (notably Margaret Thatcher) that the Conservatives had lost their governing authority. In retirement, Thatcher testified to feeling 'relief' when the 'bad loser' Heath abandoned his courtship of potential allies.[35] Evidently Enoch Powell was not the only doctrinaire anti-socialist who thought that Britain could safely be entrusted to a Labour Party committed to the most radical industrial programme in its history.

Only those who are fixated on the outcome of Britain's 'winner takes all' voting system could deny that Labour was also a loser in February 1974. The snap election caught it unprepared in terms of constituency organisation, but the fact that it boasted only 135 full-time agents, compared to the Conservatives' 363, reflected a longer-term decline.[36] A weak electoral machine probably had little impact on the level of Labour support in a contest shorn of positive enthusiasm for either of the chief protagonists. Compared to the 1970 defeat, Labour's share of the vote fell from 43.1 to 37.2 per cent. In 1964, when it had fought a Conservative government whose record (though tarnished) was fairly defensible, the party had won more than 44 per cent of the vote. When Labour had lost the 1959 general election, inspiring earnest speculations about its future as a potential party of government, it had won 43.9 per cent.

When Heath transferred the task of forming a minority government to his long-term rival, Harold Wilson arrived at Downing Street to tell the nation that 'We've got a job to do. We can only do that job as one people.' As Wilson well knew, the nation was divided as it never had been before in the post-war period. Nowhere was the schism more apparent than amongst members of his own party, some of whom thought that the inherent contradictions of the capitalist order had been exposed, while others still believed that it could be tamed and rescued along Keynesian lines. Roy Jenkins, by now the unquestionable leader of the latter faction, contemplated the February 1974 result with distinctly mixed feelings. As he reflected in his memoirs: 'In 1970 I wanted Labour to win and thought it deserved to do so. In 1974 I took a different view on both points.'[37] His reward for staying on board the Labour ship which was veering away from his preferred, consensual anchorage was one of the four 'great offices of state'; but Wilson was too canny to give him the position he craved (Foreign Secretary) and he had to trudge back to the Home Office where his progressive efforts were unlikely to improve his chances of ever taking the top job.

Tony Benn's published diary gives no indication of euphoria at the downfall of the hated Tories. Indeed, over the ensuing days, as he returned to what was essentially his old Whitehall battleground (now the Department of Industry rather than the Ministry of Technology), he was gearing up for a new fight against the institutional forces which sought to extinguish the ideological vigour he had fostered during Labour's years of opposition.[38] Benn's implicit forebodings were well founded. The inconclusive election result, and the manner in which his party leader had conducted the campaign, suggested that radical thinking would be spurned so long as Wilson remained at the helm, with a presumed 'mandate' to postpone into the indefinite future any policy initiatives which threatened a departure from a reconfigured national 'consensus' built around the social contract. As he contemplated a precarious political future, Benn could insist that the full vote-winning potential of a left-wing programme had not been subjected to a proper test, and that his party would have fared better under a leader who truly believed in the radical policies Benn had tried so hard to promote since the 1970 defeat. But Labour was back in office after a campaign which had been run along pragmatic lines, and the reasons for victory (as well as the party's governing strategy until a new election which could not be delayed for long) lay in the hands of the biggest pragmatist of them all.

Conclusion

The Labour shadow team elected by the parliamentary party in 1970 included some of Britain's most talented post-war politicians. Regardless of ideological allegiances, few could deny that Callaghan, Jenkins, Healey, Benn, Castle, Crosland and Foot were formidable figures. The team-sheet also included the sprinkling of unheralded 'utility players' who are invaluable for any successful side, as well as potential stars of the future like Shirley Williams and Roy Hattersley.

In February 1974 this 'Shadow Ministry of all the Talents' achieved the goal of all opposition parties by moving back into government. However, this could not be regarded as a reflection of Labour's performance since 1970. In part, the opposition had profited from developments which exposed and accentuated its own latent ideological divisions. It was at least equally unhelpful that its top team was riven by rivalries. Some of these (e.g. Crosland vs Jenkins) were alloyed to some extent by long-standing friendship; others (e.g. Callaghan against everyone else except Merlyn Rees) had more of the quality of personal vendettas. In sharp contrast to the successful England football team of 1966 (and the losers of 1970) Labour was led back into a government by a shop-soiled operator who was well aware that he was trusted by none of his senior colleagues and who regarded the most gifted amongst them as potential political assassins. As a weary Wilson retraced his steps over the Downing Street threshold he had first visited as a small child, both the immediate challenges he faced and the nature of the party he led made it seem unlikely that Labour would be in government for long.

6

Impossible Promises and Far-Fetched Resolutions (1979–1987)

On 28 March 1979, the Labour government was facing a vote of no confidence after just over five years in power. While initially confident they could win, the Labour whips were crestfallen when two socialist Irish nationalist MPs announced that they would be abstaining in protest of Labour's pro-unionist position in Northern Ireland.[1] Even three bottles of whisky had not been sufficient to tempt one of these MPs, who had a drink problem.[2] Labour was one vote short, but the whips had one more option. A few days earlier, the Labour MP for Batley, Alf Broughton, had suffered a heart attack and was on his death bed. He, nonetheless, volunteered to be driven in an ambulance from Yorkshire to save the government.[3] His doctors warned that the journey could kill him.[4] Labour whip Ann Taylor thought it was worth the risk: 'At least he'll die happy.'[5] The prime minister Jim Callaghan was 'squeamish' about the idea.[6] Broughton was left in Yorkshire, where he would die five days later. Seizing their chance, an alliance of Conservatives, Liberals, Scottish and Irish nationalists, and the odd Ulster unionist brought down the Labour government by one vote: 311 to 310. It was the first such defeat for any government since Labour's collapse in 1924. In the ensuing general election, Margaret Thatcher's Conservatives were victorious.

The period from 1979 to 1997 marked Labour's longest spell in opposition since it first became the Official Opposition in 1922. No one expected Labour to be out of power for so long.[7] Labour's vote share had declined by just 2 per cent in the 1979 election. Conservative gains had been made thanks to the Liberals losing nearly a quarter of their previous vote.[8] Recent history had suggested that Labour could bounce back into government.[9] Its previous spell in opposition, discussed in Chapter 5, had lasted just three and a half years. Thatcher's economic agenda, cooked up by her 'mad monk' Keith Joseph, was expected to be catastrophically damaging.[10] The new prime minister was not personally popular, with Callaghan seen as a more appealing figure.[11]

Labour's initial reaction to defeat was to turn inward. Labour supporters could not decide whether the last Labour government had been a great success against the odds or a miserable failure. For those in the labour movement who believed the latter interpretation, the main diagnosis was that the government had abandoned its socialist principles. In order to remedy this situation, the left of the Labour Party embarked on a project of wholesale reconstruction of the party's democratic machinery.

This quest for party democratisation succeeded in securing changes to Labour's constitutional structures and cemented a left-wing policy agenda, but the process required to achieve these victories nearly broke the Labour Party. It drove a wedge between erstwhile allies on the left and spurred the creation of a rival party to the right known as the Social Democratic Party (SDP), which appeared poised to eclipse Labour altogether. Labour MP Betty Boothroyd gravely referred to these developments as 'terminal dangers'.[12] Margaret Thatcher suggested, albeit hubristically, that the last Labour government might be 'perhaps the last ever'.[13] Labour's defeat in the 1983 election resulted in its lowest number of MPs since 1935 and its lowest share of the vote since 1918. After a spirited but shambolic campaign led by Michael Foot, Labour, nonetheless, managed to keep the SDP in third place and retain a significant share of seats in Parliament thanks to the first-past-the-post electoral system, ensuring its continued status as the main alternative to the Conservative Party.

Between 1983 and 1987, the Labour Party continued to face internal strife. The miners' strike of 1984–85 attracted the sympathies of the Labour grassroots, but the tactics of the leadership of the National Union of Mineworkers clashed with the moderating outlook of Labour's new leader Neil Kinnock. Equally, Kinnock turned his ire to Labour's representatives in local government. Once viewed as the party's sturdy foundations, Labour-run councils had turned into political liabilities by embarking on initiatives that were seen as detached from the everyday realities of most working-class Britons. Behind these efforts, in some cases, was a far-left entryist movement known as the Militant Tendency.

By the time of the 1987 election, Kinnock had succeeded in wresting control of the National Executive Committee and imposing rigorous discipline on the party's electioneering. The intense focus on party rules, however, meant that changes in policy were relatively slight. Although presented with a different emphasis, the basic outlines of Labour's 1983 manifesto remained in place in 1987. A third consecutive defeat emboldened the party's 'modernisers' to argue that a complete policy overhaul would be required. Labour's eighteen long years in opposition require two chapters to do them full justice. This chapter will concentrate on the years 1979–87, when the party came to the brink of destruction. Chapter 7 will chart Labour's years of recovery from 1987–97.

Assessing the Record of the Previous Labour Government (1974–1979): Discontent, Dishonesty and Disloyalty

The sequel to Labour's defeat in 1979 was 'venomous examination of the defects of the fallen government'.[14] At issue were 'rival explanations of what caused that defeat' which 'shook the party to its very foundations'.[15] These disagreements did not manifest simply over questions of campaign style, managerial competence, or even policy differences. The core question was over whether the previous Labour government had in fact been a socialist one. This appraisal was not conducted in a comradely or even particularly honest fashion. History became weaponised for factional effect.

The charge from the left of the party was that the Callaghan government had shifted its priorities from the interests of labour to those of capital. The evidence cited for this claim consisted of its policies to combat inflation through wage control, its cuts to government expenditure, and its humiliating recourse to taking on a loan from the International Monetary Fund (IMF). In 1976, the then Chancellor Denis Healey had informed the party conference that the IMF loan 'means sticking to the very painful cuts in public expenditure on which the government has already decided'.[16] He was jeered by furious delegates with calls of 'Resign!' Behind Healey, members of the left-dominated NEC looked on, shaking their heads in disgust. At that same conference, Callaghan declared: 'We used to think that you could spend your way out of a recession and increase employment by cutting taxes and boosting government spending. I tell you in all candour that that option no longer exists.'[17] To the ears of many delegates, the Labour prime minister seemed to be sounding the death knell of Keynesianism.

The election defeat of 1979 lifted the lid on what had already been a steaming cauldron of dissent among the Labour grassroots. Tony Benn, who became one of the previous Labour government's chief critics in spite of (or, he would say, because of) serving as a minister in it for eleven years, explained that 'the loyalty to the government was such that [Labour activists] stuck by the government, but as soon as the government was defeated in '79 and that bond of immediate loyalty was lifted by defeat, then, of course, all this pent up feeling began to emerge'.[18]

Following the precedent set by Ramsay MacDonald in 1924, Clement Attlee in 1951 and Harold Wilson in 1970, Callaghan did not resign immediately upon defeat. However, unlike these predecessors, Callaghan had no appetite to fight another election, by which point he would likely be in his 70s. Soon after the 1979 election, Callaghan told his preferred successor Healey that he would remain leader for eighteen months 'to take the shine off the ball'. 'Jim's last eighteen months', Healey later said, 'not only took the shine off the ball but ripped away the leather as well'.[19]

Callaghan had hoped that the sting of defeat would soon recede and that the party would unite in the common mission of removing Margaret Thatcher from 10 Downing Street. He was wrong. Instead, Callaghan became the target of eighteen months of character assassination. 'It was not a happy period', he sullenly recounted.[20] These reproaches were made most vocally at party conferences. As was custom, Callaghan sat on the stage in full view of television cameras while delegates condemned him and the government over which he had presided. At the 1979 conference, the General Secretary of the Labour Party, Ron Hayward, roared: 'I come not to praise Callaghan but to bury him!'[21] He asked: 'Why was there a winter of discontent? Because the Cabinet, supported by MPs, ignored [Trades Union] Congress and Conference decisions.'[22] Keighley MP Bob Cryer argued: 'We were not defeated at the last election because we carried out party policy but precisely because of the opposite.'[23] Voicing support for the previous Labour government was taken as a sign of inadequate socialist conviction. Left-winger Joan Lestor chided a fellow MP when she caught him applauding Callaghan during the leader's conference speech. 'What a scandalous thing to do', she hissed.[24]

Not all felt this way. Some trade unionists 'felt deeply uneasy, even guilty, about the fact that union actions in the winter of 1978–9 had contributed to the loss of support for the Labour Government'.[25] Trade union leaders had been unhappy with the wage restraint policy, but most accepted that high inflation had restricted the government's room for manoeuvre. In addition, the policies of the Labour government had appeared to be working, with Healey having suppressed inflation from over 20 per cent to 8 per cent by the time of the election.[26] The vote of no confidence in March 1979 short-circuited the life of the government by seven months, depriving it of crucial time to improve the economy before an election. With Labour out of the picture, the union leaders recognised that the British government had been taken over by, in Healey's colourful term, 'sado-monetarists'.[27]

In spite of the preferment given to him by Callaghan, Healey was narrowly defeated in the Labour leadership contest of November 1980 by Michael Foot. A figure on the party's left, Foot had nonetheless served as a loyal and effective minister in the 1974–79 government. Foot and Healey shared the common conviction that the Labour government had been successful under very difficult conditions. Foot told a group of academics: 'It is true that we wavered in allegiance to our own doctrines ... Mistakes and misjudgements certainly.'[28] Yet, he would not accept that no advances had been made. As Leader of the House in the hung Parliament of 1976–79 and in the midst of an economic crisis, Foot shepherded bills of great importance through the Commons: increases in pensions and benefits, the establishment of the Police Complaints Board, the expansion of comprehensive education, a statutory responsibility to provide housing for the homeless, universal child benefit, grants to inner cities, workplace safety legislation, grants to insulate houses, the Consumer Safety Act 1978, the creation of credit unions, nationalisation of the shipbuilding industry, phasing out pay beds in NHS hospitals, and housing security for agricultural workers.[29]

In Healey's estimation, the idea that the Labour government had betrayed its left-wing principles was one of the 'more exciting fantasies [pushed] by the drug pedlars of the Broad left'.[30] Yet, it is perhaps understandable why many in the party felt there had been a doctrinal shift, given Callaghan's dramatic pronouncements in his 1976 conference speech. Callaghan admitted in his memoirs that these lines 'made the fur fly', but defended them on the basis that they were appropriate for the circumstances of the time and not intended to be a general denunciation of Keynesianism.[31] Upon closer inspection, these remarks were allowed to overshadow Labour's achievements. Foot lamented: 'Those words have hung round our necks too long.'[32] As a result of bad-faith recriminations, Labour in opposition failed to assess properly the previous government's record. Too few were prepared to champion its successes, especially given the difficult context in which it operated. Too many were quick to condemn it. These major failings were indicative of the self-destructive behaviour of the Labour Party during this period, when it operated more often as an opposition to itself than to the Conservatives.

Strengthening the Party Machine: The Quest for Party Democracy

At the 1979 Durham Miners' Gala, Michael Foot warned his comrades not to fall into the trap of distracting themselves with internal party controversies. 'It would be tragic and unforgivable if at such a moment we turned aside from this supreme task [of defeating Thatcher] to tear ourselves in pieces if we supposed that what is needed is a constitutional wrangle within the Labour Party.'[33] Foot added: 'That was the great folly which Hugh Gaitskell committed after the electoral defeat of 1959. I trust we can escape a repetition of such a dangerous diversion today.'[34] Foot's trust was misplaced. The ructions of the early 1980s within the Labour Party would prove to be far worse and more destructive than those of the early 1960s.

Labour's initial years in opposition in this period were consumed by a laborious process of redrafting the party's rule book. The chief driver of party reform was the Campaign for Labour Party Democracy (CLPD), a grassroots organisation which had been founded in 1973 after the Labour conference voted in favour of a radical programme that included nationalising twenty-five of the biggest companies in Britain.[35] CLPD's aim was to reinforce the principle of conference sovereignty, laid out in Labour's 1918 constitution, by making conference motions binding on Labour governments.[36]

They argued for three rule changes to cement this principle. First, MPs needed to face a vote of their local party membership before each election in order to be reselected as a candidate, known as mandatory reselection. Second, Labour members and trade union affiliates should be able to vote for leader and deputy leader. Third, the NEC, which itself comprised representatives chosen by conference, ought to have the final say on the content of the party's election manifesto, not the Shadow Cabinet or the leader. It was hoped that these reforms would ensure 1) that conference motions would be translated into election manifestos, 2) that only MPs who believed in these conference motions would be allowed to stand as Labour candidates, and 3) that the party leader and deputy leader could be challenged by conference if they failed to abide by conference policy in government.

Through a combination of 'good luck, tactical dexterity, and the disunity and the extraordinary incompetence of the right', CLPD narrowly succeeded in passing motions on mandatory reselection and the election of party leaders (Figure 6.1).[37] They were not able to wrest control of the manifesto from the Shadow Cabinet, but the NEC retained a joint role in its drafting anyway.

The immediate consequences of CLPD's reforms were not as radical as the organisers had hoped. Initially, they had expected dozens of right-wing MPs to fall and be replaced by left-wingers. The left-wing MP Joan Maynard promised to keep an eagle eye out for any MPs who 'talked left but walk[ed] right'.[38] CLPD activist and future Labour MP Chris Mullin excitedly drew up a guide called *How to Select or Reselect Your MP*.[39] It

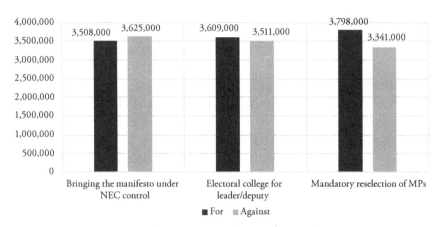

Figure 6.1 Constitutional reforms at Labour Party conferences, 1979–1980
Source: Minkin, 1992

might well have been called *How to Deselect Your MP*. Yet, most local MPs were relatively popular among members, even if they sat on the right of the party. Just eight constituency Labour parties (CLPs) deselected their MPs before the 1983 election, and most of these were older MPs who were removed for inactivity. Perhaps the most significant purge in this period was of MEPs who were deselected for not being Eurosceptic enough.[40]

The more significant reform implemented by CLPD was to change the franchise for electing the Labour Party leader, but the disruptive implications of this change would not be felt until 2010 (see Chapter 8). Until this point, the Labour leader was expected to command the confidence of a majority of the Parliamentary Labour Party. This confidence could be tested at the PLP's Annual General Meeting, as it had been against Hugh Gaitskell by Harold Wilson in 1960 and Tony Greenwood in 1961, but, since Ramsay MacDonald's defeat of John Robert Clynes in 1922, no incumbent Labour leader had been successfully removed from his post.

CLPD wanted to use conference to hold the leader's feet to the fire, but there were some disagreements over the extent to which conference should be in control of selecting the leader. Even Tony Benn bristled at the MPs' role being taken out entirely.[41] The compromise was that the Labour leader would be elected by an electoral college in which the votes of MPs, constituency parties and trade unions would be weighted in a tripartite structure.

The October 1980 Labour Party conference voted in favour of the principle of an electoral college but punted on determining the precise weighting formula. The electoral college's composition would be determined at a special conference three months later. CLPD was strategically wise to separate the vote in principle from the murky question of weighting. The vote in principle was won narrowly, made possible only due to an about-face by the small Boilermakers' Union, who had previously indicated their opposition to an electoral college.[42] Even some on the left opposed reform, voicing constitutional concerns. Michael Foot argued in the pages of *Tribune* that the new system could 'involve a serious erosion of parliamentary authority' and a 'gross assault on parliamentary rights'.[43] A Labour leader could be elected with the support of party members and union affiliates but lack the confidence of his or her own MPs in Parliament, a problem later encountered by leaders Ed Miliband and Jeremy Corbyn (see Chapter 8).

Shortly after the 1980 conference but before the special conference, Jim Callaghan resigned as Labour leader, forcing a contest under the old rules for one final time. It was in this contest on 10 November that Foot pulled off his victory over Healey by just ten votes. The following day, the Shadow Cabinet voted (8 to 7) in favour of MPs comprising 50 per cent of the electoral college and the other half being divided equally at conference between constituency parties and affiliates. Known as the 'Hattersley Compromise', this 50:25:25 formula seemed most likely to be adopted.[44]

The January 1981 special conference in Wembley was one of the most significant in Labour history. Its outcome could not have been predicted, being the result of gross incompetence by trade union leaders.[45] The Hattersley Compromise would have prevailed had the leader of the Amalgamated Union of Engineering Workers (AUEW) Terry Duffy not acted with 'appalling ineptitude'.[46] Duffy was a right-winger who believed that MPs should have a majority share of the electoral college. Because 50 per cent was not technically an absolute majority, Duffy directed his delegates to abstain on the proposal, killing it. It was 'a tactical blunder of awesome proportions'.[47] Labour MP John Silkin later joked that the mathematically inept Duffy then proposed giving unions, MPs and CLPs 40 per cent of the vote each.[48] David Lange, the future right-wing Labour prime minister of New Zealand, attended the conference as a guest of the Labour MP Austin Mitchell. Lange turned to Mitchell and exclaimed, 'This is madness.'[49]

The AUEW's abstention was a catastrophic misjudgement, which was then followed by another miscalculation. USDAW, another right-wing union, idiosyncratically proposed 40 per cent to the trade unions, 30 per cent to CLPs, and 30 per cent to the PLP. This was a much lower proportion of PLP power than the Labour right had wanted, and CLPD immediately seized upon the formula. The right-wing Labour MP Giles Radice said the USDAW formula 'was such a cock up. We had been outmanoeuvred by the left.'[50] Sid Weighell, the moderate General Secretary of the National Union of Railwaymen, later lamented that it was 'a disastrous Saturday's work'.[51] For the left, it was a triumph. CLPD's Jon Lansman enthused, 'We were bloody lucky to have won.'[52]

The following day in East London, former Labour Cabinet ministers Shirley Williams, Bill Rodgers, Roy Jenkins and David Owen announced:

'The calamitous outcome of the Labour Party conference demands a new start in British politics. A handful of trade union leaders can now dictate the choice of a future prime minister.' Labour, they declared, had abandoned 'its commitment to parliamentary government'.[53] The 'Limehouse Declaration' was widely understood to be the prelude to a new party (discussed below).[54] The Wembley conference had provided these defectors with a plausible pretext for their departure.

The Wembley conference was the low point for the Labour right. Almost immediately, right-wing trade union leaders began to organise a counter-offensive. Alan Tuffin, the General Secretary of the Communications Workers Union, said that it was 'the beginning of a lot of us [union leaders] realising we were not paying enough attention' to the internal battles of the Labour Party.[55] The following month, a group of senior union leaders began what would become monthly meetings at the St Ermins Hotel in London to coordinate their actions.[56] The following year, a group of right-wing members of the NEC began to do the same, calling themselves the Beaujolais Group due to their penchant for good food and wine.[57]

The organisational strength of the party right was soon put to the test when Labour's Deputy Leader Denis Healey, who had been elected unopposed on the day he lost the leadership to Michael Foot, was challenged under the new rules by Tony Benn. After a gruelling campaign of six months, Healey defeated Benn by 'half an eyebrow' – a margin of 50.4 per cent to 49.6 per cent – in September 1981.[58] While Healey benefited from superior right-wing organisation, some of the victory was owed to good fortune. For instance, the only two unions to consult their members (the National Union of Public Employees (NUPE) and the Fire Brigades Union) had left-wing leadership, but their members supported Healey in the consultation, depriving Benn of crucial union bloc votes.

More significantly, however, Healey's victory was due to shifting sands on the party's left. The first ballot had been a three-way contest between Benn, Healey and John Silkin, another left-wing candidate who had little chance of winning. In the first round of voting, the two left candidates' combined vote was 54.6 per cent to Healey's 45.4 per cent.[59] With Silkin eliminated, his votes ought to have transferred to Benn in the second ballot. An analysis of the two ballots indicates that some unions, CLPs and MPs declined to cast a second vote (see Table 6.1). Had these 'missing' votes gone to Benn, he would have won.

Table 6.1 Total votes cast in the 1981 deputy leadership election, indicating the number of abstentions in the second ballot

Section	Ballot 1	Ballot 2	Difference
Affiliates (40%)	6,427,000	6,352,000	**−75,000**
CLPs (30%)	626	624	**−2**
MPs (30%)	245	208	**−37**

Note: The total votes did not affect the weighting of the three electorates.
Source: Mortimore and Blick, 2018

The most significant abstentions were the thirty-seven MPs, who were mostly on the left, including NEC members Neil Kinnock and Joan Lestor. Cries of 'Judas!' rang out when Kinnock failed to cast his vote for Benn.[60] The Benn candidacy had driven a split through the Labour left. The left-wing 'Tribune' pressure group split, with the formation of a further left 'Campaign Group' of MPs. The two factions within the Labour left were known respectively as the 'soft' and the 'hard' left.

In forcing this division, Benn's challenge sowed the seeds of the destruction of the left's power. First, the contest was unnecessary, vindictive, divisive and damaging to Labour's standing in the polls. Benn professed to be the champion of true socialism against the sell-out Healey. Even those on the left thought this was far too simplistic. Jennie Lee, a Labour peer of impeccable left-wing credentials (and the widow of Nye Bevan), wrote to a fellow Labour MP: 'Tony Benn's self-righteousness gets on my nerves.'[61] Peter Shore, once a close friend of Benn, refused to endorse either Benn or Healey. He likened the Bennites to Calvinists who 'divided [Labour MPs] into the Elect and the non-Elect … They are intolerant, fanatical, and authoritarian.' Continuing the analogy, Shore charged that 'Benn's New Model Army' were 'anxious and ready for war: civil war'.[62] Michael Foot later raged, 'the responsibility for transmuting every controversy of the time into an internal Labour Party dispute rested directly with Tony Benn'.[63]

The 'soft left' began to see the right as their greater allies for the first time. This reorientation of ideological weight within the party would become extremely significant as the years progressed. Soft-left Michael Foot stood loyally behind his right-wing deputy Healey. Foot even dared Benn to abandon his challenge to Healey and seek the leadership against Foot himself. Benn later chided: 'That was quite hysterical, I thought.'[64]

For the party's right, Healey's victory demonstrated that the left could be defeated through good organisation. This was important in preventing further defections to the SDP. The right-wing rallying cry became one of 'stay in the party and fight'. When Healey had tried to make this argument to the first wave of SDP defectors in the spring of 1981, his pleas had fallen on deaf ears. 'I told them just to wait 6 months. The NEC would change', Healey later recalled.[65] After the defeat of Tony Benn, this argument had greater credibility.

In January 1982, union leaders met in Bishop's Stortford at the lavish headquarters of the Association of Scientific, Technical and Managerial Staffs led by Clive Jenkins. They agreed that there would be no further constitutional changes, no new challenges to the leadership and no purges of the far left. The agreement became known as the 'Peace of Bishop's Stortford'.[66] It marked a temporary end to the major constitutional battles, but the damage was long-lasting. The previous three years had produced a challenger party of the right, a split on the left, and given the public the impression of a party at war with itself.

In fairness to the Labour left, the argument that there should be no internal reform, lest it risk the party being distracted from the task of defeating the Conservatives, could not be entirely justified either. It meant the continued protection of a right-wing status quo. The left-wing Sheffield MP Martin Flannery argued that such a critique amounted to 'an invitation to the Left to shut up and to let the Right-wing have its way'.[67] In this respect, the left cannot be blamed for seeking reform, but it can be blamed for failing to consider the wider ramifications of the process required to achieve that reform. In particular, it is now obvious that Tony Benn's challenge to Denis Healey was a major misjudgement, not only for Labour's image but also for the left's power within the party. Its one salutary, if unintended, effect may have been stymying further defections to the SDP.

Building the Party's Relationship with the Electorate: Suicide Notes and Beds of Roses

The battles over the Labour Party constitution distracted from the party's ability to construct a winning electoral coalition following its 1979 defeat. Moreover, the constant criticism of the previous Labour government by the Labour Party itself did little to endear the public to the prospects of a future Labour government. Shadow Chancellor Peter Shore criticised the party's navel-gazing tendency. He told the Carlisle Labour Party in February 1981: 'the politics of socialism is essentially the politics of persuasion. If the Labour Party was ever to take the view that it did not need to persuade the electorate and all it needed was to demonstrate its own ideological purity, it would wither and shrink to an insignificant political force.'[68] Yet, in the immediate years after its 1979 defeat, Labour's concern about its standing in the electorate was secondary to the doctrinal disagreements within the party. The consequences of this obsessive self-regard were predictable.

The 1983 campaign was a complete fiasco. Eric Shaw described it as 'disorganised, ramshackle, and uncoordinated with no obvious strategy or central message'.[69] David Butler and Dennis Kavanagh concluded in their Nuffield Study: 'it is difficult to think of any campaign fought by a major party since the war that was more inept than Labour's in 1983'.[70] Healey admitted that 'our election campaign was the worse organised than any I have ever known'.[71]

The party had limited funds. Neil Kinnock recalls: 'The party was broke, absolutely financially smashed to pieces.'[72] As a result, Labour could not hope to match the Conservatives in numbers of paid campaign staff. It had only sixty-three full-time agents compared to the Conservatives' 320.[73] Labour was not without professional expertise, but even this advice was squandered. The party commissioned polling firm MORI and advertising guru Johnny Wright, who later called his experience 'advertising hell'. Labour posters and broadcasts were hurriedly designed and too esoteric. One poster was so literal that it was indecipherable. It depicted 'a traumatised pensioner being squashed in a gigantic metal clamp, above the headline, "Are you going to vote pensioners into 5 more years of the pinch"'. The campaign committee 'disliked us and everything we stood for', one of Wright's associates confessed. In the middle of a presentation to the NEC given by Labour's image consultants, Eric Heffer MP interjected, 'Who the hell are these fucking idiots?' When Wright visited Foot at his home to show potential poster designs, Foot laid them out on the floor and invited his dog Disraeli to choose one.[74] Labour selected the grammatically indefensible slogan, 'Think positive, act positive, vote Labour'. It was, as Foot's biographer Mervyn Jones shuddered, 'an appeal coined by someone who could not tell an adjective from an adverb'.[75]

The central campaign committee was far too large. It consisted of twenty-three members and tried to take decisions collectively, which was admirably democratic but often resulted in delay, confusion or contradiction. In the heat of a campaign, many decisions had to be taken at short notice in response to rapidly changing events. Shadow Education Secretary Neil Kinnock, who was a member of this committee, stopped attending after about four meetings, finding them to be completely unhelpful in setting the campaign's direction.[76]

Michael Foot was enthusiastic but presentationally chaotic. Barbara Castle, leader of Labour's MEPs, later fumed, 'there was Michael on telly hunched up with his collar all out of place. Why didn't someone tell him? I wanted to.'[77] There was too much emphasis on cramming in as many campaign stops in a day as possible. This resulted in poorly planned visits, with an air of chaos about them. On one 'hectic' occasion, Foot travelled around Greater Manchester on an open top bus.[78] He was pelted with eggs and tomatoes and filmed nearly being knocked off the bus as it passed under a bridge.[79] The press remarked that the bus seemed to attract foul-mouthed individuals supping from cans of beer in the middle of a working day, not necessarily the image the party wished to project.[80]

Denis Healey assessed that the entire Shadow Cabinet were given 'ridiculously heavy programmes'.[81] Kinnock had campaigned across the country to a point of near exhaustion, nearly losing his voice.[82] Days would begin at 7 a.m. at the new Labour headquarters on Walworth Road, followed by a press conference, and then touring the country all day before returning to London at midnight to catch a few hours' sleep before beginning the whole exercise again the following day. This approach meant there was little time for developing a clear, concise and consistent message.

As a result, the enthusiastic Foot would sometimes go off message, resulting in 'own goals' with time subsequently wasted on 'damage control'. One vivid occasion occurred before a packed audience in Oxford Town Hall. In an attempt to defend the honour and patriotism of the Labour Party, Foot allowed himself to get carried away by recalling a by-election which had taken place in Oxford forty-five years earlier.

'Do you know who was their Munich candidate in 1938, in effect licking Hitler's jackboots after he had tramped on Czechoslovakia?', Foot asked the 'bewildered' audience.[83] 'Lord Hailsham, who is still in this government now', Foot triumphantly revealed. These charges were put to the Lord Chancellor. 'The old boy has plainly lost his marbles. Poor old, dear old Worzel Gummidge', Hailsham mused. 'There is not a word of sanity in all that.' Hailsham pointed out that he had fought and been injured in the war, whereas 'Michael Foot never fired a shot.'[84] When asked if he would consider suing Foot, Hailsham replied magnanimously, 'Good gracious, no. I do have mercy.' Rather contentedly, he concluded: 'If he is the leader of a national party and talks like that, ha, bloody, ha.'[85]

Not all blame can be laid before Foot. A lack of unity from those who ought to have known better marred the campaign. Harold Wilson gave an interview to the *Daily Mail* which carried the headline 'Where my party has gone wrong'. Foot depressingly reflected: 'Mrs Thatcher could have approved every word. The whole piece might have been another brilliant advertisement designed by Saatchi and Saatchi.'[86] Wilson feebly claimed that because it was dark he hadn't realised that the *Mail* journalist, whom Wilson had invited into his car, was writing down every word the ex-PM said. Jim Callaghan, for his part, trashed Labour's position on unilateral nuclear disarmament at a speech in Cardiff, which was widely covered by the press.

As the campaign wore on, Labour's position worsened. This was largely to the benefit of the Alliance formed between the SDP and Liberal Party (Figure 6.2). The first MORI and Harris polls, conducted immediately after Thatcher asked for a dissolution, respectively showed Labour enjoying a 10- and 14-point lead over the SDP–Liberal Alliance. On polling day itself, Labour was just 2 points ahead. Jack Straw, the Labour MP for Blackburn, later posited that had the campaign continued for another week, Labour would have fallen into third place: 'our votes were dissolving like snow in the sunshine'.[87]

The creation of the SDP in 1981 had constituted one of the gravest threats to Labour's existence since the formation of the National government in 1931. After Shirley Williams won a shock victory at the Crosby by-election in November 1981, *Tribune* warned: 'Labour is two years from disaster … Will the growing challenge from the SDP

IMPOSSIBLE PROMISES AND FAR-FETCHED RESOLUTIONS

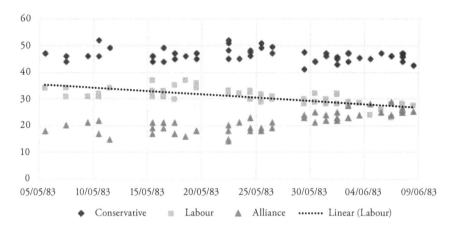

Figure 6.2 Polling during the short campaign of the 1983 election, with trendline for Labour (8 May–9 June 1983) (%)
Source: Polling dataset from https://www.markpack.org.uk/opinion-polls

push Labour back into a 1931-type position?'[88] By the time of the 1983 election, twenty-seven SDP MPs sat in Parliament: twenty-four had been elected as Labour MPs, one as a Conservative, and two (Jenkins and Williams) had entered Parliament in by-elections won as SDP candidates.

Yet, the SDP split could have been far worse. They failed to woo the right's biggest hitters, notably Healey. The SDP could not win the support of any of the unions. They struggled to build a mass membership. They couldn't even agree if they were a centrist party or a socialist party. Williams, Rodgers and Owen called for a 'new democratic socialist party'.[89] Yet, when asked by a journalist if he considered himself a socialist, Roy Jenkins chortled, 'I haven't used the word ... for some years.'[90] Ultimately, the first-past-the-post electoral system was Labour's greatest security, preventing SDP breakthroughs while preserving 209 Labour seats on 27.6 per cent of the vote. Even with their electoral pact with the Liberals, the SDP–Liberal Alliance won just twenty-three seats on 25.4 per cent.

Although Labour was out of power nationally, the party controlled local government in many of Britain's most important cities. Regional authorities – Greater London, Greater Manchester, the West Midlands, West Yorkshire, South Yorkshire, Tyne and Wear and Merseyside – were all abolished by the Thatcher government in 1986, but from 1979 to 1986 they gave some indication to the public of how Labour might wish to govern.

The most important of these authorities was the Greater London Council (GLC), established by the Local Government Act 1963 under the Conservative government of Alec Douglas-Home. It had originally been established to replace the London County Council (LCC), a Labour-dominated bastion, by expanding its reach into the Conservative-voting suburbs. Some Labour figures also supported the GLC because it meant that the inner city would benefit from the rates paid by richer suburbanites.[91]

In 1981, immediately after Labour's success in the local elections in London, left-winger Ken Livingstone defeated the incumbent leader Andrew McIntosh and seized control of the GLC. The future left-wing Labour MP Diane Abbott was excitedly standing outside the committee room in County Hall and described the emergence of the new leader in almost biblical terms: 'When they came out, Ken was leader. He looked completely different; it was the effect of power; suddenly he was transfigured! I knew he would win because we had the numbers, but I wasn't expecting the transfiguring effect.'[92] Livingstone set about implementing a left-wing agenda at County Hall, and he had strong support from the Labour membership in London to do it. In 1981, for instance, eighty-two out of ninety-two CLPs in London voted for Tony Benn to be Deputy Leader.[93] Historian Owen Hatherley argues that 'Livingstone, as much as [LCC leader Herbert] Morrison, intended London to be a microcosm of what socialist government would look like. The [Conservative] government knew this and crushed it.'[94]

The GLC promoted campaigns on behalf of women, gay people and ethnic minorities at a time when it was unfashionable to do so. The proportion of Black members of staff trebled. In the 1980s, Labour enjoyed sky-high support from ethnic minorities. In 1983, 81 per cent of Asian voters and 87 per cent of African-Caribbean voters backed Labour. In 1987, it was 67 per cent and 86 per cent respectively.[95] A Runnymede Trust study estimated, quite plausibly, that about 1 million of Labour's 8.5 million votes in 1983 had come from ethnic minorities. The report argued that these voters had stopped Labour from coming third in the national vote share and from losing up to thirty more seats.[96]

In spite of the growing importance of non-white voters in the Labour Party and in some Labour constituencies in the 1980s, Britain was still over 95 per cent white.[97] Peter Shore called the orientation of politics to non-class-based identities a 'cultural revolution', one which he felt distanced Labour from its historic base.[98] There was little attention paid by the GLC, for example, to the construction of council housing. In contrast, the GLC arts department funded grassroots projects, such as using ratepayers' money to fund a reggae record called 'Kill the Police Bill'.[99] In its 1983/84 financial year, the GLC allocated £6.9 million to its women's committee to spend on pro-gender equality initiatives.[100] John McDonnell, who served as the GLC's chair of finance, reflected: 'It was revolutionary ... It's no wonder Mrs Thatcher closed us down. It challenged the establishment.'[101] The GLC became Thatcher's prototype of a 'loony left' council. Conservative MP John Hunt labelled Livingstone a 'Marxist mad hatter'.[102] Other councils were similarly branded by the press as 'loony left'. About 150 councils, nearly all Labour-run, declared themselves to be 'nuclear-free zones'.[103] Nottinghamshire council sponsored 'non-competitive sports days'.[104] Sheffield City Council had a 'peace budget' of £250,000 to fund local efforts related to peace, such as peaceful song-writers, anti-nuclear amateur dramatics, pro-peace clothing makers and arts and crafts with a peaceful message.

In 1985, Neil Kinnock and the NEC concluded that Labour needed professional help to improve the party's image among the electorate. That autumn, the television producer and grandson of Herbert Morrison, Peter Mandelson, was appointed as Labour's director of communications. Mandelson immediately commissioned a consultancy firm to test Labour's image, just as one might test a new product. The investigation found that Labour's policies were seen as 'beyond the pale' and that the party was 'associated with minorities' yet also seen as 'old-fashioned', a seemingly contradictory charge.[105]

Mandelson's 'Shadow Communications Agency' deployed 'commercially-derived techniques' to develop a slicker campaign appeal.[106] Yet, this advice sometimes went too far in the other direction. Neil Kinnock was instructed that he could no longer smoke his pipe, drink a pint, or give extemporaneous remarks. Barbara Castle thought this was a grave mistake. She condemned those 'who made him look like a bank clerk ... He wasn't breathing the oxygen he so desperately needed.'[107] Equally, while Mandelson had a good eye for visual production and slogans, his understanding of policy was shallow. Bryan Gould, the Shadow Cabinet minister who would run Labour's 1987 campaign, felt that Mandelson was 'a limited political thinker who was surprisingly wooden when it came to ideas'. While Mandelson could be well-focused strategically, his political insights were 'stunningly banal'.[108]

Mandelson enlisted the talents of an Islington-based artist, Michael Wolff, to give Labour a makeover. 'Labour need to drop the word "party"', Wolff proposed, 'and get rid of the depressing and crass use of red and yellow.'[109] Kinnock suggested the addition of a red rose, a common symbol in social democratic parties in Europe. Mandelson was delighted with the rose, which he believed gave Labour 'a new corporate identity'. He wrote in 1987 that Labour's abandonment of its red flag logo helped to 'reinforce the impression of an innovative party shedding past associations'.[110] The party's electoral fortunes slowly began to improve. In April 1986, Labour won Fulham in a by-election, its first gain off the Conservatives since 1982.

The 1987 campaign had an entirely different feel to that of 1983. Labour's polling position held steady as the campaign wore on (Figure 6.3). Analysing all of the polling data available from May and June 1987, there was a modest positive trend in Labour's favour, whereas

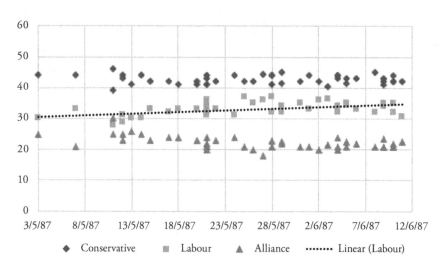

Figure 6.3 Polling during the short campaign of the 1987 election, with trendline for Labour (2 May–11 June 1987) (%)
Source: Polling dataset from https://www.markpack.org.uk/opinion-polls

the SDP–Liberal Alliance failed to make headway. In effect, the Labour versus Alliance trend was the reverse of 1983.

The verdicts on the 1987 campaign were almost as positive as those of 1983 had been negative. The historian Martin Pugh assessed: 'Labour fought the best campaign in 1987.'[111] Feeling within Labour was much more positive as well. Bryan Gould described Labour's campaign as 'slick and professional'. It was 'successful in every sense, except that we lost'.[112] Peter Mandelson called the campaign 'brilliant', but he felt it showed that Labour needed to change its policies in a more right-wing direction. He asked rhetorically after the election: 'If the Labour Party can run the best campaign in history and still lose by over a hundred seats, why bother?'[113] These sentiments presaged the dramatic shift in party policy which will be discussed in Chapter 7.

Managing Relationships with the Trade Unions: Miners and Militants

The rise of left-wing trade unionism in the 1970s had important consequences for the centre of political gravity in the Labour Party. The unions controlled 90 per cent of the votes at conference and their representatives made up a sizeable proportion of the National Executive Committee. Historically, union leaders were mostly deferential to the party leadership, and the size of union representation within the party's institutions had typically been to the leader's advantage. However, the growing assertiveness of a left-wing grassroots within the union movement jeopardised their stabilising role. As will be discussed in this section, the Militant Tendency was initially dismissed by some left-of-centre unions as a non-threat, but as the harsh impact of its sectarianism on their members became clear, hitherto left-wing public sector unions shifted allegiance on the NEC. In so doing, they provided an essential ballast to the Kinnock leadership.

Another relevant development was a change in the quality of union leadership for the worse. The formidable leaders Jack Jones (TGWU) and Hugh Scanlon (AEU) gave way to lesser figures. In Denis Healey's estimation, 'Moss Evans was a very inadequate substitute for Jack Jones' at TGWU. 'He had no leadership qualities and little loyalty to the Labour Party.'[114] Terry Duffy, who replaced Scanlon at AEU, was of unreliable judgement, and his incompetence resulted in unnecessary defeats, as was shown so visibly at Wembley. The most famous union leader of the decade was Arthur Scargill, the president of the National Union of Mineworkers. Scargill was charismatic but a poor tactician.

The miners' strike of 1984–85 is perhaps the most famous in British history after the General Strike of 1926. The political stakes were high. Miners had brought down Conservative governments before, most notably in 1974. Joan Maynard MP argued that Thatcher's tactic was 'you had to start with the strongest. If you broke them, you were laughing because all the others went down like ninepins.'[115] Her left-wing NEC colleague Eric Heffer explained: 'I knew that the defeat of the miners would be a defeat for the entire working-class movement. The miners *had* to win.'[116]

The NUM was one of Britain's most powerful unions, given the essential importance of the energy supply. Miners were a sympathetic subject, described by the former Conservative prime minister Harold Macmillan in a 1984 speech as 'the best men in the world'.[117] Yet Scargill, an inflexible and combative Marxist, proved a useful villain for the Thatcher government. For Labour, the dispute pulled the party in two directions. On the one hand, there was enormous sympathy for the miners and their families among Labour Party members. On the other hand, the strike had been called without a ballot and some of the tactics on the picket lines veered into intimidation, admittedly in the face of egregious police violence and state repression. The ultimate defeat of the miners in 1985 was 'a watershed' which 'led to a loss of confidence' on the trade union left.[118]

Yet, while the miners' strike was an emotionally significant episode, as well as one of key symbolic resonance for the wider union movement, its political impact on the Labour Party was rather muted. The more significant development in trade union relations during this period occurred surreptitiously on the National Executive Committee. After the Wembley conference of 1981, as has already been discussed, right-wing trade union leaders began to prepare a counter-offensive against the Labour left. In the eyes of the historian Dianne Hayter, 'the trade unions – founders of the Labour Party – came to its rescue'.[119] Perhaps equally significant, however, was a showdown with the far-left Militant Tendency in Liverpool that drove left-leaning union officials away from the hard left and into alliances with the Labour right on the NEC by 1986.

The Trotskyist Revolutionary Socialist League was founded in 1955, and later organised itself around the *Militant* newspaper, founded in 1964. Between 1965 and 1986, the number of Militant activists rose from 100 to 8,100.[120] They called themselves a 'tendency', meaning a 'way of thinking', in order to protect themselves from expulsion from the Labour Party. By the 1980s, the newspaper had sixty full-time staff and an annual conference, giving the impression that the newspaper was a front for a party within a party, which was prohibited by Labour Party rules.[121]

Militant supporters sought to use the Labour Party as a vehicle for achieving their revolutionary socialist goals. They managed to get supporters elected to the NEC, using the youth section as an initial foothold, and as Labour MPs. Demonstrating the breadth of their support in the Labour grassroots, in 1985 at least 100 CLPs, sixty-five trade union branches, fifteen women's sections, 107 Young Socialist branches and nine university Labour clubs passed motions condemning an NEC inquiry into the activities of Militant.[122]

The hotbed of Militant was in Liverpool, where the group controlled the district Labour Party's executive. Although eleven to sixteen councillors (out of a total of 99) were in Militant, the process of selecting and deselecting councillors was in the executive's hands.[123] Therefore, even councillors who were not of the 'tendency' held their seats at Militant's mercy. As a result, Militant effectively ran Liverpool City Council.

In 1984, the council threatened to set an illegal budget because it could not make up a budgetary shortfall due to rate caps. This resulted in the Thatcher government agreeing to send £20 million in additional support.[124] The following year, the council tried the same tactic, but this time the Thatcher government refused to budge, telling the council it needed to balance its books as required by law. The council then decided it would set a 'legal' budget, but in order to balance the budget, it would sack the entire city workforce. On 27 September 1985, it voted to issue ninety-day redundancy notices to all 35,000 city workers. Labour leader John Hamilton announced: 'We are saying to the government, you have 90 days.'[125] If the government didn't send more money, 'then Liverpool will suffer and will be plunged into the depths of poverty and disaster …

The responsibility lies on the shoulders of the Cabinet and 10 Downing Street.'¹²⁶

It was intended to be a bluff. The Labour councillors obviously did not want to make all of the city's workers unemployed but hoped a bailout would emerge like the year before. One of the council's difficulties was that the public sector NALGO union had instructed their members not to distribute the redundancy notices.¹²⁷ So council officials secretly hired a fleet of twenty-seven taxis to deliver the redundancy notices instead.¹²⁸ On hearing this news, Neil Kinnock said privately to his chief of staff Charles Clarke, 'I've got the bastards; this is where I go in.'¹²⁹

A fortnight later, the Labour Party gathered for its annual party conference in Bournemouth. Without mentioning the words 'Liverpool' or 'Militant' once in the entire speech, it was obvious against whom Kinnock was directing his ire with perhaps the most famous few lines of his career:

> I'll tell you what happens with impossible promises. You start with far-fetched resolutions. They are then pickled into a rigid dogma, a code, and you go through the years sticking to that, out-dated, misplaced, irrelevant to the real needs, and you end up in the grotesque chaos of a Labour council – a LABOUR COUNCIL – hiring taxis to scuttle round a city handing out redundancy notices to its own workers. I am telling you, no matter how entertaining, how fulfilling to short-term egos, you can't play politics with people's jobs and with people's services or with their homes.¹³⁰

The right-wing of the party adored the speech. Denis Healey oozed, 'I think it was a superb speech which has changed the centre of gravity inside the Labour movement and set us firmly on the road to power.'¹³¹ The left-wing reaction was rather different. Liverpool MP Bob Parry fumed, 'Kinnock showed today that he is the biggest traitor since Ramsay MacDonald. He is the man who kicked Liverpool in the teeth when it was down on the ground.'¹³² Tony Benn described Kinnock's speech as 'virulent and unfair'.¹³³ In his diary, Benn confessed that when he left the conference hall, he broke down in tears.¹³⁴

The reality is that Liverpool City Council was doing precisely what Kinnock had accused them of. The city council *had* hired taxis to deliver redundancy notices to its own workers. Liverpool MP Eric Heffer, who had stormed out of the conference hall as Kinnock launched his tirade, insisted that the redundancies were 'a tactic to put pressure on the government'.[135] Yet, in this admission, Heffer implicitly admitted that the council *was* playing politics with people's jobs and services.

Even more so than Tony Benn's deputy leadership contest, the Militant affair split the Labour left. Left-wing politicians and union leaders were appalled by the behaviour of Liverpool City Council. They encountered a 'rude awakening' on their visit to the city as part of the NEC Inquiry into Liverpool District Labour Party.[136] Sheffield council leader David Blunkett met Liverpool council leader John Hamilton, who was under intense pressure from his Militant-controlled district party. Blunkett, who is blind, could 'feel him physically shaking, and his chair shaking, with fear'.[137] NUPE's Tom Sawyer said after meeting with members of his union who had been denied jobs or promotion due to ideological impurity: 'I felt terribly naïve actually and stupid; I had never seen this in my life.'[138] The defection of Sawyer, who had been a loyal union organiser for Benn during the 1981 Deputy Leader contest, was particularly significant. Kinnock apparently told his team at the time, 'from now on "majority" is spelt S-A-W-Y-E-R'.[139]

Holding the Conservative Government to Account: Friedman and the Falklands

There is a certain irony that during this period of intense internal division within the Labour Party, there was a strong consensus across Labour on the moral wickedness of the Thatcher government, especially its economic policy. Michael Foot wrote that the 1979 election had 'let loose on the nation a mass of iron ladies, Selsdon men, and mad monks', a reference to Margaret Thatcher and the free-marketeer Conservatives Nicholas Ridley and Keith Joseph, respectively.[140] Peter Shore, Labour's Shadow Chancellor, wrote scathingly of monetarism in 1983: 'The gullible, inexperienced, and ideological Conservative politicians who in 1975 displaced Mr Edward Heath swallowed, hook, line, and sinker, the theoretical doctrines … of Dr Milton Friedman and Professor Hayek.'[141]

Initially, it seemed like the Conservative government would self-destruct. After Labour had reduced inflation to 8 per cent, it peaked at 22 per cent in 1980. Unemployment in 1982 reached over 3 million, double what it had been under the previous Labour government. In 1980, Labour achieved a 13 per cent swing in the Southend East by-election, nearly overturning a 10,000 Conservative majority. Yet, distracted by its internal battles, the Labour Party did a poor job of holding the Conservative government to account for its economic failure. Foot later assessed, 'our Tory opponents watched in gleeful disbelief and gratitude'.[142] He reflected that the years of his leadership ought to have been a prime opportunity 'to destroy the Tory Government. Instead, we turned it into a period of futility and shame.'[143] The Labour NEC organised mass marches across the country to protest high unemployment. An initial march in London proved successful, but marches in Cardiff and Birmingham turned into 'fiascos' as members of the far left arrived, heckling Labour MPs off the stage for being pseudo-socialists.

One area where Labour provided inconsistent opposition was over the Falklands conflict of 1982. The background to the conflict is worth examining, as it is often ignored in narratives of the conflict which lionise Margaret Thatcher as a steely (or iron) leader of great conviction. In the 1970s and early 1980s, the *HMS Endurance*, an armed survey ship, patrolled the waters around Argentina. As prime minister, Jim Callaghan had been given advice to withdraw the *Endurance* for cost reasons, but Callaghan 'turned it down flat'. In December 1981, General Leopoldo Galtieri seized control of the presidency of Argentina in a military coup. Astonishingly, the following month, Thatcher ordered the withdrawal of *Endurance*, in spite of strong protests from Falkland Islanders. The islands were left with no military protection except for the few ceremonial guards assigned to the Governor. On 9 February 1982, Callaghan warned Thatcher, 'the Government's decisions to withdraw and pay off *HMS Endurance* when she returns from the South Atlantic is an error that could have serious consequences'.[144] Two months later, the Argentinians took the islands without meeting any armed resistance.

Labour requested that Parliament be recalled, to which Thatcher acquiesced, on 14 April 1982 – the first Saturday sitting since the Suez crisis. Michael Foot launched into an impassioned defence of the Falkland Islanders' right to be British:

> There is no question in the Falkland Islands of any colonial dependence or anything of the sort. It is a question of people who wish to be associated with

this country and who have built their whole lives on the basis of association with this country. We have a moral duty, a political duty and every other kind of duty to ensure that that is sustained.

Foot excoriated Thatcher for having 'betrayed' the Islanders.[145] It was one of Foot's greatest parliamentary performances, among many, and deeply embarrassing for the Thatcher government. One Labour MP reflected: 'The fact is, at that stage, Mrs Thatcher was more subdued than he was.'[146]

Yet, almost immediately, Foot came under fierce criticism from his own MPs. During the debate, Judith Hart and Tony Benn disagreed with their leader, suggesting that some kind of settlement could be reached with the Argentine leader, but Foot replied, 'they put too great a store on General Galtieri's good nature'.[147] At the next meeting of the Shadow Cabinet, Foot was denounced by Eric Heffer: 'Now we had a war and Michael Foot was as responsible for it as Mrs Thatcher. His speech was thoroughly jingoistic.'[148] At the next meeting of the PLP, Labour MP Tam Dalyell chastised Foot for his bellicosity. Foot retorted, 'I know a fascist when I see one.' In 1940, Foot had been one of the authors of the famed *Guilty Men* pamphlet which exposed the moral bankruptcy of fascist appeasement. Here again, in General Galtieri's expansionism, Foot found another such enemy who needed to be met with force. He insisted that the Falkland Islanders 'are faced with an act of naked, unqualified aggression, carried out in the most shameful and disreputable circumstances'.[149]

Under pressure, Foot pulled back and softened his rhetoric for the rest of the war, just as Thatcher ratcheted up her own. It could have been a great patriotic rallying cry for Labour, exposing the outrageously vulnerable position in which the Conservative government had placed the Falkland Islanders just months earlier. The Falklands could have been to Foot what Suez had been to Gaitskell (as described in Chapter 4). Yet it became once again a moment for internal Labour division. Ultimately, Labour's failure to speak with a clear voice on the Falkland conflict allowed Thatcher to snatch political victory from the jaws of defeat, and it became one of the great crowning successes of her premiership, when in fact it ought to have been seen as one of her greatest mistakes.

Forming a Clear Policy Agenda: The EEC and CND

The Labour Party's preoccupation with internal power struggles precluded policy development. After Labour conferences cemented a left-wing programme in the conferences of 1979, 1980 and 1981, the party's policy commitments remained stable throughout this 1979–87 period. Labour's 1983 manifesto entitled *The New Hope for Britain* was characterised unhelpfully by the right-wing Labour MP Gerald Kaufman as the 'longest suicide note in history'. The manifesto was, effectively, a collection of recent conference motions compiled into one document with little concern for their coherence.[150]

Yet, after the 1983 election not much changed.[151] Neil Kinnock later admitted: 'In policy alteration and modification terms, we barely moved.'[152] The only substantive policy change he was able to get through the NEC's home policy committee was for Labour to agree to the sale of council houses if the revenue was used for new builds and renovation of the existing stock. He claimed that the only way even this change was possible was thanks to representatives of opposing trade unions conveniently disappearing when key votes were being taken. The council house vote succeeded thanks to 'Alec Kitson [TGWU] going out to the toilet and Sam McCluskie [National Union of Seamen] going out for a smoke, thus giving me a majority of one'.[153]

More than any others, two policies defined Labour's image in the 1980s. The first was Labour's support for leaving the European Economic Community. The second was its support for dismantling Britain's nuclear arsenal. Neither policy was particularly popular with the British electorate at the time, yet because of the core socialist principles involved – namely, democratic control over national economic planning, and world peace – there was little appetite among Labour members, MPs or leaders to budge on these important topics.

In October 1980, 71 per cent of Labour conference delegates voted to leave the EEC. Brexit, as we now call it, was Labour Party policy. At the 1981 conference an even larger margin, 84 per cent of delegates, voted in favour of leaving. Hardly any Labour activist was a 'remainer'. Following the conference votes, the NEC began serious discussions to flesh out Labour's withdrawal policy. Unlike David Cameron, who blocked efforts to prepare for Brexit before the 2016 EU referendum, the Labour Party considered it vitally important to assess the future relationship between the UK and EEC *before* the withdrawal process began.

In December 1981, an NEC delegation of Labour MPs went to Brussels to discuss Labour's plan for withdrawal with the European Commission. They were led by Judith Hart, a left-wing Labour MP and chair of the NEC. Hart was a passionate advocate for anti-colonial causes, and she regarded the EEC as a 'neo-colonial' project. The Labour negotiators met with a dozen members of the Commission. 'On the whole the discussions were both serious and fruitful and conducted in an atmosphere of considerable friendliness', the Labour internal report stated. 'It was quite noticeable', however, that the only 'hostility that was shown came from the British officials'.[154]

The Labour negotiators discussed a lengthy list of topics with the Commission: trade, industrial policy, technical standards, agriculture and food, Ireland, the social fund, employment, energy and oil, Euratom, international development, the legalities of withdrawal, and a negotiation timetable. The conclusion of Hart and her team was rather cheery: 'The overall impression that the delegation gained from the meetings was that whilst there were clearly a range of problems which needed to be settled prior to British withdrawal, none of these problems were insurmountable.' While there were some areas which needed to be ironed out and 'many of the officials questioned the validity of our economic analysis of the future for the UK outside the EEC', the Labour negotiators were gratified that their visit, 'if nothing else, served to convince the Commission that the Labour Party was serious about its policy on withdrawal'.[155]

After the 1983 election defeat, there was a gradual massaging of Labour's pro-leave position. The party would first seek reform of the EEC. It would not accept, as Kinnock put it, 'anything less than Gaullist reformism'.[156] But, if the EEC refused to reform fundamentally, then the party would withdraw from the organisation. This position allowed for a kind of peace within the party. Labour's pro-Europeans were pleased to see the party move away from outright withdrawal, while the party's Eurosceptics, chastened by the 1983 rout, saw it as a necessary, if regrettable, compromise with the electorate. Even Bryan Gould, a Eurosceptic, wrote in a briefing note in November 1985, 'we must also recognise the nervousness of the British electorate about any talk of withdrawal'.[157]

The party's 1987 manifesto reflected the compromise: 'we will stand up for British interests within the European Community and will seek to put an end to the abuses and scandals of the Common Agricultural Policy'. Labour warned that it would 'reject EEC interference with our policy for national recovery and renewal'.[158]

The second contentious policy area was defence. Just 23 per cent of the British public supported unilateral nuclear disarmament in 1984.[159] Yet, it was a policy supported by a majority of the Labour rank and file. The 1983 manifesto claimed to be both unilateralist and multilateralist, with the confusing formulation: 'We must use unilateral steps taken by Britain to secure multilateral solutions on the international level. Unilateralism and multilateralism must go hand in hand if either is to succeed.'[160] Gerald Kaufman was scathing of this language, sarcastically calling it a 'lovely little formula agreed by Denis [Healey] and Eric [Heffer]'. When exposed to public view, 'it was like in *Great Expectations* when the curtains were opened in Miss Havisham's room. The moment the light came in, everything crumbled.'[161]

From 1983 to 1987, there was little evidence of change under Labour's new leader Neil Kinnock. Kinnock had been a member of the Campaign for Nuclear Disarmament since 1961. His first public engagement as party leader in October 1983 was addressing a CND rally. It was said that his beloved wife Glenys once threatened to leave him if he changed his position on nuclear weapons. In the lead up to the 1987 election, Denis Healey was able to secure a personal promise from Mikhail Gorbachev that the Soviet Union would dismantle the same number of missiles as Britain if Britain chose to do so unilaterally. While hailed by Labour as a great victory, US Ambassador Charles Price scoffed: 'that would mean when Britain reduced from 64 missiles to zero, the Soviets would drop from about 10,000 to 9,936'.[162] Thus, Labour's position on nuclear weaponry in 1987 was remarkably similar to that of four years earlier. It entailed dismantling Polaris, cancelling Trident, closing the St Mawgan and Poseidon submarine bases, and removing all cruise missiles from Greenham Common.

Conclusion

Truly, Labour walked in the valley of the shadow of death in the early 1980s. The party committed two major errors. The first was to adopt an overly critical posture towards the previous Labour government. While it is important to have a frank assessment of a government's failings, this must be done with consideration given to the relevant context in which the government was operating. Too many in Labour judged the prior government against an ideal set of economic circumstances in which it did not operate. Its second failing was to become overly preoccupied with internal party rule changes that were not designed to strengthen the party but pursued merely for factional advantage. While it was legitimate for the left of the party to criticise Labour's oligarchic leadership structures, the zero-sum fashion in which these criticisms were achieved nearly derailed the party entirely.

The focus on these changes consumed an enormous amount of the party's energy – so much so that it had little time to focus on its relationship with the electorate, policy development or even holding the government to account. Dianne Hayter is correct to say that 'between 1979 and 1982, the issue of democracy and power in the party became dominant, virtually making the substantive issues secondary'.[163] The most significant change for the party occurred on its governing National Executive Committee. The left split, with the 'soft' left finding common cause with the right against the 'hard' left; by the mid-1980s, this had provided the Labour leader Neil Kinnock with the first pro-leadership majorities on the NEC in over a decade. Edward Pearce writes with some justification that the reorientation of Labour's NEC preceded the arrival of Peter Mandelson: it 'came before red roses and mattered more'.[164]

7
Thatcher's Greatest Achievement?
(1987–1997)

For the Labour activist John O'Farrell, 'the consolation in 1983 was that it was so obvious why we had lost. 1987 felt even worse because we'd got it right and [the electorate] still hated us almost as much.' 'For all our red roses, slick broadcasts, glossy leaflets and Red Wedge Billy Bragg concerts', O'Farrell lamented, 'Labour had increased its vote by around 3 measly per cent.'[1]

O'Farrell would not have been consoled by reflecting on Labour's previous post-war experience of a third consecutive defeat. There were, though, interesting parallels with the 1959 general election, when Labour had also notched up an unwanted hat-trick after another eight-year period of Conservative government. Back in 1959 there had been no red roses and the radical balladeer Billy Bragg was crying in his cradle rather than singing on stage; but the party was judged to have run a successful campaign thanks not least to skilful media performers like Anthony Wedgwood Benn. In 1987, as in 1959, defeat was held to have strengthened the leader rather than weakening him, apparently vindicating Neil Kinnock's belief that Labour had not yet 'got it right' and would never convince voters that it deserved another chance unless it continued to adapt.

There was one positive difference between the two elections: in 1987, Labour posted a net gain of twenty seats, whereas in 1959 its tally had been reduced by nineteen. However, the voting figures presented a more demoralising picture for Kinnock and his party. In 1959, Labour candidates had won more than 46 per cent of the popular vote. The corresponding figure in 1987 was 30.8 per cent. By post-war standards, this level of support was 'measly' to say the least. It was not much consolation that the SDP–Liberal Alliance, which had threatened to outrun Labour for second place in 1983, saw its vote share fall to 22.6 per cent, and was reduced by the effects of first-past-the-post to just twenty-two MPs.

In the 1992 general election Labour regained further ground, securing an additional forty-two seats and raising its vote share to 34.4 per cent. Yet the realisation, early on election night, that the party was destined for yet another spell in opposition came as a shock even to its most defeatist supporters, who had regarded the 'hung' Parliament predicted by the BBC's exit poll as the worst possible outcome.

Five years later, Labour's prospects had improved beyond recognition and it was obvious long before the 1997 general election that the party would finally get another chance to govern. When the Conservative prime minister, John Major, faced his reckoning with the voters, Labour returned 418 MPs – twenty-five more than in the totemic 1945 contest. What seemed to have become a party of perennial opposition had turned the tables on its Tory tormentors, who were left facing an overall Labour majority of 179 and had lost all of their elected representatives outside England. If Labour's parliamentary position had been transformed, the party itself had undergone radical changes over the preceding decade. After the 1959 general election, Hugh Gaitskell's allies had argued that Labour was being held back by its outmoded name.[2] Having driven through more far-reaching reforms than even Gaitskell ever contemplated, his 'modernising' successors of the 1990s settled for an informal terminological adjustment. Whatever label might have appeared on the ballot paper in his Sedgefield constituency, as Tony Blair prepared to enter 10 Downing Street in the early hours of 2 May 1997 he promised that 'we ran for office as New Labour, we will govern as New Labour'.

In 2002, after Blair's party had won a second victory of similar seismic proportions, Baroness Thatcher identified the creation of New Labour as her greatest achievement: 'we forced our opponents to change their minds'.[3] While the extent of 'Thatcherite' influence over New Labour's philosophy and policies remains controversial, there were equally dramatic changes in the party's organisation and ethos which gave its leader much more centralised control than Thatcher had ever enjoyed over the Conservatives.

Wooing the Electorate

An alternative to Thatcher's explanation for the emergence of New Labour was that, very belatedly, the party had responded to changes in the British electorate which had been detectable even in the late 1950s. In the wake of the 1987 defeat the party conference had instigated a policy review, which was informed by a report (*Labour and Britain in the 1990s*) based on a variety of sources, including the findings of what became known as 'focus groups'. The results – predictably enough for a party which had just suffered a resounding defeat in a third consecutive general election – were disheartening, as summarised in a terse bullet-point: 'Labour has been losing votes amongst all classes.' However, the implications of the detailed research were ambiguous. If social influences were the main determinant of voting behaviour, the authors concluded, support for Labour would have fallen 'by around 6 per cent between 1964 and 1987. In fact, the reduction in Labour's vote was 13.3 per cent.' Furthermore, 'similar [demographic] changes had taken place in other West European countries, without a similar decline in the vote of parties on the left'.[4]

This implied that, even on the (well-founded) view that social class was no longer a reliable indicator of voting preference in the UK, there was still a sizeable constituency which was likely to incline towards Labour for demographic reasons; but in recent decades the party had failed to convert these reserves of inherent sympathy into electoral support. The report's qualitative findings offered several reasons for this failure. In 1987 the main objection raised by non-Labour voters was a fear that the party's 'loony left' would gain control, or at least continue to cause damaging divisions. The assumption that Labour was dominated by the trade unions was another reason advanced by those who had snubbed the party in 1987 – indeed, this factor seemed to have acted as a more potent deterrent among former Labour voters than within the electorate as a whole. While fewer respondents testified to concerns about the party's economic competence, presumably the people who nominated the influence of the 'loony left' and trade unions as their primary reasons for rejecting Labour suspected the combined influence of those divisive elements would be unhelpful to the party's economic stewardship.

On this evidence, Labour's main problems concerned the party 'brand' and were thus remediable. If it could persuade the public that it was united and free from 'extreme' influences, there was all to play for despite detrimental demographic change. As if anticipating Thatcher's claim to have created New Labour, the report emphasised that 'the population has *not* become "Thatcherite" in lots of ways that matter to the Labour Party'. Even among those who withheld their support from the party in both 1983 and 1987, there was general approval for 'a better welfare state (even at the cost of tax increases), redistribution of income, [and] an attack on unemployment'.[5] In 1989, an academic study of 'the Thatcher effect' reinforced these findings, recording that the attempt to foist Thatcherite values on the British public had been 'a crusade that failed'.[6] However, from the perspective of Labour's strategists, this made it all the more exasperating that, in 1987, the party had failed to translate anti-Thatcherite sentiment into a winning formula for a third time.

In the aftermath of the 1987 contest there seemed to be two potential routes out of opposition for Labour. The first was to keep the script much as it was, but to ditch the leading actor – Neil Kinnock, who had campaigned to the best of his considerable ability, but had palpably failed to demonstrate his prime ministerial potential beyond die-hard Labour supporters. However, in 1987 most of the latter were ready to accept that Kinnock, like Gaitskell in 1959, had lost an election despite 'winning' the campaign. The other potential route raised questions about the extent of the necessary re-write. Loyalists like O'Farrell had considered that Labour's pitch to the voters had looked passable, at worst, on the page. But perhaps the party had comprehensively misjudged the audience? After all, in 1983 Kinnock had delivered an eloquent public warning that the re-election of Margaret Thatcher would bring dire consequences to those who were young, ill or growing old. Either Kinnock's forecast had been overblown, or too many voters had felt immune from the misfortunes affecting people in those categories. Even before 1987, prominent members of Kinnock's entourage had begun to evince a kind of heroic defeatism in their evaluation of the electorate. What if the respondents to superficial surveys had taken the costless course of saying something self-flattering while thinking something entirely different? From this perspective, it became possible only to believe opinion polls on public attitudes when they conveyed a bleak message, and even to take delight in qualitative research which exposed 'Old' Labour's weaknesses. For example, the ultra-modernising pollster Philip Gould relished memories of November 1985, when 'some of the finest researchers in Britain presented ruthlessly damning findings on the unelectability of Labour'.[7] At the time, Labour was level with the Conservatives in the headline opinion polls, and about to go ahead thanks to the government's self-created crisis over the sale of Westland Helicopters.

Although the Shadow Communications Agency (SCA) established by Gould conducted various kinds of research, focus groups – in-depth discussions with around eight people at a time 'in unassuming front rooms in Watford, or Edgware or Milton Keynes or Huddersfield' – were given priority because 'they enable politicians to hear directly the voters' voices'.[8] In reality, the physical presence of Gould and his team of earnest interlocutors was bound to distort the 'voices' of the denizens of far-flung Watford and Edgware. Unsurprisingly, the modernisers were able to uncover ample evidence of what they had been looking for – a citizen body which was long on 'aspiration' and vanishingly short on idealism. Gould distilled his findings into a string of stereotypes which would have sounded comfortingly familiar to readers of right-wing tabloid newspapers:

> Most people work very hard and usually both parents [evidently lone parents were thin on the ground in Milton Keynes and Huddersfield] work. They often feel insecure about their jobs, and are always worried about crime, the NHS, and schools for their children ... They want politicians who are tough, honest and courageous, and who govern with principle. That is why they respected Margaret Thatcher, and in the end lost faith in John Major. The public want leaders who lead, they want governments that tough it out.[9]

Labour's task, then, if it wanted to reconnect with the voters, was to find out what they really wanted and then offer it to them. This, it was thought, should be reasonably straightforward, since Gould's investigators had disclosed that all voters wanted essentially the same things and, being 'more demanding' than in previous post-war decades, would be dissatisfied with anything less. It was at least equally important to find a leader who could emulate Thatcher's sense of certainty while echoing the voice of the people as vouchsafed by the focus groups. Since Kinnock was receptive to the modernisers' messages, they tended to discount survey evidence which highlighted his weaknesses. Unsurprisingly, Gould was cold-shouldered by John Smith, whose leadership (1992–4) acted as a temporary impediment to the modernising juggernaut. But as a prominent member of Tony Blair's retinue, Gould's claims to the parentage of New Labour are more persuasive than those of the much-admired Thatcher.

Electoral Infrastructure: The Millbank Machine

Gould's prospectus for electoral victory implied a centralisation of the Labour Party machine; only members of the leader's inner circle really needed to 'hear directly the voters' voices', since conversations conducted on the doorstep by party candidates might lead to the airing of unhelpfully heterodox views. By the time of the 1997 general election, the impression of centralised control had been symbolised by a shift of the party's headquarters to a suite of offices over two lower floors of the sky-scraping Millbank Tower, not far from the Palace of Westminster. By a happy augury, this daunting edifice had appeared on the bank of the Thames in 1963, just before Harold Wilson led Labour back to office and proclaimed that it could harness the white-hot transformative forces which were afoot. At that time the party was still based in its original premises, shared with the Transport and General Workers' Union in Transport House on Smith Square, within easy heckling distance of Conservative Central Office. In 1980, Labour HQ had shifted somewhat quixotically to Walworth Road, south of the river. After John Smith's death the party renamed this building after him, before fleeing at the first opportunity to the more forbidding Millbank. Those who suggested that the name should move in tandem with the party's offices were ignored: as Peter Oborne has written, 'Smith, who would have hated Millbank and everything it represented, was rapidly becoming a non-person' for Labour.[10] John Smith House is now a hostel for cost-conscious London tourists.

By 1997 the unstoppable technological revolution hailed by Wilson had brought considerable benefits for any political party which sought to secure the overall direction of its campaigning activities. The ubiquity of the telephone meant that London-based operatives could now interrupt the evening television viewing of key voters in marginal constituencies, by-passing the endeavours of volunteer constituency workers brandishing antiquated clip-boards. In 1997 telephone banks were augmented by fax machines and the computer, which allowed the central party to compile lists of supporters and 'swing' voters in distant seats. Peter Mandelson,

Kinnock's Director of Communications between 1985 and 1990 and a key member of Blair's electioneering entourage despite becoming (in 1992) a carpetbagging MP for Hartlepool, slaved over his computer to devise a 'message grid' for the 1997 campaign. According to Gould's nostalgic account: 'Each day was allotted a separate page, with simple sections typed into the margin, including details of the morning and afternoon press conferences, the whereabouts of Tony Blair, the main photo of the day and key broadcast appearances of shadow Cabinet members.'[11] It was as if the Machiavellian Mandelson, who had worked in television before being hired by Kinnock, was sculpting the script for an electoral docudrama (while hoping that any real drama would be kept to a minimum).

The party invested more than £2 million in Millbank, and at the time of the 1997 election its offices housed around 250 staff, organised into a number of 'units'. The best-publicised of these was the 'Rapid Rebuttal Unit', which was tasked with countering Tory attacks. It enjoyed the assistance of a computerised database known as 'Excalibur', financed to the tune of £300,000 by an entrepreneur whose fortune had been amassed from a home-furnishing company called 'Fads'. King Arthur would have had little need for 'the sword in the stone' if his opponents, like the Conservatives of 1997, were already dead in the water. But the much-hyped investment was probably justifiable for the extra aura of efficiency that it lent to the New Labour machine.

New Labour's anxiety to 'rebut' Conservative allegations was more than matched by an allergy to unforced errors. Media appearances were carefully rationed to minimise the opportunities of any shadow minister hoping to burnish a reputation for independent thinking and unguarded speech. The need to deny the oxygen of publicity to such unruly figures was illustrated by a spectacular 'off-message' moment in August 1996, when the dissident frontbencher Clare Short characterised Tony Blair's unelected advisers as 'the people who live in the dark. Everything they do is in hiding.' Blair's public image, she felt, had been damaged by an 'obsession with the media and focus groups'.[12] In one respect, at least, Short's accusation was unfair. Philip Gould, the focus-group fanatic, could with justice be said to have 'lived in the dark' since he attracted little public notice until after the 1997 general election, when he broke cover with a self-congratulatory account of his part in the New Labour success story. Another highly influential person who lurked in relative obscurity was Charles Clarke, who had served as Kinnock's chief of staff between 1985 and 1992 and, after a hiatus while Smith was leader, resumed his behind-the-scenes influence under Blair. Clarke became well known to journalists and political 'anoraks', rather than a recognisable public face, during the opposition years. However, Clare Short was probably also referring to individuals who were much better known – Mandelson, whose nickname 'Prince of Darkness' belied a prominent public profile, and an even more important Blair ally, his pugnacious press secretary Alastair Campbell.

Even before New Labour's landslide win in 1997 and the unprecedented decision to give him authority over civil servants, Campbell had become notorious as the party's alleged 'control-freak' in chief. Ostensibly he sought to shun the limelight, protesting that effective media aides should never become part of the stories they spin; but his good intentions in this respect were undermined by his supreme proficiency in the role he had been allotted by Blair, whose dependence on his companionship and advice ensured that when Labour returned to office he was recognised as the real 'deputy prime minister'. Formerly political editor of the *Daily Mirror*, Campbell was ferociously loyal both to institutions and to individuals; but if any conflict should arise between them, his instinctive preference was for the latter over the former. In his published diaries, for example, his evaluations of Clare Short reflect his fear that her critical commentary could derail the Blair project, whether or not they showed a genuine concern for Labour's longer-term prospects. The index entries for Short are peppered with barbed remarks such as 'incoherent on *Today* programme', 'gives another self-indulgent interview', etc.[13]

Thanks not least to Campbell's efforts, by the time of the 1997 election only 34 per cent of voters thought that Labour was divided, compared to the 84 per cent who took the same view of the Conservatives.[14] This was no mean achievement, since the workings of the Millbank machine were marred by deep-seated resentments which were bound to blossom into bitter faction-fights. In 1996 Mandelson was given the title of Shadow Minister for Electoral Planning, in recognition of his grid-generating propensities. However, responsibility in this field was shared with the Shadow Chancellor, Gordon Brown, who nursed an understandable grudge against the Prince of Darkness for his part in engineering a smooth succession for Tony Blair after John Smith's death in 1994. It used to be thought that 'divided parties don't win elections'; the experience of 1997 showed that parties which conceal their divisions from the public can win by a landslide.

The 1997 result was not entirely due to the ruthless vote-harvesting Millbank operation. The targeting of 'winnable' seats – ninety were selected in 1997 – reflected intelligence gained by the old-fashioned method of canvassing, conducted by human operatives who cared about their constituencies rather than the overall national outcome which preoccupied Labour's centralisers. Thanks to Tony Blair's membership drive, by 1997 New Labour had recruited far more of these localised 'spotters' to direct the computer-generated fire from Millbank. Party membership in 1992 had been around 280,000; five years later, with Blair's enthusiastic encouragement, it had risen above 400,000. John O'Farrell had a choice in 1997 between canvassing 'the rock-solid Labour Vauxhall, or my former constituency of Battersea just down the road'.[15] By his own admission, he did little work in either seat but his contribution was not missed; Battersea, lost to the Conservatives in 1987, was comfortably regained, while Vauxhall (vacated by the radical economist Stuart Holland in 1989) gave Kate Hoey almost two-thirds of the vote.

Holding the Government to Account

The mingled grief and frustration arising from a string of electoral defeats was accentuated for Labour by an acknowledgement that its parliamentary representatives could do nothing to prevent the passage of policies which were felt to be unusually divisive, even vindictive. Arguably the anguish was acutest during the 1987–92 Parliament because MPs were powerless in the face of repeated legislation which curtailed the political influence of their extra-parliamentary allies in the trade unions and in local government; other opposition movements, like the All Britain Anti-Poll Tax Federation established in 1989 to coordinate peaceful resistance to a radical and regressive change in local government finance, were tainted by association with law-breaking and (what was worse) the Militant Tendency (see Chapter 6).

In the parliamentary fight against Thatcher's 'flagship policy' of the Poll Tax – whose inequities had received inadequate scrutiny from

Labour in the 1987 election campaign – the party had to hope for help from dissident Conservative MPs. Their votes proved insufficient to prevent the implementation of the obnoxious measure, and they provided a further disservice to Labour by giving additional impulse to Michael Heseltine, a vocal critic of the tax whose challenge to the unpopular Thatcher precipitated her replacement in November 1990 by the more pragmatic John Major. Although Major quickly shot Labour's Poll Tax fox by finding a less controversial (though still regressive) alternative, after the 1992 general election his brand of 'Thatcherism with a human face' was tainted by various miscalculations. In 1993 the government paved the way for railway privatisation – 'the Poll Tax on wheels' as it was aptly dubbed (by a Conservative MP) – but the Tory whips were able to railroad through Parliament yet another example of dogma-driven legislation.

Labour could certainly have been more effective in holding the government to account over the Poll Tax. An explanation, rather than excuse, for the central party's poor performance was its sensitivity to any matters relating to local government and its readiness to concede media charges that Labour councillors must, by definition, be 'left-wing loonies'. A prime example of Labour's dilemmas in holding the Conservatives to account after the 1987 election was its response to the notorious Section 28 of the 1988 Local Government Act, which sought to prevent councils from 'promoting' homosexuality after a slew of distorted stories in right-wing tabloids. Caught off-guard when the designedly offensive clause was proposed at the committee stage of a Bill which was chiefly concerned with the way in which local authorities commissioned public works, Labour's spokesperson Jack Cunningham indicated that his parliamentary colleagues would seek some amendments while supporting its general purpose. For the sponsoring government minister, Michael Howard, Cunningham's implicit endorsement of the rationale for Section 28 was a gift which kept on giving through the Bill's subsequent legislative stages.[16]

In other matters, Labour frontbenchers were less inhibited in their attempts to persuade the public (if not the Tory-dominated House of Commons) that there was a viable alternative to Thatcherism's potent brew of neo-liberalism and reactionary moralising. In his response to Nigel Lawson's controversial tax-cutting budget of 1988, for example,

John Smith (then Shadow Chancellor) stormed that a package which bestowed additional rewards on the already-rich disclosed 'the Thatcher vision of society, in which unfairness, inequality and injustice march side by side. The decent majority will react to what they have seen in the Budget. It is a Budget too far. It is the beginning of the end of Thatcherism.'[17] If his closing claim proved somewhat premature, Smith had at least spoken on the assumption that polling evidence of misgivings about Thatcherism was trustworthy; his own private assessment was that there had been 'a big, deep shift away from Thatcher and her values ... including in the City [of London]'.[18] Smith's indignant rhetoric was topped by that of his colleague Gordon Brown: 'No Budget this century has given so much to so few people. No Budget this century has seen such a huge redistribution of wealth from poor to rich. No Budget this century has so offended the decent instincts of people who are far more altruistic and far less selfish than the faction that now rules over us.'[19] By 1996 Brown's lines of attack had shifted from moral indignation to complaints about the government's economic incompetence, and a petty disagreement with the Chancellor, Kenneth Clarke, about the precise extent of Britain's decline in 'the world prosperity league'.[20]

Long before the commencement of 'live' broadcasts in 1990, Prime Minister's Questions – which was staged twice a week until the format was 'modernised' by Blair – had become a slugfest for media consumption rather than an opportunity to extract meaningful information from the executive branch. For all his crowd-pleasing oratory on public platforms, after 1987 Neil Kinnock continued to attract very mixed reviews with his gladiatorial jousts with Thatcher. Although the sobriquet of 'the Welsh Windbag' demeaned his detractors more than himself, when confronted with jeering Tories in the Commons Kinnock too often seemed willing to live down to it. He even lent inadvertent assistance to one of Thatcher's most memorable displays at the despatch box, on 30 October 1990 after her return from the Rome European Council. Having derided Kinnock as 'Little Sir Echo' for comments which implied reluctance to stand up for Britain's interests, Thatcher proceeded to deliver her response to plans for closer European integration: 'No, no, no'. This occasion proved to be a 'double-whammy' for Labour: it added to the rising discontent with Thatcher among Conservative moderates, thus giving extra credence to the case for dumping a leader who had become an electoral liability, while leaving the impression that the opposition had indeed become 'too soft' on Europe. This criticism would have amazed Labour MPs at the time of the 1983 general election when the party was committed to withdrawal from the EC. By 1987 it had accepted membership, while declaring its intention to safeguard crucial British interests and singling out the Common Agricultural Policy (CAP) for criticism. In short, Labour had shifted to the same fence-sitting approach which the Conservatives had adopted under Thatcher – it would 'stay in Europe', but as an 'awkward partner'.[21]

The mood within the Labour movement became more 'communitaire' between 1987 and 1992, thanks not least to a speech at the 1988 TUC conference by Thatcher's *bête noire*, the former French Socialist economics minister and current president of the European Commission, Jacques Delors. Apart from outlining the general case for European unity – a vision which few delegates shared – Delors emphasised the potential for the EC to act as a vehicle for restraining, and perhaps even reversing, the Thatcherite attack on workers' rights. In a passage which was barely noticed at the time, Delors attempted to mollify the misgivings of any ethnic nationalists in his Bournemouth audience by insisting that the process of European integration would not erode the sense of identity felt by most Britons; indeed, he claimed, developing European institutions would enable the English, the Scots, the Welsh and the Northern Irish to preserve their distinctive characteristics more effectively than if they accepted the umbrella concept of 'Britishness'.[22] Less than two weeks later, Margaret Thatcher retaliated by lighting the blue touchpaper of English nationalism with her Bruges speech. In effect, Thatcher reinforced Delors' appeal to the TUC by claiming that the Europeans were trying to undo her (dubious) achievement of 'rolling back the state'. However, Thatcher also presented the EC as a project to create a monochrome, homogeneous European identity – the very notion which Delors had disclaimed in his TUC speech. The President of the European Commission had anticipated New Labour's Rapid Rebuttal Unit almost a decade in advance, and gone one better: he had rebutted Thatcher's allegation before it had been delivered.

As Delors' warm reception at Bournemouth testified, the Labour Party was not just converted into a pro-European party at elite level. Nevertheless, few members of the grassroots party were 'born again' like

Kinnock, who had campaigned for withdrawal from the EEC in 1975 and became a member of the EU Commission twenty years later. John Smith, his successor as leader, had been one of the few strongly and consistently pro-European Labour MPs who had not gravitated towards the SDP. The tone of the 1992 Labour manifesto had been even more Euro-friendly, including an endorsement of the European Exchange Rate Mechanism (ERM) as a means of controlling inflation. In the subsequent campaign to succeed Kinnock, Smith's opponent Bryan Gould, the Shadow Environment Secretary, had criticised the party's ERM policy but his sceptical perspective attracted limited support.

Backing ERM membership on the terms finally accepted by Thatcher (just before her deposition in November 1990) turned out to be politically damaging – but for the Conservatives rather than Smith or Labour. In September 1992 the UK was forced to suspend its membership of the mechanism – permanently, as it turned out – removing the centrepiece of the government's economic strategy and destroying its reputation for competence of any kind. This dramatic development compounded Major's parliamentary vulnerability; despite winning a record number of votes in the 1992 general election, the Conservative majority in the Commons had been reduced to just twenty-one, emboldening rebels on the government benches. It also offered Smith a chance to demonstrate his debating skills. While Kinnock had found it difficult to adjust to Major's relatively emollient style after facing the abrasive Thatcher for more than seven soul-sapping years, Smith considered the new prime minister to be a decent man who had been over-promoted.[23] When Parliament was recalled on 24 September 1992 to debate the economic situation arising from what quickly became known as 'Black Wednesday', Smith branded Major 'the devalued Prime Minister of a devalued government'. As Major himself later conceded, Smith had been left with 'an open goal'; but at least the opposition leader had hit the back of the net, unlike Kinnock who on such occasions (e.g. Westland) invariably contrived to miss the target or trip over his own bootlaces. The impression that Labour had suddenly become a government-in-waiting was not lost even on the Conservative cheerleaders at the *Daily Mail*, which announced that 'Yesterday was the day Her Majesty's Opposition found its voice.' The press verdict was as painful for the departed Kinnock as for Major; *The Times* editorial exclaimed, 'What a difference a change of leader makes!'[24]

Ironically, after three parliaments in which Labour had lodged unavailing and virtually unheeded protests against legislation which it condemned, in 1992 it found itself the beneficiary of a policy which it had endorsed in its recent manifesto. Smith, however, had attributed the crisis to government mismanagement rather than attacking the principle of ERM membership; before the storm broke he had advocated a revision of sterling's value in relation to the over-mighty German *deutschmark*. Accusations of opportunism seemed more justifiable when, in July 1993, Labour tabled a Commons amendment to a government motion which sought to confirm Britain's 'opt-outs' from the social elements of the 1991 Maastricht Treaty. Effectively, by insisting that the Treaty should not be ratified by Parliament until Britain signed up to its 'social chapter', Labour was playing into the hands of so-called 'Eurosceptics', within its own ranks as well as on the government side, who wanted to prevent its ratification in any form. In private conversation, however, Smith insisted that the social chapter was non-negotiable, since 'Europe is about people, not just about business and markets.'[25] After the government had been defeated by 324 votes to 316, Major had to resort to the 'Old Labour' device of a vote of confidence in order to force his mutinous troops back into line. In the weeks before Smith's death (in May 1994), the embattled pro-European premier had been forced to adopt the attack-lines which Thatcher had used against Kinnock, branding his opponent 'Monsieur Oui, the poodle of Brussels'. Unlike Thatcher, Major instantly regretted his own 'gratuitous and graceless accusation'.[26]

Whatever the direct practical impact of Labour's tactical manoeuvres, they contributed to a general feeling that the government had lost its authority and was now 'in office, not in power', as ex-Chancellor Norman Lamont, the ERM scapegoat, memorably put it. In this context, the bare record of parliamentary defeats was less important than the measures which had to be abandoned because Conservative rebels were now much more willing to collaborate with a newly invigorated Labour opposition. Thus, for example, shortly after the ERM crisis Michael Heseltine's proposal for swingeing pit closures prior to the privatisation of the coal industry aroused a perfect storm of resistance from Conservative MPs in affected areas, who hated the minister for his role in toppling Thatcher as well as feeling that the programme of cuts would betray miners who had stayed at work during the strike of 1984–5. Right-wing press coverage of this new fiasco was a surreal re-run of key clashes in the 1980s, with Heseltine, once feted as the Defence Secretary who defied the revived CND, now cast as the villain, while Arthur Scargill, the previously demonised NUM President, was presented as a champion of the underdog. Nevertheless, in 1994 the remaining fragments of Britain's coal industry were privatised. Another Heseltine initiative – selling off Royal Mail – was dropped in 1994 after meeting backbench resistance. Again, this was only a stay of execution for a service whose importance as an arm of the state had been recognised as long ago as 1516. After 1997 New Labour extended Royal Mail's 'commercial independence', before full privatisation by the Cameron–Clegg coalition.

Between Smith's death and the 1997 election the basic lesson did not change: in terms of accountability, oppositions are only 'good' insofar as governments are 'bad', and the misfortunes of the latter are often connected only tangentially to the activities of opposition parties. A parliamentary exchange of April 1995 between Major and Smith's successor Tony Blair is a case in point. Blair's performance on this occasion introduced a line which is often seen as testimony to the effectiveness of New Labour as a party of opposition – 'I lead my party, he follows his.' However, when the context is considered this celebrated put-down loses some of its lustre. Major, after all, had just replied to accusations that the Conservatives were hopelessly divided over Europe by pointing out that Labour had plenty of its own 'Euro-rebels'. This was demonstrably true, but those members of the public who took notice of Prime Minister's Questions were more likely to be interested in the divisions which were making the government's position untenable than in Labour's internal agonising over the European project and its implications for 'national sovereignty'. Blair might have been a less distinguished lawyer than John Smith, but his experience at the Bar had augmented his inherent theatrical abilities. He took full advantage of the situation by delivering, with perfect timing, a form of words which not only made Major look weak but also seemed to overturn years of media allegations that Labour was divided. Since Blair's memorable riposte was best understood as a deliberate exercise in missing the point, Prime Minister's Questions on 25 April 1995 marked the apogee of opposition by soundbite.

After Black Wednesday, John Major's government faced the most effective and damaging opposition in British political history. Yet the deadliest blows were landed by the media, not the Labour Party. Blair and his allies were beneficiaries of the kind of press coverage which had made Kinnock's life a misery; in place of endless stories about the 'loony left', the public was treated to daily tales of Tory 'sleaze', often in the same right-wing newspapers. This dramatic shift could be seen as a New Labour achievement, rewarding Tony Blair's efforts to bring outlets like *The Sun* onside. However, the new feeding frenzy had other origins – a public feeling that it was 'time for a change', reinforced by resentment of John Major for not being Margaret Thatcher. In 1992, with their usual media support, the Thatcherless Tories had prevailed with the tacit message: 'Life's been pretty grim under the Conservatives. Don't let Labour make it even worse.' By 1997 there were few reasons even for loyal Tories to dispute the modest forecast in the opposition's campaign song: 'Things can only get better.'

Policy Development and Relations with the Unions: Coming to Terms with 'Thatcherism'

Typically, inquests into Labour defeats have been dominated by critics of the leadership. The situation in 1987 was different, partly because the leadership itself was only too keen to press for policy changes, but also due to its new dominance of the NEC which had previously given dissidents a powerful institutional platform (see Chapter 6). After an NEC meeting of July 1987, Tony Benn wondered why he bothered serving on that body; 'and when anyone comes to ask why the Labour Party died I've described it in my diary today'.[27] In that year's Shadow Cabinet elections Benn trailed the eighteen-strong field, just behind a new candidate, Tony Blair. Benn's subsequent agreement to challenge Kinnock for the party leadership (with Eric Heffer standing as Deputy Leader against the incumbent, Roy Hattersley) divided the dwindling forces of the left; the result – a crushing defeat in October 1998, which Benn described as 'appalling' – merely advertised the strength of the current regime.[28] In retirement, Hattersley hailed the contests as 'the end of Bennism as a force within the party'.[29] For understandable reasons, he overlooked the enduring attraction to Labour activists of a key element of Benn's appeal. A powerful cult of personality had been built around him, not least because of his insistence that political principles were far more important than individual personalities. Nearly two decades after what Hattersley hailed as 'the end of Bennism', this aspect of the Bennite formula worked to the advantage of one of his most loyal parliamentary allies, Jeremy Corbyn.

Although the party's upper echelons were not wholly persuaded by Kinnock's modernising project – it was still possible to discern a loosely affiliated group of 'soft-left' sceptics after 1988 – the majority broadly agreed that Labour must try to nullify the negatives which allegedly prevented it from gaining a sympathetic hearing even for attractive policy ideas. The most grievous electoral liability – the impression that the party was riddled with leftist lunatics – had been dealt with quite effectively by 1992 thanks to Kinnock's well-publicised purges. But the Conservatives could still discredit Labour through its relationship with the trade unions. The attempt to reform the unions' role, which had stalled under Kinnock, resumed in earnest after he stepped down. During his 1992 leadership campaign John Smith signalled support for a significant reduction of union influence over conference decisions and candidate selection. Nevertheless, in his contest against Bryan Gould, Smith won almost all (93.6 per cent) of the union vote, strengthening his credentials as a catalyst for compromise.

During the 1993 party conference Smith had to concede ground before securing agreement from the unions; for example, they would still play a key role in leadership elections and the choice of parliamentary candidates, while a reduction in the proportional weight of the 'bloc vote' at conference (from 90 to 70 per cent) barely affected their status as pivotal policy players. Yet although this was a long way from the One Member, One Vote (OMOV) arrangement favoured by the modernisers, it was of considerable symbolic importance. If the unions had been as dominant in Labour's counsels as the right-wing media claimed, no deal would have been possible. However, for the modernisers this could only be a provisional settlement; their impatience with Smith's flexible approach was compounded by his declaration that the issue had been resolved and that the party should shift its focus from constitutional quibbles to policy development.

On that front, the modernisers had already made considerable progress without stooping to compromise. The fruits of Kinnock's policy review were harvested into a series of documents – *Meet the Challenge,*

Make the Change (1989), *Looking to the Future* (1990) and *Opportunity Britain* (1991), which were endorsed by successive party conferences. The first-named policy statement – whose evocative title failed to disclose the identity of the challenge its contents were designed to meet, and which inspired an unwonted exercise in satire from Tony Benn – ushered several of Labour's sacred cows into the slaughter-house.[30] Apart from abandoning Kinnock's oft-repeated personal commitment to unilateral nuclear disarmament in favour of multilateralism, it hedged the prospect of renationalising the public utilities sold off by the Conservatives with insuperable obstacles, while addressing the operations of the free market in terms which would have struck even a liberal like John Maynard Keynes as unduly lyrical. The remaining questions, apparently, concerned the extent to which governments should play a 'regulatory' role in economic activity, or whether the idea of an 'enabling state' would frighten City of London financiers as excessively interventionist. After the party's new-found faith in market forces had been discussed at the NEC, Benn concluded that Labour 'has accepted the main principles not only of capitalism but of Thatcherism'.[31]

The ready approval of *Meet the Challenge* by conference 'convinced the leadership that, on a number of issues, it had been unduly circumspect'.[32] The modernisers – temporarily, as it turned out – were off the leash. In 1989 the rapidly rising Tony Blair (now Shadow Employment Secretary) announced that a future Labour government would not reverse the Conservative ban on union-only workplaces (better known as 'the closed shop'). As soon as *Meet the Challenge* had been endorsed by the 1989 conference, Kinnock 'made the change', demoting the moderate moderniser Bryan Gould from the economically sensitive post of Shadow Secretary for Trade and Industry and replacing him with Gordon Brown, whose raging contempt for Thatcherism expressed after the 1988 budget was already starting to subside.

Unfortunately for the modernisers, the policy changes they had made failed to 'meet the challenge' of attracting sufficient votes from the British electorate in 1992. For John O'Farrell, when yet another overall Conservative victory was confirmed, 'it felt like having the inside of your stomach kicked out'. From his understandably jaundiced perspective: 'Deep down if voters do not want to vote for you then any excuse will do: an embarrassing bit of rock-star posturing at a political rally in Sheffield, nonsense about the disintegration of the United Kingdom, or a few scare stories about tax.'[33] In policy terms, O'Farrell was complaining that the Conservatives had exaggerated the threat to the integrity of the UK posed by devolution to Scotland, Wales and Northern Ireland (which, in the 1970s, Neil Kinnock had passionately opposed) and, ably abetted by the mendacious media, amplified the 'Shadow Budget', which John Smith had unveiled as a modest attempt to undo some of the fiscal unfairness inflicted by Thatcherism, into 'Labour's Tax Bombshell'.

These factors might have had a depressive effect on the Labour vote in 1992. The orthodox view is that Kinnock's 'rock-star posturing' at Sheffield, when the ebullient Labour leader released too much of the emotional tension built up during his prolonged campaign to make his party 'electable' again, had little effect on the outcome because it came too late to sway many voters, and that Labour's private polling had already suggested that it was heading for defeat.[34] The verdicts of a two-member 'focus group' of Labour MPs were mixed. Heartened by Kinnock's repeated use of the word 'socialism' at the Sheffield rally, Tony Benn merely recorded that 'The people who went enjoyed it.' However, Giles Radice, on the right of the party, wondered how the 'vulgar' event would be received by those who had not reached a final decision.[35] Certainly the notion that voters were amenable to last-minute persuasion had occurred to the editor of *The Sun* newspaper, which ran with a puerile front-page attack on Kinnock on election day and subsequently claimed 'It's *The Sun* wot won it'.

In truth, the most likely explanation for Labour's fourth consecutive defeat is that as an opposition party it had incurred the usual and well-deserved fate of every over-keen suitor. Apart from an evident anxiety to meet 'Thatcherism' at least halfway when framing its policy proposals, parts of the 1992 Labour manifesto also suggested an acceptance that the party's opponents had won an underlying battle of philosophical ideas. The standard Thatcherite argument that the pursuit of equality was incompatible with the preservation of liberty had been contested by Bryan Gould and Roy Hattersley before and after the 1987 election.[36] Nevertheless, the party's electoral appeal was still based around social justice and improved public services, which made it arresting that the 1992 manifesto opened with an announcement that 'at the core of our convictions is a belief in individual liberty'. Whether or not this statement would have sounded convincing to voters who remembered the 1983 party manifesto, it was difficult to square with the very recent NEC rejection of Ken Livingstone's argument for an equalisation of the age of consent.[37] To propitiate entrepreneurs who were temporarily dissatisfied with services normally provided by the Conservative Party, the 1992 document followed up unsubtle and well-publicised pre-election attempts to build bridges with key figures in the City of London by affirming that Labour could provide 'a government which business can do business with'. The manifesto even coupled claims about Labour's 'practical commitment to freedom' with reassurance about the party's devotion to Britain's armed forces.

Although John Smith did not live long enough to flesh out a full policy agenda, he did establish a Social Justice Commission, announced in December 1992 to coincide with the fiftieth anniversary of the Beveridge Report. Closely associated with the Institute for Public Policy Research (IPPR) think tank – one of the most constructive initiatives of the Kinnock years – the Commission's findings could command the credibility associated with semi-independent research while offering the advantage of deniability in the unlikely event that they included anything outlandish. As it was, although Tony Blair was attracted by some of the Commission's proposals (which included the abolition of mortgage tax relief and the introduction of repayable university tuition fees), he reportedly commented that 'Some of this isn't New Labour enough.' While the Blairites found it useful to advertise their links with fashionable 'think tanks' (notably Demos, founded in 1993), the notion of serious arm's-length policy advice did not outlive John Smith.[38]

For his best-remembered move in the quest for 'electability', Blair resumed the Kinnockian task of depriving the Tories of easy targets. For decades, critics had depicted Clause IV of Labour's constitution as nothing more than a source of embarrassment to the party in government, and an obstacle to its transference from opposition to office. The retention of a constitutional party commitment to nationalisation seemed more anomalous than ever during Kinnock's policy review, when shadow ministers had sought respectable reasons *not* to take privatised utilities back under state control. However, even for party members who were beginning to doubt some elements of the pre-Thatcherite 'mixed economy' (e.g. a state monopoly in telecommunications), the Clause held enormous symbolic importance. For Blair himself, the replacement of the 1918 wording with a 'modernised' text, after a special conference held on 29 April 1995, was much more than symbolic; having routed the forces of 'Old Labour' on this ultra-emotive issue, he had no reason to fear resistance in other crucial policy areas.

The policy implications of the revised Clause IV were (deliberately) obscure: it affirmed Labour's belief

> that by the strength of our common endeavour we achieve more than we achieve alone, so as to create for each of us the means to realise our true potential and for all of us a community in which power, wealth and opportunity are in the hands of the many, not the few, where the rights we enjoy reflect the duties we owe, and where we live together, freely, in a spirit of solidarity, tolerance and respect.

Compared to the libertarian tropes which had littered the 1992 party manifesto, some of this could even be interpreted as a swing back to the left. But within a few weeks of winning his Clause IV battle Blair had demonstrated his true valuation of 'the few', compared to 'the many', by jetting to Hayman Island to address Rupert Murdoch and assembled News Corporation executives. Introducing Blair to his lackeys, Murdoch joked that the flirtation could result in them 'making love like two porcupines – very carefully'.[39] Only one participant was leaving himself vulnerable to a nasty prick, but Blair saw no need for precautions; as he later reflected, when given an invitation of that kind, 'You go, don't you?'[40] He could have claimed a prior engagement, to the annual Miners' Gala held in Durham near his Sedgefield constituency. But, as he might have put it, when asked to encounter representatives of the traditional working class, 'You find other things to do, don't you?' In the previous month Blair had found space in his diary to break bread with the owner and editors of the *Mail* group ('not our kind of people', according to Alastair Campbell, who nevertheless found the 'very right-wing' *Daily Mail* editor Paul Dacre 'almost likeable').[41]

In fact the jaunt to the Australasian island was unnecessary, because Blair had already conveyed the essential message to his fellow porcupine. He and his modernising coadjutor, Gordon Brown, had followed up their Clause IV victory with speeches marking a capitulation to post-Thatcherite economic verities. The conquest of inflation, rather than the re-establishment of something approaching 'full employment', would be their priority in office. To that end, a Labour government would go even further than Thatcher in augmenting the role of the Bank of England in setting interest rates, one of the state's key levers in affecting economic activity.[42] It was not until January 1997 that Brown decided to spike one of the few remaining Tory guns, announcing that he would preserve existing rates of income tax – including the ones for higher earners which he had condemned so splenetically back in 1988 – and would adhere to the Major government's parsimonious public spending targets for at least two years.[43] As the party machine prepared to move into Millbank, everything possible was being done to lighten the workload of its Rebuttal Unit.

In its thirst for victory, by 1997 the Labour Party had cured its propensity to air ideological washing in public fora. The draft manifesto, given the hyperbolic title *New Labour, New Life for Britain*, was approved by a ballot of party members, confirming Blair's preference for 'a plebiscitary form of leadership' and providing him with a level of support (around 95 per cent) which would have satisfied most leaders of that ilk.[44] The 'New Life for Britain' would be difficult to distinguish from the old one, since the document conceded even more ground to the post-Thatcherite agenda, on health and education. The published version repeated and embellished the 'many, not the few' conceit from the new Clause IV, claiming that 'New Labour is the political arm of none other than the British people as a whole' and garnishing it with a populist reference to 'an elite at the top increasingly out of touch with the rest of us'. What seemed at the time to be a costless shot at the Tories took on a different aspect when, during its dying days in government, New Labour attracted extra odium from the parliamentary expenses scandal. Elsewhere, there was a significant departure from Clause IV, which had characterised Labour as 'a democratic socialist party'. New Labour preferred to face the electorate as 'a broad-based movement for progress and justice'.

Many keyboards have been pounded by journalists and academics in the quest to capture the ideological essence of New Labour. The wisest course might be to play it safe, as Blair's party did in 1997 by boiling its pitch to the nation down to five modest and measurable pre-election pledges which were printable on a small card. Not even Margaret

Thatcher – who once, bizarrely, labelled Kinnock 'a crypto-Communist' – could have dreamed up a definition of 'democratic socialism' which might accommodate New Labour; the inclusion of those words in the new Clause IV was another reason for describing it as misleading rather than meaningless. There have been several well-intentioned attempts to spatchcock 'Blairism' into the social democratic tradition. However, that interpretation was unpersuasive to one well-placed observer: Tony Blair himself. Shying away from the inoffensive social democratic label, Blair favoured alternatives such as the 'Third Way' associated with the writings of Anthony Giddens and with other political figures, notably Bill Clinton. If the third way is meant to denote a *via media* between socialism and neo-liberalism, it would be plausible to regard it as synonymous with social democracy, which accorded a significant role to the profit motive as a driver of economic growth. Indeed, there are plausible reasons for reconciling Labour's 1992 election platform with other European variants of social democracy.[45] However, the party had been pushed into that 'revisionist' position – which in practice had driven its policies for most of its history, notwithstanding Clause IV and all – by senior figures in Kinnock's entourage who would have preferred it to move much further in a Thatcherite direction. John Smith sought to arrest Labour's version of 'the great moving right show', and might have consolidated a genuine social democratic approach even if he would have been hesitant to adopt it in name.[46] His early demise left the field open for New Labour, whose positive enthusiasm for market forces led it to embrace the Private Finance Initiative (PFI) – a one-way bet for unscrupulous private-sector operatives – and to endorse the 'light-touch' approach to financial regulation which, under Brown, created the conditions for the Conservatives to return to office and for Labour to rediscover the dubious delights of opposition.

Conclusion

On a superficial review of Labour's record over the decade after 1987, one might conclude that the party finally perfected the art of opposition by gradual stages and, ten years later, reaped the rewards for learning appropriate lessons the hard way. An alternative, though still charitable interpretation, could conclude that the party based its learning on an understandable mistake. Ignoring the cliché that changes of government occur due to the blunders of incumbents, rather than the virtues of opposition parties, Labour embarked on a course which, under Tony Blair, made it into a movement that left nothing to chance. When Blair proclaimed that his party would 'govern as New Labour', he meant that it would continue to act as if it was still in opposition, engaged in a perpetual election campaign against insidious elements – 'the forces of conservatism', which Blair excoriated in his speech to the 1999 Labour conference to explain away his first government's failure to inaugurate the promised 'New Life for Britain'.

From that mistaken perspective, it was natural for Blair to confide that his chief goal after New Labour's 1997 landslide was to repeat the feat next time round. To paraphrase Billy Bragg's best-known song, he wasn't looking for a new England; he was just working for a second term. Along with his allies, he reshaped Labour into a 'catch-all' party – a temporary political outlet for fair-weather friends. The New Labour 'big tent' was always likely to be excessively susceptible to high winds, and had collapsed long before the 2010 general election. With the advent of David Cameron as head of a coalition with the Liberal Democrats, the political wheel had come full circle. If Thatcher was right in rating New Labour as her greatest achievement, Cameron, the 'heir to Blair', was a self-styled imitation of her imitator.

8

In New Labour's Shadow (2010–2024)

Labour's longest period as the Official Opposition, from 1979 to 1997, was followed by its longest uninterrupted period in government, from 1997 to 2010. During this time, the Labour Party won substantial majorities in three consecutive elections, and Tony Blair became Labour's longest-serving prime minister. The central question for Labour in the period of opposition that followed these electoral triumphs was how to confront the legacy of that Labour government.

The creation of New Labour, discussed in the previous chapter, represented both a symbolic and a substantive break from previous Labour governments and oppositions. Although the contrast with 'Old Labour' was sometimes overstated, the party's economic model defied traditional socialist articles of faith. Specifically, New Labour accepted a light touch to financial regulation and preserved the Conservatives' privatisation of industry and public services. It also surrendered control of monetary policy to an independent Bank of England, a proposal even John Smith called shocking.[1] However, the Labour government used buoyant tax revenues to fund welfare expansion and drive significant investment in the public realm, often in joint projects with the private sector. A relaxed immigration system ensured a steady supply of low-wage labour with weak bargaining power, acting as a mechanism to hold down inflation.[2] This model produced ten years of unbroken economic growth, rising prosperity, stable inflation and successful public services.

Yet, the New Labour project was fatally undermined by its own foreign and economic policies. Two events in the 2000s echoed into the 2010s and shaped the Labour opposition in profound ways. The first was the Blair government's decision to join the US invasion of Iraq in 2003. Although probably informed by the successful 'liberal' military interventions in Kosovo and Sierra Leone, the case for the war was weak and ultimately found to be baseless.[3] The Blair government's cajoling of MPs to support the war split the Labour Party, with a large minority of Labour MPs and party members fiercely opposing their own government. It spelled the end of the sense of optimism and confidence that had characterised the rise of New Labour. The subsequent disaster of the war, with hundreds of thousands dead and a destabilised Middle East, only reinforced the feelings of betrayal.

The second event was the financial crisis of 2007–8. The New Labour economic model had been constructed on what Labour leader Ed Miliband would later characterise as a 'Faustian pact with business'.[4] To the British Chamber of Commerce in 2000, the Chancellor Gordon Brown announced that New Labour offered 'a Britain where there is not stop-go and boom-bust but economic stability; a Britain which is business-friendly ... which rewards the innovator and risk-taker'.[5] Under New Labour, poverty fell and public services, especially in health and education, saw significant investment, but inequality grew, labour power decreased, and wealth became ever-more concentrated around London. Unbroken economic growth came to a crashing halt soon after Brown became prime minister in 2007. At the next general election in 2010, the party secured just 29 per cent of the vote, its second lowest since 1918.

In the spasms of defeat, the Labour Party found itself in an extraordinary leadership contest between two brothers, Ed and David Miliband, the sons of the Marxist academic Ralph Miliband who famously posited that the Labour Party was a dead-end for socialism.[6] Both had served in the previous government, but David presented himself as the heir to New Labour, whereas Ed advocated its demise. Trade unions, using their power in the electoral college bequeathed to them by the 1981 Wembley conference (see Chapter 6), deprived David of the leadership in spite of his support from a modest majority of Labour MPs and members.

Although Ed Miliband's candidacy was predicated on a rejection of New Labour, his need to hold the party together after his surprising and underwhelming victory resulted in an uneasy compromise with the party's right. While he continued to voice his critique of New Labour's foreign and economic policies, Miliband was unable to repudiate them convincingly, due both to his own involvement in the previous government and to the extreme fiscal caution of his Shadow Chancellor Ed Balls.

In an effort to demonstrate his independence from the unions, Miliband entered into the quagmire of internal party reform. He abolished the electoral college, handing the power of electing the leader to party members, members of affiliated trade unions, and anyone else who paid a nominal fee on the promise that they believed in the party's values. Paradoxically, Miliband's attempt to weaken union influence required the approval of the unions because they held 50 per cent of the vote at party conferences. Rather than a defeat for union power, the reforms unintentionally offered the potential for stronger union influence, while reducing MPs' influence to the nomination stage only, a reform that even Tony Benn thought was too radical in the early 1980s.

The strategic ineptitude of those on the party right who advocated for these reforms became clear after Labour's defeat in the 2015 election, following which Miliband resigned immediately. Once again, the Labour selectorate chose a candidate who rejected the foreign and economic policies of the previous Labour government. Jeremy Corbyn, a Bennite backbencher for thirty-two years, had been a consistent critic of the war in Iraq, financial deregulation and fiscal austerity. Corbyn offered a return to the old-fashioned socialist principles of the pre-New Labour period. Unlike Miliband, the Labour right totally disavowed Corbyn, which ironically left him freer to put his principles into policy, especially after surviving a leadership challenge one year into the role.

The first test of this programme was the 2017 general election. To everyone's surprise, Labour's share of the popular vote climbed 10 percentage points, the highest increase in one election since 1945. For the first time since 1997, Labour gained seats, including a net of twenty-two from the Conservatives, which deprived the prime minister Theresa May of her majority. Had the SNP not lost twelve seats to the Conservatives, Labour could have had the numbers in Parliament to form a government.[7] The 2017 election saw the highest turnout since 1997. A higher share of the eligible electorate voted Labour under Corbyn in 2017 than in any election since 1997. While these records did not erase the fact that Labour was unable to form a government,[8] they poured cold water on the idea that a socialist programme was necessarily a vote loser.

The buoyancy of the 2017 victory was deflated in the next two years by Labour's ineptitude in responding to Britain's greatest policy challenge of the twenty-first century: implementing the 2016 vote to leave the European Union. Immediately after the referendum, Corbyn called for the initiation of the process to leave the EU, and in the 2017 election the Labour Party promised to respect the Leave result. At that election, one in four Leavers voted Labour, and two-thirds of Labour MPs represented Leave-voting constituencies.[9] However, the hung Parliament after the 2017 election gave some Labour MPs the (false) hope that they could block the referendum result. While Corbyn and his inner circle resisted these manoeuvres initially, they eventually succumbed in the face of the threat of dozens of Labour MPs forming a breakaway party.[10]

In the 2019 election, Labour promised a second referendum with the aim of overturning 'Brexit'. The result was predictably catastrophic for Labour, erasing nearly all of the gains of the 2017 election. Labour won 32 per cent of the vote (higher than Brown or Miliband), but it suffered disproportionate losses in its 'heartland' seats which had supported leaving the European Union. A few months later, after Corbyn's resignation, the indefatigably pro-EU Labour membership rewarded the architect of Labour's second referendum policy, the Shadow Brexit Secretary Keir Starmer, with the party leadership.

Starmer's leadership had a rocky start, with the COVID-19 pandemic producing a kind of 'rally around the flag' effect for the Conservative government of Boris Johnson.[11] In May 2021, Labour lost Hartlepool to the Conservatives on a 16-point swing from the already poor 2019 result. It was the first time Labour had lost the seat to the Conservatives and only the second time since 1982 that a government had gained a seat at a by-election. Yet, a year later, Starmer's fortunes improved when Conservative ministers deposed Johnson in response to accusations that he and his advisers had broken their own COVID lockdown rules. With this stroke of luck, followed by the unprecedentedly brief and disastrous forty-nine-day premiership of Liz Truss, Labour's poll-rating skyrocketed.

Starmer had been elected on a series of pledges to continue Corbyn's socialist programme. Yet, he spent his time as Leader of the Opposition abandoning nearly all of them. Commitments to ending tuition fees, bringing rail and utilities into public ownership, and abolishing the welfare cap on families with more than two children were jettisoned. For a party that had sought to bury New Labour under Miliband and Corbyn, Starmer demonstrated his willingness to dig up its corpse and apply electroshock therapy in the hope that he could reprise the Blair electoral miracle.

Assessing the Record of the Previous Labour Government (1997–2010): No Heir to Blair

After Labour's defeat in 2010, Gordon Brown resigned, sparking a four-and-a-half-month contest to replace him. The frontrunner was David Miliband, who as Foreign Secretary in 2009 had contemplated challenging the unpopular prime minister. At the time, David consulted his brother Ed, who was Energy and Climate Secretary. Ed apparently advised David to hold fire; his moment would come after the general election.[12] So, it was to the surprise of many, including David himself, that Ed announced his own candidacy for leader three days after his brother.[13] Former Health Secretary Andy Burnham, who had announced his candidacy the previous day, was shocked: 'I had, perhaps from a northern working-class sensibility, assumed that Ed wouldn't stand against his brother because I would never. I can't get my head around that.'[14] Ed Miliband was accused of political 'fratricide', a charge from which he never recovered reputationally.[15]

While something of an oversimplification, the Ed versus David contest became a referendum on New Labour itself. David was supported by key members of the New Labour establishment, including Peter Mandelson and (albeit covertly) Tony Blair. Ed Miliband's candidacy was premised on bringing New Labour to an end. He wrote in a Fabian essay during the campaign: 'To win next time, it is the New Labour comfort zone that we must escape … It is my rejection of this New Labour nostalgia that makes me the modernising candidate.'[16]

Ed Miliband's disavowal of New Labour drew plaudits from the party's left. Many supported the left-wing Diane Abbott but then gave their crucial second preferences to the younger Miliband. The left-wing MP John McDonnell supported Ed over David, later explaining: 'we could see that Ed Miliband was different … He understood the traditions of the party … he actually understood he had to have radical policy change.'[17] The grandfather of the Labour left, Tony Benn, preferred the younger Miliband, who had done work experience in Benn's parliamentary office as a student, praising Ed for his principles and thoughtfulness.[18] There was clearly a strong sense from the 'old guard' that New Labour had deviated from the party's core principles, even among the 'old' right.[19] From this perspective, Labour's former Deputy Leader Roy Hattersley breathed a sigh of relief when Ed defeated David: 'At last the Labour Party has a leader who is both capable of winning the next general election and actually believes in the principles of social democracy.'[20] Even Hattersley's old right ally, the late leader John Smith, was placed in the Ed camp by his widow Elizabeth, who enthused, 'I identify with Ed's values and principles, and I know that John would have done so too.'[21] When Ed Miliband was elected, Neil Kinnock is alleged to have roared, 'We've got our party back!'[22]

There were two issues at the heart of Ed Miliband's critique of the previous Labour government. The first was its economic model. At his announcement speech, Miliband complained, 'We have lost our radical edge.'[23] In an August 2010 *Guardian* article, he elaborated: 'New Labour's political economy – highly flexible, liberal markets and a stronger welfare state – achieved great things', among them continuous economic growth, low inflation, and high tax revenues that funded generous redistribution and good public services. However, he argued that the model had serious drawbacks, including exposure to market volatility and high levels of inequality. 'We need a different approach', Miliband insisted.[24] Andrew Murray, later an adviser to Jeremy Corbyn, congratulated Miliband for having 'grasp[ed] that 2008 had mortally wounded the economic model underpinning the 1997 triumph'.[25] In his victory speech, Miliband announced: 'You saw the worst financial crisis in a generation, and I understand your anger that Labour hadn't changed the old ways in the City which said deregulation was the answer.'[26] Patrick Diamond writes: 'It was under Ed Miliband's leadership that the "New Labour as neoliberalism" narrative gripped the party.'[27]

The second issue was the Iraq War. For journalists Francis Beckett and Mark Seddon 'the short answer' to the puzzle of Ed defeating David 'is that … David voted for the war in Iraq'.[28] Two of the leadership candidates had voted for the war: David Miliband and Andy Burnham. Diane Abbott had voted against. Neither Ed Balls nor Ed Miliband were yet MPs in 2003, but Balls did not disavow the war. On the other hand, Ed Miliband denounced the invasion and implied, perhaps implausibly, that he had expressed his concerns at the time to his former boss Gordon

Brown.[29] In his victory speech, Ed was emphatic: 'I do believe that we were wrong. Wrong to take Britain to war and we need to be honest about that.' The television cameras panned to Labour's Deputy Leader Harriet Harman smiling and warmly applauding. Sitting next to her, David hissed: 'You voted for it. Why are you clapping?'[30]

While the party membership had tolerated New Labour, it never really embraced it. Manuel Cortes, leader of the TSSA union, believed that by 2010 'New Labour had run its course. Why did the average member of the Labour Party go along with New Labour? Because it could win general elections. The moment it couldn't, it was dead in the water.'[31] Contemporary data from the polling firm YouGov reveals that in 2010 Labour members saw themselves as left of New Labour. On a -100 to +100 left-wing to right-wing scale, the average Labour member placed themselves as -51 (firmly centre-left). They placed Blair as +9 (marginally right-of-centre), David Miliband -2 (centre), and Ed Miliband as a -31 (moderately centre-left).[32] Ed Miliband's ideological positioning was more congruent with that of the party membership than either his brother or Blair (see Figure 8.1).

However, even though party members saw themselves as even more left-wing than Ed, they ultimately favoured David because he was seen as more 'electable', thus appealing to members' desire to win back power. David won 44 per cent of members' first preferences and 54 per cent of their final preferences. This willingness to compromise on ideological affinity in exchange for electoral viability was not entirely surprising given that party members had been told for years that a left-wing policy programme was a vote loser. As a result of these anxieties, Ed Miliband's team referred to the contest as a 'David versus Goliath' struggle, before having to clarify, rather confusingly, that Ed was David and David was Goliath.[33] Ultimately, as will be discussed in

Ideological placement	-100	0	+100
Labour members	-51		
Ed Miliband		-31	
David Miliband		-2	
Tony Blair		+9	

Figure 8.1 Average left (-100) to right (+100) ideological placement, according to Labour members, 2010
Source: Bale, 2015

the next section, it was the union movement which provided Ed with the fatal slingshot.

When Ed was elected, GMB leader Paul Kenny proclaimed: 'New Labour is gone. It is a product of history. It can join Madame Tussauds now.'[34] Symbolic of this change, the new.labour.org web domain was stripped of the 'new'. At the 2011 party conference, Ed Miliband was cheered for saying, 'I'm not Tony Blair.'[35] Miliband continued to criticise the previous Labour government during the 2015 general election campaign, reaffirming, 'I thought we needed to move on from New Labour because ... I thought on issues like Iraq [and] inequality, we got it wrong.'[36]

For those on the party right, Miliband's rejection of New Labour was a serious strategic misjudgement. In their view, the party membership might not have liked New Labour, but the public did. One former Cabinet minister said after Miliband's election: 'Ed is a therapist, not a leader. He will make the Labour Party feel good about itself again, but that's not important to the country.'[37] Tony Blair later ruminated, 'I wasn't sufficiently aware of the degree of repudiation, funnily enough, until much later', but in hindsight Blair believed Miliband's criticisms to be 'bad' and 'politically damaging'.[38] In spite of her loyal applause, Harriet Harman believed Miliband's attacks on New Labour were wrong. She later lamented: 'We'd failed to embark on a persistent and dogged exposition of our achievements in government, which served to assist those who wanted to denigrate our record and lend passive support to the highly successful Tory mantra, "Why give the car keys back to the people who crashed it?"'[39] Harman's diagnosis is half correct. The mistake was not in making criticisms of New Labour but in failing to develop a convincing alternative.

After Miliband's resignation in 2015, the shadow of New Labour hung over the leadership contest to replace him. Beckett and Seddon argue that members were looking for a candidate who shared Miliband's diagnosis but, this time, championed policies which would provide the cure.[40] For his part, Jeremy Corbyn entered the Labour leadership contest with no ambitions of winning. On the day he announced his candidacy, at 100–1 odds, Corbyn candidly told the *Guardian*: 'We had a discussion among a group of us on the left about how we might influence the future development of the party ... We decided somebody should put their hat in the ring in order to promote that debate. And unfortunately, it's my hat in the ring. Diane [Abbott] and John [McDonnell] have done it before, so it was my turn.'[41]

Corbyn's success shocked the political world, but its underlying reasons were much the same as they had been for Ed Miliband's victory five years earlier. First, Corbyn was anti-war and had voted against the invasion of Iraq.[42] Like Ed Miliband (but with greater credibility), this set him apart from the other contenders who, in the cases of Burnham and Yvette Cooper, had voted for the war and, in the case of Liz Kendall who was elected in 2010, unapologetically defended the invasion.[43] Second, Corbyn was a credible critic of both New Labour financial deregulation and the fiscal austerity of the Conservatives. Corbyn had been consistent, whereas New Labour architect Peter Mandelson denounced Ed Miliband as a hypocrite:

> Even though he was absolutely part of the Gordon Brown Treasury and its financial reforms, [Ed] laid the deregulation of the financial markets at our door and by implication that we had precipitated the financial crisis. That took some nerve … His own complicity in New Labour policies while working with the Treasury went unacknowledged.[44]

Corbyn, who had not served in any frontbench role before becoming party leader, could avoid accusations of complicity or hypocrisy. These factors, more than any other, secured his leadership. The fact that the continuity New Labour candidate Kendall secured just 4.5 per cent demonstrated that, from the perspective of Labour members, the New Labour project was truly dead.

After Corbyn resigned as leader in 2020, none of the leadership candidates pledged a return to New Labour. The winner, Keir Starmer, maintained the same posture as Miliband and Corbyn. Starmer was elected on a series of radical pledges, including a sweeping extension of public ownership, the abolition of tuition fees, an enormous council house building programme and the reversal of various Conservative welfare cuts. Starmer 'presented himself as the natural successor' to Corbyn.[45] Only elected as an MP in 2015, he was not 'a New Labour heirloom' in the way that the ex-New Labour ministers Miliband (*frère et frère*), Balls, Cooper and Burnham inescapably were.[46]

Yet, Starmer spent much of his time as Leader of the Opposition waking the old ghosts of New Labour while burying the charred remains of the Corbyn leadership. First, he withdrew the party whip from his predecessor over accusations of insufficient contrition for antisemitic comments made by Labour members when Corbyn was leader. Then, he abandoned nearly all of the bold pledges on which he had been elected leader.[47] Instead, he appointed key advisers from the New Labour years to his team.[48] The pinnacle of Starmer's peace with New Labour was a July 2023 appearance with Tony Blair at the former prime minister's eponymous institute, a combination of a charity, think tank and consultancy. Blair's speech was, according to one journalist, 'a bit of a snooze' – 'a 10-minute stump speech that somehow felt twice as long' – but the former PM provided Starmer with his imprimatur: 'We'll be in good hands with you.'[49]

Managing Relationships with the Trade Unions: A Parliamentary Bust-Up

During the New Labour years, several unions, including the RMT which had founded the Labour Party, disaffiliated in protest of government policy.[50] The remaining unions exercised influence on internal party decisions in exchange for their continued financial support. The buoyant economic circumstances, declining union membership and the legacy of Thatcher's anti-union laws (which New Labour retained) limited the capacity of unions to influence politics through their industrial muscle like they had done in the 1970s. To bolster their strength, smaller unions merged to create a handful of 'super unions'. The most important of these were UNISON, Unite and the GMB. In 2010, 62 per cent of Labour's income came from unions, 23 per cent from Unite alone.[51] The mergers gave a small number of union leaders greater say in the direction of the Labour Party than their counterparts in the previous, more pluralistic industrial landscape.[52]

The revival of union power in the Labour Party would not come through strike action but through the electoral college reforms implemented at the Wembley conference in 1981. Although the system gave members of affiliated unions and socialist societies one third of the vote for leader, their power had not previously been demonstrated. Until 2010, every Labour leadership election held under this system had been won in a landslide. In 1983, 1988, 1992 and 1994, the winning candidate won all three sections of the college and secured victory on the first round of voting. In 2007 only one candidate, Gordon Brown, secured enough nominations to stand, and was elected unopposed.

In a close contest, however, the union vote could potentially be decisive. Recognising this, on 14 July 2010, the general secretaries of the four biggest unions – Unite, UNISON, the GMB and the CWU – met for dinner at the Commonwealth Club off the Strand.[53] They agreed that they needed to stop David Miliband. One of the men at that meeting revealed: 'Once it was decided that he was the Blairite continuity candidate, he was dead in the water.'[54]

Under the electoral college, affiliated unions were entrusted with issuing ballots to their members. The party instructed the unions that they 'should not include any information in the ballot envelope indicating support for individual candidates'.[55] In a creative response to the rules, the GMB and Unite put photos of Ed Miliband *on* the envelope, rather than *in* it. The unions gave material support to Ed Miliband's campaign and allegedly constrained other candidates from communicating with their members.[56]

The final result was the clearest demonstration of union power in the selection of a Labour leader since TGWU leader Ernest Bevin forced George Lansbury to resign in 1935 in favour of his deputy Clement Attlee (see Figure 8.2). The fact that Ed Miliband had been the choice of union members but not of party members or MPs caused Ed, in the eyes of GMB leader Paul Kenny, to 'have an insecurity to a certain degree about his leadership'.[57] This insecurity was not immediately addressed until a curious set of circumstances unexpectedly changed the course of Labour history two years later.

On 22 February 2012, Eric Joyce, Labour MP for Falkirk, had drunk too much. A former army major and Scottish judo champion, Joyce arrived at the Strangers' Bar in Parliament at 10 p.m. and growled, 'there are too many fucking Tories in here'. Joyce began to sing and sway, causing some drinkers to issue rebukes. The turning point in the evening occurred when Andrew Percy, a Conservative MP, asked Joyce if he could borrow a spare bar stool.[58] 'Then he flipped', recalled one witness. Joyce erupted in fury, headbutting Conservative MP Stuart Andrew, leaving him with a bloodied nose. 'Poor Stuart was just having a quiet pint and

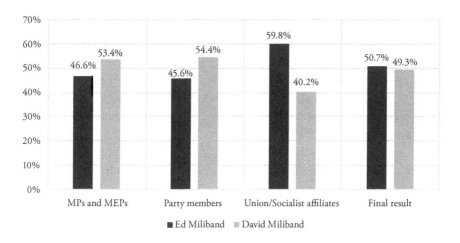

Figure 8.2 Results of the 2010 Labour leadership election, final round
Source: https://www.theguardian.com/news/datablog/2010/sep/26/labour
-leadership-results-election

minding his own business, and Eric headbutted him. Stuart was just in the wrong place at the wrong time', recounted a bystander.[59] Phil Wilson, a Labour whip, jumped in to try to restrain his colleague but was forcefully struck. It wasn't until the Conservative MP Jackie Doyle-Price bravely placed herself between Joyce and his intended male victims that his pugilism subsided and he was restrained by five parliamentary security officers. As Joyce was led away in handcuffs, he lashed out once more and broke a window.

Joyce lost the Labour whip, creating a vacancy in Falkirk. The CLP chair was Unite's shop steward at the local Grangemouth refinery. In a CLP of fewer than 200 members, Unite recruited over 100 of its own members into the Labour Party. As was customary, the union paid for their first year's party subscriptions. None of this was against the rules, but the Labour right decried the attempt to 'stitch up' the selection for a Unite candidate. General Secretary Len McCluskey defended his union's actions: 'Labour needs more trade unionists in Parliament, as opposed to seats being handed out on a grace-and-favour basis to Oxbridge-educated "special advisers".'[60]

Miliband reacted to the furore by trying to demonstrate that he was tough on the unions. At his invitation, the former union leader and party General Secretary Ray Collins proposed a series of reforms to the party's relationship with the unions. The Collins Review recommended that unions' affiliation fees be determined by a member opt-in process rather than calculated by unions' overall membership size. This move could result in a substantial financial loss to Labour, which drew a third of its income from union subscriptions. For example, the GMB's direct funding to Labour collapsed from £1.2 million to £150,000.[61] Ironically, this reform would only empower union leaders more. Before the Collins Review, when members of affiliated unions paid a political levy, this money would go directly to the Labour Party in the form of affiliation subscriptions. Now, members could choose whether their money went to Labour or to their union's independent political fund. Money from the latter could, in turn, be donated to the Labour Party but this was now at the discretion of the union leadership, who could use the possibility of a generous donation as leverage against the party.

In addition, the Collins Review abolished the electoral college. The reforms created a Labour leadership franchise consisting of three eligible types of participant: ordinary Labour members, members of affiliated trade unions, and 'registered supporters'. Unlike before, there would be no difference in weight between these three categories. Once again, Collins's reforms unwittingly opened the path to *greater* union influence. Under the electoral college, the union vote was capped at one-third, but after its abolition, the proportion of votes coming from affiliated unions was theoretically unlimited. Beckett and Seddon point out that, 'quite by error, Ed Miliband had presented a great opportunity to the unions' to influence the choice of leader.[62] Union leader Manuel Cortes claimed that Miliband was a terrible negotiator: 'What started off as being an attempt to disenfranchise unions ended up in what I thought was a very good deal for unions.'[63]

As of yet, the unions have not been able to wield greater influence through the new electoral system. In the three leadership contests between 2015 and 2020, as Figure 8.3 shows, union voters made up just under 20 per cent of all votes cast, compared to their 33 per cent influence between 1994–2010 and 40 per cent between 1981–92. Nonetheless, there are far more eligible union affiliates than Labour members, and a savvy candidate, with strong union backing, could potentially mobilise them.

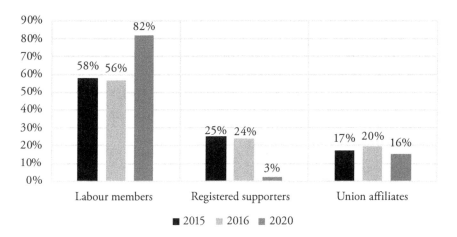

Figure 8.3 Breakdown of voter types in Labour leadership elections, 2015–2020
Source: https://labour.org.uk/people/leadership-elections-hub-2020/leadership-elections-2020-results

Unions became even more significant under Jeremy Corbyn's leadership. The fact that Corbyn commanded the support of many of Labour's unions in the 2015 leadership contest was crucial for his victory. He was backed by Unite, UNISON, TSSA, BFAWU and the CWU. The more moderate GMB declined to endorse any contender, which in itself was a victory.[64] The unions had taken a strong interest in a Corbyn candidacy because the previous five years of industrial action had resulted in few gains. Moreover, the Conservative government at this very point had announced they were pursuing further anti-union legislation which would make strike action even more difficult. Union leaders and members turned to politics once more, just as they had done after the failure of an industrial strategy in 1926, as discussed in Chapter 1.[65]

While Corbyn had a generally positive relationship with the unions, there were some moments of strain. Notably, Corbyn had been a lifelong opponent of nuclear weapons and served as vice-chair of the Campaign for Nuclear Disarmament. Britain's nuclear defence industry funded thousands of well-paid, unionised jobs. Unite was well-organised in the nuclear sector.[66] Corbyn continued to say that he personally could not imagine any circumstances in which he would deploy nuclear weapons, but Shadow Foreign Secretary Emily Thornberry explained that the Cabinet would come to a collective view on their deployment: 'We will make those decisions together and Jeremy listens to his colleagues.'[67]

Under Keir Starmer, relations with the unions soured. As the economy reeled from rampant inflation following the COVID-19 pandemic, union members took to the streets to seek higher wage settlements on a scale of industrial action not seen since the 1980s. Starmer instructed members of the shadow frontbench not to appear on picket lines, an historically unprecedented step.[68] In the summer of 2022, half a dozen Labour frontbenchers faced disciplinary action for visiting picket lines. In a long-running rail workers' dispute, Starmer announced that he was 'against the strikes' and sacked a shadow transport minister for supporting them.[69] Defending this position, Shadow Foreign Secretary David Lammy said 'a serious party of Government does not join picket lines'.[70] The comment reflected a profound historical illiteracy, with numerous examples of Labour government ministers in the 1970s, 1990s and 2000s having visited picket lines to show solidarity with striking workers.[71]

Lammy's comment was indicative of a mindset among some Labour strategists that the party would lose an election if it were seen as being too close to the unions, much like Ed Miliband's advisers feared. Yet this reflected an outdated analysis of politics. Britain was no longer living in the shadow of the 'Winter of Discontent' of the 1970s or facing untrammelled trade union power. By the 2020s, British living standards had been squeezed to an unprecedented degree by the long-term impacts of the financial crisis, David Cameron's austerity policies, and post-COVID inflation. Yet, in summer 2023, the Labour National Policy Forum 'watered down' previous commitments to strengthen trade union rights 'in a bid to woo business', raising questions about the Labour opposition's commitment to providing a transformative alternative to the Conservatives in advance of the next election.[72]

Strengthening the Party Machine: The Rise and Fall of Party Membership

One of the most significant developments of Labour's time in opposition after 2010 was the ballooning of its membership numbers. Under

New Labour, the party membership steadily atrophied. Labour entered office with 405,000 members; it left with about 150,000, a 61 per cent decline.[73] Not unrelatedly, the party was deeply in debt. In 2010, Labour could only afford a third of the paid staff that it had during the 2005 election.[74]

The leadership contest of 2010 stopped the decline and produced a slight recovery, but Labour never managed to reach even 200,000 members at any point under Ed Miliband (see Figure 8.4). Labour's membership at the start of 2015 was still lower than it had been ten years earlier, at the height of the Iraq War. The 2015 leadership contest resulted in a 40 per cent increase in one year. By 2017, Labour's membership had reached over 560,000, higher than it ever was under New Labour. This much-increased membership enhanced Labour's campaign capacity.[75] Because most new members had joined to support Jeremy Corbyn, they also shifted the internal balance of power, an unsurprising consequence of entrusting members with electing the leader.

Both Ed Miliband and Jeremy Corbyn became leaders without the support of most of their MPs or even a majority of their Shadow Cabinet. Just twelve MPs admitted to voting for Corbyn in 2015.[76] Corbyn contended with a near-constant internal rebellion by Labour

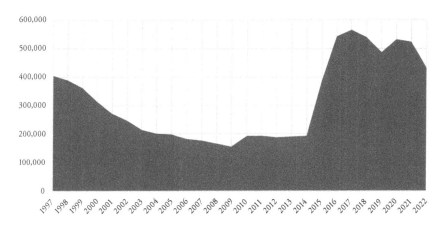

Figure 8.4 Labour Party membership, 1997–2022
Source: Membership of Political Parties in Great Britain, *House of Commons Library*, https://commonslibrary.parliament.uk/research-briefings/sn05125

MPs and peers. Lord Mandelson declared quite openly, 'I work every single day in some small way to bring forward the end of his tenure in office.'[77] The most serious threat to Corbyn's leadership occurred in June 2016, just after the British public voted to leave the European Union. During the weekend after the referendum, nineteen members of the Shadow Cabinet resigned, as did twenty-eight junior shadow ministers and eleven parliamentary private secretaries. It was a coordinated effort to remove Corbyn by his senior team, anticipating the successful overthrow of Boris Johnson by his own ministers in July 2022. Yet, unlike Johnson, Corbyn 'simply refused to resign'.[78] When a delegation of soft-left MPs came to Corbyn to tell him to quit, Shadow Chancellor John McDonnell emerged exclaiming, 'no way. It's not going to happen.' McDonnell later recalled, 'a couple of them burst into tears and all that sort of thing ... I just said this is not happening. We're not doing any of that. Get used to it.'[79]

In a task that is admittedly easier from opposition than in government, Corbyn replaced the resigning frontbenchers with as many loyal MPs as he could find. Because of the scale of the resignations, Corbyn was forced in some cases to ask shadow ministers to take on multiple roles, often with limited or no junior shadow ministerial support. Even decrepit, perennial backbenchers were dragged into service. After twenty-six years on the backbenches, the eighty-one-year-old MP Paul Flynn suddenly found himself as Shadow Welsh Secretary and Shadow Leader of the House of Commons. Flynn, who was old enough to remember delivering leaflets in the 1945 general election, thanked Corbyn for his 'job creation scheme for geriatrics'.[80]

The evening after the shadow ministerial resignations had run their course, a vote of no confidence was moved against Corbyn at the PLP meeting, which he lost: 172 to forty with twenty-two not voting.[81] Margaret Hodge, who moved the motion, admits that after this defeat, 'we just assumed he'd resign' but even with nearly three quarters of his MPs voting no confidence in him, Corbyn once again simply refused to go.[82] Unlike in the Conservative Party, a vote of no confidence in the leader has no constitutional status in the Labour Party, and it turned out to be a paper tiger.

A formal leadership challenge was then launched, with the little-known, soft-left MP Owen Smith as the candidate. The saviour of the Corbyn leadership was the party membership. Under the electoral college, a determined and overwhelming proportion of MPs opposing Corbyn could have delivered the leadership to Smith, but thanks to Miliband's reforms, MPs could not remove Corbyn so long as he held firm and the members continued to back him.

Part of the reason Corbyn was confident that he retained members' support was due to the organising activities of the pro-Corbyn organisation known as Momentum.[83] Momentum had been set up the month after Corbyn was elected leader to provide him with the backing in the membership that he would not find in Parliament.[84] It was led by Jon Lansman, who had been a key player in the Campaign for Labour Party Democracy in the 1970s and 1980s (discussed in Chapter 6). By 2017, Momentum had 150 branches, fifty staff and 23,000 members.[85]

Margaret Hodge later admitted, 'we miscalculated'. She had thought that after the vote to leave the EU, 'young people in Momentum would be cross about the referendum and wouldn't support him'.[86] She overestimated the extent to which young members were motivated by EU membership rather than issues like unemployment, austerity and housing. John McDonnell later quipped, 'as plotters they were fucking useless'.[87]

The 2016 leadership challenge had two effects, both unintended by his adversaries. The first was that it strengthened Corbyn's position in the party. Corbyn's support increased from 60 per cent to 62 per cent. So, while only 17 per cent of MPs had voted confidence in him, three fifths of members remained loyal. This dynamic put anti-Corbyn MPs in a vulnerable position. Members began to raise the possibility of deselecting his internal opponents. These plans were largely aborted by a combination of the leadership and unions losing their nerve and the unexpected 2017 and 2019 elections.[88] The failure of mandatory reselection proved a missed opportunity for Corbyn to entrench his power over the PLP.

The second consequence, more directly beneficial for the party machine, was an enormous funding windfall. The source of this largesse was the registered supporter scheme, introduced by Ed Miliband under his ally Peter Hain's 'Refounding Labour' report and passed by party conference in 2011 to no notice or acclaim. Any member of the public who paid a nominal fee, set by the National Executive Committee, was entitled to vote for leader as long as they ticked a box to say they believed in Labour's aims and values. In 2015, the NEC set the fee at £3, and over 105,000 individuals took part, raising over £300,000 for the party. Jeremy Corbyn won 84 per cent of their first preferences. In a blatant attempt to price out Corbyn's supporters, in 2016 the NEC raised the fee to £25. Their plan failed; 121,000 registered supporters paid the higher fee, even more than in 2015. Unexpectedly, the revolt against Corbyn raised nearly £3.5 million for the Labour Party.

These funds were deployed when Theresa May called a snap election seven months later. One Labour Party insider recalled, 'We don't usually have that [spare cash].' At the start of an election campaign, 'We usually have to start fundraising. This was put to one side and kept for a general election. All the costs of a general election, new computers, new cars – all this sort of stuff – we could afford it on day one.'[89] As a result, before legal spending limits kicked in, Labour spent £2 million on campaign advertising in every constituency except for the seventy-five safest in the country.[90]

Forming a Clear Policy Agenda: Vote Labour and Win a Microwave

Ed Miliband's criticisms of New Labour in the 2010 leadership contest did not translate into a robust policy alternative. The political economist Helen Thompson drew a contrast in early 2015 between Miliband's bold rhetoric and weak policies: 'Miliband's political language is the discourse of crisis and the desperate need for structural reform of the economy to reduce inequality … Yet, there is nothing in the policies he has thus far offered … that would remotely amount to a radical economic programme aimed at addressing what is purportedly so badly wrong.'[91] As Andrew Murray assesses, Labour's shrunken offer in 2015 'essentially harkened back to the recent past – with no vision of economic transformation'.[92]

Instead, Labour was committed to Conservative spending plans, deficit reduction and a public sector pay freeze. The 2015 Labour manifesto contained a series of poorly joined up 'retail' offers, which were derided by the American political strategist David Axelrod as amounting to little more than 'Vote Labour and win a microwave'.[93] In the wake of the 2015 defeat, Labour MP Jon Cruddas condemned his party's 'minimalist, safety-first offer'.[94]

There were two explanations for the failure of Labour to develop a radical alternative. The first was perceived electoral necessity. A left-wing alternative was believed to be electorally unpopular and, therefore, Labour needed to make policy compromises with the electorate if it hoped to win power. As discussed later in this chapter, Shadow Chancellor Ed Balls was convinced that there was no appetite in the public for a tax-and-spend manifesto. Second, some on the party right were ideologically opposed to a socialist programme altogether, whether or not it was popular; in 2015, Tony Blair told the New Labour pressure group Progress: 'I wouldn't want to win on an old-fashioned leftist platform … Even if I thought it was the route to victory, I wouldn't take it.'[95] Miliband's precarious position as leader depended on their beneficence.

David Kogan is correct to assess that 'the problem with denying New Labour was that there had to be a strategy to replace it and a united opposition to deliver the messaging'. Ed Miliband had neither. He was given contradictory advice. One key strategist, Stewart Wood, told him to be bold; another, Spencer Livermore, advised caution. Miliband ended up saying one thing but doing another. 'Labour's 2015 manifesto', Patrick Diamond writes, 'hardly marked a fundamental departure from the 2010 government's policies'.[96] It is, therefore, no surprise that Labour only managed to win just over 30 per cent of the vote, a pitiful improvement on Gordon Brown's 29 per cent five years earlier.

By the time Jeremy Corbyn became leader, there was a real hunger for policy change within the party. The new Shadow Chancellor John McDonnell instructed: 'Get ready; start preparing now … if you don't get this right, the left will be out for another generation. For God's sake, we've got to get ready.'[97] McDonnell began developing an ambitious economic alternative, drawing on the expertise of socialist economists. McDonnell called this his 'New Economics' project and ran both closed and open seminars on left economics. The Shadow Chancellor even edited a book entitled, *Economics for the Many*.[98] In contrast to the intellectual flaccidity of New Labour and the Miliband era, the McDonnell Shadow Treasury team elicited a genuine exchange of radical new ideas that fed into both the 2017 and 2019 party manifestos.[99] In 2019, McDonnell pledged to 'rewrite the rules of our economy'.[100]

Labour's 2017 manifesto, *For the Many, Not the Few*, just shy of 25,000 words, will go down in the annals of Labour history as among its most famous, alongside its celebrated 1945 manifesto and its less esteemed 1983 'suicide note'. The manifesto proposed raising taxes to fund an expansion of the welfare state, nationalising utilities and rail, strengthening workers' rights and building hundreds of thousands of council homes. When these proposals were leaked to the press, the news 'electrified Labour's campaign'.[101]

The 2017 manifesto was not a far-left document out of step with Labour's ideological traditions.[102] It returned the party to its ideological norm, correcting the rightward aberration of the New Labour manifestos, the most right-wing in Labour's history.[103] Ideologically, the 2017 manifesto was comparable to those of the 1940s–70s as well as the 1992 manifesto (see Table 8.1). It was to the right of the losing 1983 manifesto and the winning February 1974 manifesto, which Corbyn had helped to shape with his involvement in *Labour's Programme 1973*, a conference document of numerous left-wing pledges passed in advance of the 1974 elections.[104]

The biggest policy challenge facing the British state in the 2010s was the task of British withdrawal from the EU. Although principally a test for the government, the issue of 'Brexit' became an increasingly thorny predicament for Labour, especially after the Conservatives lost their majority in the 2017 election.

Brexit aroused conflicting issues for the Labour Party. Two thirds of Labour voters supported Remain, but two thirds of Labour MPs

Table 8.1 Ideological placement of Labour's manifestos

More left-wing than 2017	Ideologically similar to 2017	More right-wing than 2017
1951, 1955, February 1974*, 1983	<u>1945</u>, 1950, 1959, <u>1964</u>, October <u>1974</u>, 1979, 1992	<u>1966</u>, 1970, 1987, <u>1997</u>**, <u>2001</u>, <u>2005</u>, 2010, 2015

Note: Elections won by Labour are underlined. *most left-wing manifesto; **most right-wing manifesto.
Source: Allen and Bara, 2019

represented Leave-majority constituencies. The overwhelming proportion of the Labour membership supported remaining in the EU, but significant figures in the Corbyn circle, including Corbyn himself, were highly critical of the supranational organisation which entrenched capitalism through its treaties. These views could be found elsewhere in the Labour Party, notably in the socially conservative 'Blue Labour' movement established by the Labour peer and academic Maurice Glasman.[105] Although meant as a criticism, Matt Bolton and Frederick Pitts were basically correct to argue that both 'Corbynism and Blue Labour see the world in essentially national terms. Both sense opportunity in Brexit to reinstate the sovereignty of the nation-state against global capital.'[106]

Initially, there was enthusiasm in Corbyn's leadership team for Brexit. On 15 November 2016, John McDonnell declared: 'Labour accepts the referendum result as the voice of the majority, and we must embrace the enormous opportunities to reshape our country that Brexit has opened for us. In that way we can speak again to those who were left behind and offer a positive, ambitious vision instead of leaving the field open to divisive Trump-style politics.'[107] However, Shadow Brexit Secretary Keir Starmer was said to be 'absolutely furious' and 'seriously pissed off' about the remarks.[108] McDonnell was 'spooked' by the hostile reaction within the PLP to his speech, with whispers of further internal sabotage if the top brass spoke too positively about a left-wing Brexit programme.[109]

Jon Trickett MP, a member of the Shadow Cabinet's Brexit strategy committee, proposed that Labour set out an alternative left-wing vision of Brexit based on socialist and internationalist principles. At one meeting, he urged: 'Jeremy, pick up the phone and speak to people like Lula in Brazil or Correa in Ecuador. Use Brexit to create new internationalist alliances. If you make the case for an anti-racist Labour Leave option, the [Labour Party] membership won't cling to Remain; they'll come to you.'[110] Trickett's theory had some supporting evidence. In the summer of 2016, Corbyn, who advocated for the immediate triggering of withdrawal from the European Union, decisively defeated Owen Smith, who offered a second referendum to stop Brexit. However, McDonnell and Corbyn's adviser Seumas Milne avoided a full-throated Left Brexit policy because it would have involved stirring up a hornet's nest in the PLP and sacking Keir Starmer, one of the few members of

Corbyn's Shadow Cabinet who had campaigned for Smith.[111] At a 2017 strategy meeting, Diane Abbott warned Corbyn: 'He [Starmer] doesn't want Brexit done. He wants you done so he can become leader.'[112]

In the months after the 2017 election, Milne and Andrew Fisher, another Corbyn adviser, produced a pro-Leave Labour programme called 'Brexit: A New Approach'. At a January 2018 meeting of the Shadow Cabinet Brexit strategy sub-committee, Corbyn began to read out the proposal's key policies. Starmer erupted: 'Enough. This is completely outrageous', and threatened to resign if the document became Labour's Brexit policy. John Hilary, the former director of the charity War on Want, had been asked by Corbyn's office to develop a comprehensive 'trade justice' policy as an alternative to EU customs union membership, yet, within weeks, Starmer announced that Labour would seek customs union membership, contrary to the wishes of the Labour leader and his close advisers.[113]

As early as 12 November 2018, Starmer was telling the media 'Brexit can be stopped', which was in contravention of Labour Party policy and the wishes of the Labour leadership.[114] After the 2019 European elections, he publicly embraced a second referendum policy and promised to campaign for Remain. Corbyn's political secretary told Starmer that from an electoral standpoint this policy was so obviously damaging that 'not even an A-level politics student would formulate [it]'.[115] That summer, Boris Johnson was able to excoriate Corbyn for abandoning his democratic and socialist principles:

> At last, this long-standing Eurosceptic, the right hon. Gentleman, has been captured. He has been jugulated – he has been reprogrammed by his hon. Friends. He has been turned now into a remainer! Of all the flip-flops that he has performed in his tergiversating career, that is the one for which I think he will pay the highest price.[116]

As Johnson predicted, Labour suffered a serious electoral penalty for its second referendum policy. The biggest swings against Labour in 2019 were in Leave-voting constituencies, matching the local election results earlier that year.[117] Although Corbyn in 2019 won a higher share of the vote than Ed Miliband in 2015 or Gordon Brown in 2010 (and a higher share of the eligible electorate than Tony Blair in 2005), Labour succumbed to its worst result in terms of seats since 1935. This was due to Labour disproportionately underperforming in the pro-Leave constituencies it needed to hold and to gain in order to win government. Commentators who claim that Labour's defeat was due to a failure to woo Europhile Liberal Democrats show a marked misunderstanding of the electoral geography of Leave and Labour voters under the first-past-the-post system.[118]

Corbyn's inner circle believed that it was impossible to develop a bold, socialist programme within the European Union, but they failed to make the case to the party membership, partly out of fear of backlash from non-Corbyn-supporting Labour MPs. Labour's eleventh-hour switch to an anti-Brexit position in 2019 aggravated working-class voters, who overwhelmingly voted Leave, and projected the image of a political class who patronisingly thought they'd voted the 'wrong way' the first time around. The second referendum policy remarkably enabled Boris Johnson to steal the left-populist clothes that should have been Labour's. Johnson exclaimed in 2019: 'The reality now is that we are the party of the people. We are the party of the many, and they are the party of the few.'[119]

Building the Party's Relationship with the Electorate: The Base Weakens

Between 2010 and 2019, Labour fought four elections, all unsuccessfully, with a high level of volatility between them. Labour's vote ranged from a low of 29 per cent in 2010 to a high of 40 per cent in 2017. The party won an historically good result in Scotland in 2010 but suffered a near-wipe-out there just five years later. In England and Wales, Labour made inroads with working-class voters in 2017 but lost them two years later, along with seats that Labour had held for generations.

In some respects, the 2015 result was the most devastating because it was both bad and unexpected. In 2010 and 2019, it was obvious that Labour would lose, but in 2015 Ed Miliband was convinced he would become prime minister, if not of a majority-Labour government then of a Labour-led coalition or minority.[120] The fact that the Conservatives won a majority, their first since 1992, was a crushing blow, compounded by Labour losing all but one of its forty-one seats in Scotland.

The collapse of Labour in Scotland can be largely explained by the Scottish National Party (SNP) capturing nearly all of the Labour voters who had voted to leave the United Kingdom in the 2014 independence referendum.[121] Labour had campaigned strongly against independence ('No'), yet 35 per cent of Scots who voted Labour in the 2010 election voted for independence ('Yes'). A staggering 90 per cent of these pro-independence Labour supporters switched to the SNP in 2015. In contrast, Labour held onto the vast proportion of its 'No' voters, with just 13 per cent defecting to the SNP.

The 2017 election result stands out in recent history as something of an anomaly (see Figure 8.5). The assumption that a left-wing manifesto would destroy the party's electoral prospects had been taken as an article of faith. The *New Statesman* editor Jason Cowley wrote a week before the election: 'Whether it loses 30, 50, or 70 seats, the Labour Party is heading for a shattering defeat under Jeremy Corbyn.'[122] Instead, Labour made a net gain of thirty seats, the only time since 1997 it had made gains. The party won its highest share of the popular vote since 2001. The 2017 election generated the highest turnout since 1997. In fact, as a share of the eligible electorate, which is sensitive to turnout, Corbyn's 2017 result (27.5 per cent) outranked Blair's 2001 result (24.2 per cent), too.

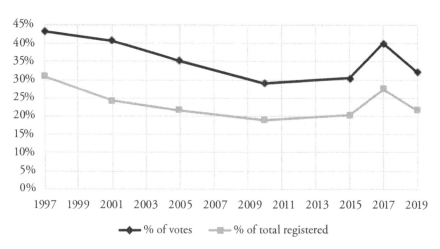

Figure 8.5 Labour's share of eligible voters and total votes cast, 1997–2019
Source: Mortimore and Blick, 2018

In their book, *The New Politics of Class: The Political Exclusion of the British Working Class*, political scientists Geoffrey Evans and James Tilley argue that Labour's lurch to the right under New Labour left working-class voters politically homeless. This was expressed not by such voters switching to the Conservatives but rather by them dropping out of the electoral process entirely.[123] In 2017, Labour improved its performance across all classes, but Evans and Tilley show that its support among working-class voters improved the most (Table 8.2).[124]

In 2019, Labour stood on an equally bold manifesto as 2017 and with nearly identical leadership, yet it declined 8 points in the popular vote and lost sixty seats. What explains the difference between these two elections? The key change was Labour's position on leaving the European Union. In 2017, both Labour and the Conservatives had pledged to implement the Leave result, effectively neutralising the issue. John McDonnell credits this as the great achievement of Labour's 2017 campaign: 'We were the anti-austerity party ... We were effective in having a simple anti-austerity message and then a policy programme where each policy reinforced that message.'[125]

By 2019, Labour had decided not to implement the 2016 referendum, in spite of having promised previously to respect Leavers' choice. Instead, Labour encouraged voters to 'think again' with a second referendum that contained the option of ignoring the earlier vote. Although, as a share of the popular vote, Labour performed better in 2019 than Brown in 2010 or Miliband in 2015, it lost far more seats. All but two were in constituencies that voted Leave. In areas that supported Leave by greater than 60 per cent, the swing against Labour was 16.5 per cent. It is evident that Labour's second referendum pledge was electorally catastrophic in these parts of the country.

Table 8.2 Class voting in the 2015 and 2017 elections: Support for Labour

	2015	2017	**Change**
Managers and employers	28%	31%	**+2**
Professional salariat	40%	41%	**+1**
Routine and clerical workers	34%	41%	**+7**
Manual workers	39%	44%	**+5**

Source: Evans and Tilley, 2017

Beyond Brexit, there were two other issues that contributed to Labour's loss in 2019. The first was that Jeremy Corbyn was a more personally unpopular figure. He had been severely weakened by accusations of insouciance and even complicity in light of allegations of rampant antisemitism among the Labour membership. Corbyn had asked the civil liberties campaigner Shami Chakrabarti, along with two vice-chairs (Baroness Royall and Professor David Feldman, director of the Pears Institute for the Study of Antisemitism at Birkbeck) to investigate. The Chakrabarti Report made no definitive finding on the scale of antisemitism within the Labour Party but provided recommendations for Labour to be a more welcoming party and clearer procedures to expel those who engaged in racist abuse.[126] Corbyn's critics argued his response was not tough enough.[127]

The second issue which damaged Labour in 2019 was the Conservative Party's changing approach to public finances. Two years' earlier, as has been said, the election was fought on fiscal policy. Theresa May pledged fiscal prudence, whereas Labour championed an expansionary fiscal programme. Under Boris Johnson, the Conservatives abandoned a dogmatic commitment to austerity and offered a variety of bold public spending pledges. These deprived Labour of a clear economic dividing line.

The 2017 election was an inconvenient result for Corbyn's critics. They wanted 'to revive the myth of 1983' that a left-wing programme was a vote loser.[128] They had to wait until 2019 for this narrative to ring true. The irony, of course, is that the Labour right had been the key pushers of the policy that cost Labour so many of its heartland seats in that election.

Holding the Conservative Government to Account: Five Faces of Power

In just over six years, from 2016 to 2022, the United Kingdom was led by five prime ministers: David Cameron, Theresa May, Boris Johnson, Liz Truss and Rishi Sunak. The volatility in the Conservative Party leadership had little to do with the Labour Party's ability to hold these figures to account. Cameron resigned after he lost the EU referendum. May was forced out by her backbenchers. Johnson was toppled by his frontbenchers. Truss self-imploded. On the two great policy challenges of the post-2010 period – the management of the British economy and Brexit – Labour's opposition strategy was inept.

On the economy, between 2010–15 and 2020–24, Labour expressed strenuous criticism of the Conservatives' poor economic management but repeatedly held back from offering a structural alternative. As Shadow Chancellor, Ed Balls imposed, in his own words, 'rigid discipline' on Labour's spending commitments. He instructed his staff to scour speeches and press releases from frontbenchers 'to root out any spending commitments'.[129] Balls committed to following the Conservative-led government's spending pledges and even promised that Labour would run a budget surplus.[130] This meant accepting the Conservatives' 1 per cent public sector wage freeze, which was deeply unpopular with the 44 per cent of Labour members who worked in the public sector.[131] The Shadow Chancellor was, in effect, committing a future Labour government to years of further fiscal austerity. According to one commentator, these spending pledges ran contrary to Ed Miliband's own instincts, but, due to his own weakness within the PLP, Miliband had become 'a prisoner of the party right'.[132]

By his own admission, Balls chose fiscal austerity out of political expediency rather than genuine conviction. He wrote in his memoirs: 'my economic instinct was to set out a clear alternative to [Chancellor] George Osborne ... [But] my political antennae said this was an argument that just could not be won.' In Balls's view, the political climate had not shifted drastically since 1992, when Labour's 'Shadow Budget' was mercilessly attacked as a tax 'bombshell' by the Conservatives. In Balls's estimation, 'whenever Labour talked about more public investment ... the public just heard more borrowing, more risk, and higher taxes. So, I took a slower, more defensive approach.'[133] He admitted: 'with political and economic logic pulling in opposite directions, I decided that if we had a chance of winning the election, I had to put politics first.'[134] Writing in 2016, Balls was still convinced his political judgement was sound: 'Arguing for a detailed jobs plan paid for by more public borrowing just wouldn't have worked.'[135]

Other members of the Shadow Cabinet, however, disagreed. Jonathan Ashworth, Shadow Cabinet Office Minister, saw this caution as politically self-defeating: 'the problem was that we ran a campaign for five years focused on stagnating wages and on the lack of economic growth and then when it came to the general election, our economic policy was not radically different enough from Conservative policy'.[136]

After Ed Miliband's resignation, Harriet Harman returned as Labour's acting leader. She shared Balls's belief that Labour needed to demonstrate to the public that it was economically credible, meaning rigid fiscal discipline. This led Harman to instruct Labour MPs to abstain on the new majority-Conservative government's welfare bill, which slashed £12 billion in benefits payments. Forty-eight Labour MPs rebelled; Corbyn was the only leadership contender among their number.[137] His ally John McDonnell said during the debate: 'I would swim through vomit to vote against the bill. And listening to some of the nauseating speeches tonight, I think we might have to.'[138]

The welfare vote was probably the 'precise moment that ... Andy Burnham lost the election ... If Burnham had voted with his instincts that day, he would probably be Labour leader.'[139] A poll conducted by YouGov between 17 and 21 July (i.e. just as the candidates were declaring their positions on the welfare bill) revealed that Corbyn and Burnham were neck-and-neck among Labour members (50 per cent each in a head-to-head), but Corbyn was leading Burnham among registered supporters and union affiliates.[140] By early August, after the welfare vote, Corbyn maintained his lead amongst non-members and surged ahead with members at 56 per cent to Burnham's 44 per cent.[141] Arguably, 'Harman probably did more for Corbyn's victory than any other Labour MP.'[142] Extraordinarily, she devotes no attention to the welfare vote in her autobiography in spite of the fact that it was probably the most important political decision of her career.

The second challenge for Labour in holding the government to account was over Brexit. Here, straightforward opposition was not an option. In the 2016 referendum, Labour campaigned to remain, but polls showed that (like in Scotland in 2014) one in three Labour voters backed the contrary position. These Labour Leavers were disproportionately concentrated in Labour's fragile base of working-class seats in the North of England, the Midlands and Wales. Corbyn believed that Labour needed to accept the verdict of the referendum, and a three-line whip was imposed on Labour MPs to trigger the Article 50 process of leaving the EU. In the 2017 election, as we have seen, both Labour and the Conservatives pledged to implement Brexit, effectively neutralising the issue and, instead, turning the election to a battle over fiscal policy. Winning between them 82.3 per cent of the vote, the 2017 election was the first time that more than four-fifths of voters had supported Labour or the Conservatives since 1979.

After the 2017 election, the Conservatives formed a minority government. Initially, Corbyn's team proposed maintaining the Brexit truce. Andrew Murray suggested that Labour do a deal with Theresa May for cross-party Brexit negotiations in the national interest, but the idea was belittled by Shadow Home Secretary Diane Abbott as 'the Ramsay MacCorbyn plan'.[143] Between 2017 and 2019, an increasing number of Labour MPs, who were emphatically pro-EU, tried to conspire with small parties and a rump of Conservative rebels to force a second referendum, supported by an organisation named 'the People's Vote' campaign.

In spite of these machinations, in April 2019, Labour came excruciatingly close to agreeing a deal with Theresa May's government. May had repeatedly failed to pass her Brexit deal due to the rebellions of her own MPs, both those who wanted a cleaner break with the EU and those who were against the idea of leaving altogether. Number 10 invited Labour and the trade unions into negotiations to name their price. Len McCluskey, the Unite General Secretary who was part of the negotiations, claimed that an agreement had been nearly reached when it was spiked by Shadow Brexit Secretary Keir Starmer. In McCluskey's estimation, Starmer 'frankly just didn't want a deal'.[144] Indeed, he threatened to resign if a deal was reached.[145]

Such a posture was strategically inept. Had Labour struck a deal in April 2019, it would have defused the Brexit issue before the next election. Labour could have abstained; Theresa May would have passed her Brexit deal and shouldered all the blame and responsibility for what came next. It was highly likely Labour could have split the Conservative Party, as John Smith had so deftly done in his decision to abstain on the Maastricht Treaty in 1993.[146] May would have been an unpopular, wounded incumbent like John Major. In these circumstances, it is perfectly possible that Labour could have won the next election. The fact that once Keir Starmer became leader in 2020 he immediately dropped any discussion of returning to the EU suggests that his strategists came to realise (or perhaps always knew) that their approach was an electoral folly.

Conclusion

Labour had two viable options after its defeat in 2010: it could have either rejected or embraced the New Labour project. Ed Miliband rejected the project intellectually but preserved it in practice. With his Shadow Chancellor Ed Balls urging deficit reduction and other MPs further to the right calling for Labour to be even more fiscally restrictive, Miliband offered a bold diagnosis but weak medicine. This was 'contradictory' and 'ended up pleasing nobody'.[147] It was like telling a patient they had cancer but only offering them a cup of tea to aid recovery. Miliband himself admitted years later, 'I probably fell between two stools. I should have been more radical.'[148]

Patrick Diamond argues that 'New Labour's main legacy was shifting the party sharply to the Left more than at any previous moment in its history.'[149] Much of this was of New Labour's own making. The anti-New Labour coalition in the Labour Party comprises young people, idealistic baby boomers and public sector workers. New Labour's failure to build new housing while also encouraging an open international labour market has made it increasingly difficult for young people to acquire stable housing and start a family. Diamond, a defender of New Labour, nonetheless admits that it is 'difficult to dispute that the intergenerational divide was in part New Labour's legacy'.[150] Baby boomers had fallen out of love with New Labour over the Iraq War, spin and sleaze. They were looking for their idealism to be restored with a more ethical direction. Public sector workers, who in 2015 comprised a staggering 44 per cent of Labour's membership, had been radicalised by the squeeze on their living standards due to the 1 per cent public sector pay freeze.[151]

Ed Miliband's trenchant critic Peter Mandelson makes an astute assessment of his leadership: 'His abiding aim was to delegitimise and kill off New Labour without replacing it with any alternative, coherent, cogent thinking of his own.'[152] It took Miliband to kill off New Labour, but it took Corbyn to provide the alternative. That alternative achieved one of Labour's most dramatic electoral improvements in its history, attracting 3.5 million more voters to the Labour side than just two years earlier.[153] Rather than build on this result, however, the next two years saw Labour's position unravel almost entirely due to the self-inflicted wound of its strategically inept posture towards the process of withdrawal from the European Union, as well as Corbyn's worsening personal unpopularity.

After a rocky start, Keir Starmer managed to improve Labour's polling position to heady heights, not seen since the eve of Labour's 1997 election landslide. Like in 1997, in 2024 the Conservatives encountered a serious 'cost of governing' penalty. As in the 1990s, Labour adopted a strategy of tight discipline and extreme policy caution, hesitant to offer any policies that could be seen as 'socialist'. But, the picture today is different from the 1990s. The economy is weaker, the global environment is more precarious, public memory of the 'Winter of Discontent' has faded and the prospects for the next generation are bleaker. Labour may benefit from 'not being as bad' as the Conservatives, but the challenge after opposition is to govern. For that, Labour needs a programme that meets the scale of the challenges of the moment.

Conclusion

In an era of unremitting social and technological change, it is all too easy to conclude that those who refuse to study the lessons of history will simply be saving themselves from a pile of unprofitable reading. Specifically in relation to Labour as a party of opposition, it might be thought that 'the lessons of history' are digestible without serious enquiry. The party is at its best when it can fight elections broadly united behind coherent and radical programmes which reflect a more general mood within the British electorate – even those who have previously voted for other parties. Ominously for Labour, though, the 1945 election, which best conforms to that model, was contested in unusually helpful circumstances; senior figures had given distinguished service to a war-winning coalition government, making it very difficult for any Conservative to claim with credibility that Labour was lumbered with too many impractical idealists. As such, 'history' suggests that the ideal scenario for Labour as an opposition party is a set of circumstances which, hopefully, will never be repeated.

Of the other occasions when Labour has moved from opposition into government, four followed general elections which provided the party with insufficient parliamentary support to implement its preferred policies. Labour formed minority governments in 1924 and 1929 without having used the preceding periods in opposition to prepare coherent programmes of reform. This was not the case when the party narrowly regained office in 1964; but, apart from its precarious position in the House of Commons, it was hamstrung by an economic situation which was even worse than its leaders had supposed and which continued to dog the government after its comfortable re-election in 1966. Labour won more seats (though not more votes) in February 1974 than a Conservative administration which had been overwhelmed by a series of crises whose gravity was only too obvious; although the Labour manifesto claimed that the party was proud to pursue 'Socialist aims' even amid exceptional difficulties, the document included pledges (notably in relation to state ownership) which the leadership was unlikely to honour even if Labour had achieved a comfortable majority in the second (October) 1974 contest. The majority won by New Labour in 1997 was more than 'comfortable', outweighing even the fabled 1945 landslide. However, that triumph brought to an end eighteen years of impotent opposition, during which the Conservatives under Thatcher and Major had been able, so far as they dared, to prosecute a neo-liberal assault on key aspects of the Attlee governments' legacy. For New Labour, the price of a return to office was the acceptance of a 'post-Thatcherite' consensus and the abandonment of key commitments, extending far beyond the partly symbolic revision of Clause IV. Arguably, instead of assuming that Labour would surf back into office on the back of public demands for a new approach, Tony Blair had spent his time as Leader of the Opposition making unnecessary concessions to a Tory tide which had receded even before Labour suffered a fourth consecutive defeat in 1992. His determination to conciliate right-wing views, rather than confront them, overshadowed those elements of the 1997 manifesto which came near to the (new) Clause IV characterisation of Labour as a 'democratic socialist' party. The 1945–51 Labour governments used their parliamentary positions to secure lasting reforms against the odds; given its opportunities, Labour's record between 1997 and 2010 is one of deliberate under-achievement in domestic matters, leaving aside its ill-starred intervention in America's 'War on Terror'.

A superficial view might suggest that Labour has not been particularly proficient in the art of opposition, yet even if that were shown to be true it would be worth examining the party's various attempts and asking why its general performance has been poor. In his classic study of British political parties, R.T. McKenzie argued that Labour and the Conservatives shared more characteristics than their supporters would care to admit. Both epitomised what Roberto Michels had called 'the iron law of oligarchy': irrespective of any claims to transparent debate and grassroots input, decisive influence on key matters of policy and organisation is reserved for an elite leadership group.[1] Whatever the justice of McKenzie's analysis, it paid inadequate attention to a crucial contrast in the *ethos* of Britain's major parties.[2] Traditionally, Conservatives have seen themselves as members of a 'natural party of government' and readily accept that their leaders are actuated by 'an appetite for power'.[3] Applying the same shorthand characterisation, Labour could be depicted as a natural party of opposition, driven by a disposition to dissent. Labour, after all, was founded as a 'challenger party' in two respects: far from joining the Liberals in a 'progressive alliance', it had to supplant them in order to find a competitive berth within a two-party system; and its purpose was to supersede an established order (in terms of socio-economic factors as well as political orthodoxy) which had been shaped by its much longer-established partisan rivals.

If Labour has generally exhibited an oppositional ethos, this is a product at least in part of the ways in which allies of the status quo have manoeuvred in their determination to thwart the threat from the left. The 'bankers' ramp' of 1931 is only the most spectacular instance of financial muscle being applied unhelpfully to a Labour government.[4] In addition, from the Zinoviev Letter to the character assassinations of Kinnock, Miliband and Corbyn, the right-wing press has consistently excelled as the Conservative Party's dirty-tricks department, working to prevent Labour from forming governments and, when those efforts have failed, obstructing its intentions in office or belittling its achievements.

Differences in ethos between Labour and the Conservatives are exemplified by their respective choices of leader. Winston Churchill (1940–55) had defected to (and back from) the Liberals; Harold Macmillan (1956–63) had refused to take the government whip in the 1930s, as a protest against its appeasement of Mussolini. Both of these 'rebels' were eventually installed as leaders of the Conservative Party when it was already in office, having in the meantime assuaged any doubts that (whatever their private feelings) they would prove to be unstinting upholders of the party's interests. By contrast, in 1980 Michael Foot, the political heir of Nye Bevan, was elected as Labour leader despite overwhelming evidence that he was happier as a champion of friendless causes than an administrator; his long previous record as a principled dissident made him wholly unsuited to the task of restoring the discipline his party urgently needed in 1980. In much more recent times, the Conservatives have chosen as their leaders Iain Duncan Smith, who never knowingly obeyed the party whip in votes concerning 'Europe', and Liz Truss, whose enthusiasm for EU membership had undergone an abrupt and career-enhancing transition, and whose resemblance to Churchill began and ended with a spell of passionate Liberal partisanship. Both were removed from office before they could lead their party to electoral disaster. The Labour Party's ancestral fondness for unruly elements was verified in sensational style in 2015, when it chose Jeremy Corbyn as its leader, and subsequently sustained him in that position through two elections (and a referendum) despite his nugatory support within the PLP.

The Corbyn example might suggest that Labour would prefer to lose under an idealist than to win office with a pragmatic politician at the helm. Read a different way, Corbyn's stickability confirms another difference between Labour and the Conservatives: whatever the qualities of the incumbent leader, Labour has proved much more reluctant than the Conservatives to force a change, even after demoralising electoral defeats. Hugh Gaitskell (in 1959) and Neil Kinnock (1987) both enjoyed enhanced positions within the Labour Party after election campaigns which failed in their main objective but were judged to have been well conducted. On other occasions the party has been all too eager to dissect the records of Labour administrations in a search for symptoms either of insufficient faith in their leaders, or evidence of outright 'treachery' of the kind exhibited by Ramsay MacDonald in 1931.

The notion that the Labour Party has an oppositional ethos does not mean that party members relish opposition. All too often, as recorded in this book, Labour has indulged in introspection, mistaking procedural battles at party conference or within the NEC for landmarks in the quest for public approval. It took too long to address the democratic deficit epitomised by the union bloc vote, and when that institutional idiosyncrasy was addressed, it allowed the 'sovereign' annual conference to lapse into a rubber-stamping ritual rather than a forum for constructive debate even in a reduced advisory capacity. In its treatment of parliamentary dissidents it has never stumbled upon a 'Goldilocks' formula, veering instead between excessive indulgence (extended, on occasion, to grassroots 'entryists') and a draconian approach to discipline. Until recently, the Conservative Party could find ways to reduce the chances or consequences of counter-productive public altercations with erratic ex-leaders like Ted Heath and even Margaret Thatcher; by contrast, Labour's current management went out of its way to pick quarrels with Jeremy Corbyn, who had enjoyed far more lenient treatment when, as a recalcitrant backbencher, he lambasted New Labour's foreign policy.

At the time of writing (October 2023), the next general election looks like being Labour's to lose – a feat, admittedly, which would not overtax its historic capacity for self-inflicted damage. The party is palpably disunited in most things except its determination to return to office. As in the New Labour years, rather than welcoming open debate, the leadership extends limited tolerance towards 'off-message' ruminators. Instead of using traditional Labour principles as its sheet anchor for policy development, the party under Sir Keir Starmer has preferred to offer tentative modifications to the tried and distrusted practices of successive Conservative governments since 2010, basing its approach on a New Labour template and giving the top team, after a reshuffle in September 2023, a distinctively New Labour look. In February of that year, Sir Keir committed his party to 'five missions for a better Britain'. The long-term aspirational agenda was far removed from New Labour's carefully calibrated pre-landslide pledge card. Yet it followed, by just a few weeks, a speech in which the prime minister, Rishi Sunak, made 'five promises' for the coming year. The policy priorities of the rival leaders were dissimilar, but critics within both of their parties had begun to detect a degree of synchronicity in their approaches to post-Brexit Britain. The notion that the long-departed spirit of 'Mr Butskell' has been revived in the form of Sir Kishi Starmak seemed less fanciful in September 2023 when Sunak opened a heavily leaked speech with an attack on Westminster's short-termist approach to policy-making. This was exactly the sentiment which Starmer had expressed in February, when announcing Labour's 'five missions'; the difference was that Sunak felt able to denounce short-termism before devoting the remainder of his speech to an opportunistic bid for electoral support from motorists, endangering his own stated long-term goals on the reduction of carbon emissions.[5]

Whatever the depth of its commitment to long-term policy thinking, the current Labour leadership has kept its cards carefully concealed, giving rise to suspicions that it has no intention of deploying any aces even against a beaten and befuddled opponent. Before the October 2023 party conference, even New Labour stalwarts like Lord Mandelson and Alastair Campbell – not unfriendly critics – expressed concern about the inadequate policy work being conducted by Starmer and his team.[6] The leadership's 'mood music' is equally muted. Whatever the justice of causes espoused by its trade union allies, the central party pursues a consistent policy of holding them at arm's length while pocketing their money, raising only muffled protests against the Sunak government's refusal to negotiate. From this perspective, it looks possible that Labour could suffer another transition from opposition to government with all of the deficiencies which hampered it in 1924, 1929, 1964 and 1974, and shorn of the shallow, short-lived optimism of 1997. In addition to its own inadequate process of policy formulation and its underlying disunity, if successful in the next election it will inherit social, political and economic problems comparable (at least) to those of 1964 and 1974.

However, there is a reasonable chance that an uninspiring Labour opposition could 'over-achieve' once returned to office. The lessons of recent history show that when a Labour government fails to capitalise on its opportunities the result is a decade or more of essentially sterile party infighting. But when such a government establishes a connection with the people it aspires to represent – those who, as John Smith claimed in 1988, 'are far more altruistic and far less selfish' than Thatcherites (and Blairites) assumed – and constructs a convincing narrative for radical change while genuinely meaning what it says, it is not impossible for Labour, once back in office, to generate a mood similar to that of 1945, and to forge a robust approach to policy-making which extinguishes the last vestiges of post-Thatcherite assumptions.

For some Labour supporters who voted for Brexit, Starmer is the wrong leader to head a government of that kind. However, at the time of writing, there is no reason to be sure that he is *not*; for this former Director of Public Prosecutions, the jury is still out and it would be wrong to deliver a final verdict until he has undergone the ultimate test of governmental responsibility. The current cost of living crisis has exposed unequal life-chances which New Labour left unaddressed and which, among young people in particular, were accentuated by the Coronavirus pandemic. In its response to COVID-19 the Conservative government was forced to be creative, and found the public generally supportive. Whether or not his views have shifted dramatically rightwards since his early days, Starmer seems to be the kind of politician who would be willing to embark on a more radical programme for change (for example, in relation to the renationalisation of key public utilities) if he detects unmistakable signs of public support once Labour is back in office.

When Robert McKenzie argued that Labour, in organisational terms, was really not very different from its Conservative adversary, he was aware of the increasing prominence of party leaders in British political conflict (and, having contributed to BBC election coverage, he was in a good position to gauge the media's importance in enhancing their role). McKenzie's ghost would have been gratified to note the increasingly leader-centric nature of our survey of Labour's history as an opposition party which, initially, tried to contravene 'the iron law of oligarchy' by eschewing the notion of any designated 'leader' (see Chapter 1). However, the increasingly 'presidential' media coverage of British politics, which Labour could scarcely have avoided, has coincided with a diminution of public interest in the work of politicians at lower levels. Voters regularly complain that their elected representatives in general are 'out of touch', and this perception is bound to affect Labour more than the Conservatives since the latter have rarely apologised for their estrangement from the real-life experiences of average voters. Labour duly incurred more damage than the Conservatives from the parliamentary expenses scandal which came (in 2009) hard on the heels of the financial crash; it just seemed more egregious for representatives of an ostensible party of the underprivileged to be using taxpayers' money to subsidise lavish lifestyles, even if their individual expense claims invited less ridicule than Conservative subventions for the maintenance of ornamental duck ponds and castle moats.

More generally, Labour has been harmed by the increasing prominence in its parliamentary ranks of 'career politicians' – those who leave university for positions as special advisers and are then selected for winnable seats, without serving any kind of apprenticeship outside the foetid milieu of Westminster intrigue. Again, this development has more worrying implications for Labour than for the Conservatives – it was, after all, a Conservative who characterised political promotion as the ascent of a greasy pole rather than a means of changing the world – and its active encouragement by New Labour is another sign that the party lost its way between 1994 and 2010. In both major parties, time-servers who make themselves useful to incumbents now rise through the ranks, while persons of principle are purged. In government, Labour was at its best under Attlee who, like Abraham Lincoln, harnessed the abilities of a gifted but disputatious 'team of rivals'.[7] Harold Wilson was too suspicious of would-be political assassins to emulate Attlee, but Labour's frontbench under his leadership continued to feature numerous individuals who were eminently capable of holding high office and became well-known public figures because of their personal qualities as well as their prominent postings. During the New Labour years, too many ministers seemed anonymous and thus essentially interchangeable. In opposition it is always more difficult to establish a public profile, but it would not be unkind to suggest that few senior Labour office-holders today bear comparison with the phalanx of distinguished and distinctive characters who served until the early 1980s.

Even by Labour's varying standards, the party has not been particularly effective in opposition since 2010. Either by choosing the wrong leaders or by failing to reach settled, coherent positions on monumental issues like austerity and Brexit, it does indeed seem to have paid insufficient attention to the lessons of the past. While earlier developments in the party's history might now seem impossibly distant, it could have profited from a much closer examination of its varied experiences in opposition. If British voters have conceded that Labour is electable again, this is very largely a reaction against the evident unfitness of the Conservatives. However, the record shows that parties can win something which deserves to be called a 'popular mandate' even on that negative basis. Party members who keep the red flag flying in their hearts still have grounds for hoping – if not wholly expecting – that Labour back in office will prove to be much more than the lesser of two evils.

Notes

Introduction

1 This was Peter Snow's description of the programme when he introduced it as part of BBC Parliament's *Harold Wilson Night* on 16 February 2013.
2 Fletcher, 2011.
3 Ball and Seldon, 2005; Heppell, 2012.
4 Quoted in Campbell, 2014, 210.

1 In Pursuit of an 'Insane Miracle' (1922–1929)

1 'Noisy Crowds in the Streets', *Manchester Guardian*, 16 November 1922.
2 'Gay London Crowds Watch the Returns', *New York Herald*, 16 November 1922.
3 'Noisy Crowds in the Streets', *Manchester Guardian*, 16 November 1922.
4 'Premier's Whip for the Treaty Bill', *Evening Standard*, 18 November 1922.
5 'Mr JR Clynes in New Role', *Daily Herald*, 21 November 1922.
6 Quoted in Murphy, 1948, 109.
7 Ridley, 2021, 421–2.
8 Morrison, 1960, 112.
9 Attlee, 1954, 107.
10 Howell, 2002, 339.
11 Laybourn, 2000.
12 Donoughue and Jones, 2001.
13 Ramsay MacDonald to John Muir, 11 July 1928 (quoted in Howell, 2002, 40).
14 Howell, 2002, 20.
15 Morrison, 1960, 93.
16 *London Labour Party Circular*, June 1918 (quoted in Donoughue and Jones, 2001, 103).
17 *London Labour Chronicle*, June 1921 (quoted in Donoughue and Jones, 2001, 63).
18 Labour was the fourth largest party elected at the general election but because the first two parties formed a coalition (Conservatives and Lloyd George Liberals) and the seventy-three Sinn Féin MPs refused to take their seats, the fifty-seven Labour MPs were technically the largest opposition party.
19 Reid and Pelling, 2005, 45.

20 Some (e.g. Fletcher, 2023) argue that William Adamson acted as the first Labour Leader of the Opposition, but this point is disputed. Adamson never carried the same status in Parliament, the party or the country as MacDonald did in 1922. Douglas writes, 'Adamson did not press his claim for Opposition leadership' (1971, 141).
21 Ramsay MacDonald to Oswald Mosley, 21 February 1928 (quoted in Howell, 2002, 71).
22 Quoted in Howell, 2002, 383.
23 Quoted in Howell, 2002, 384.
24 See Squires, 1990. Saklatvala would later be imprisoned for sedition due to a speech he gave during the General Strike of 1926.
25 'Honouring a Bolshevik', *Hackney Gazette*, 25 July 1927. These two-bedroom flats, renamed Cambridge Court, now sell for over half a million pounds.
26 Reid and Pelling, 2005, 46.
27 Stephens, 1981, 78f.
28 In the 1960s, the paper mutated into *The Sun* and was bought by Rupert Murdoch in 1969.
29 Ramsay MacDonald to Clifford Allen, 16 September 1924 (quoted in Gilbert, 1965, 180).
30 Winston Churchill, Letter, *The Times*, 18 January 1924.
31 Quoted in Self, 2006, xxiii.
32 Attlee, 1954, 88.
33 Quoted in Marquand, 1977, 304.
34 Oswald Mosley to Ramsay MacDonald, 8 November 1927 (quoted in Howell, 2002, 71).
35 Quoted in Howell, 2002.
36 McKenzie, 1963, 306–7, 347–52.
37 MacDonald Diary, 3 December 1924 (quoted in Howell, 2002, 33).
38 https://www.parliament.uk/about/living-heritage/transformingsociety/towncountry/towns/collections/labhousing1/housea2
39 Shepherd, 2002, 209.
40 Reid and Pelling, 2005, 47.
41 Paton, 1936, 227–8.
42 Ramsay MacDonald to John Paton, 22 April 1926 (quoted in Howell, 2002, 269).
43 Shepherd, 2002, 211.
44 The LSE has digitised all of them from 1884–2000. The 1920s tracts can be found at: https://digital.library.lse.ac.uk/collections/fabiansociety/tracts1919-1939.

45 Howell, 2002, 67. See Minkin, 1992, 19–20.
46 Ramsay MacDonald, 'The Work of the ILP', *Forward*, 27 March 1926. See also HC Deb 8 December 1926, vol. 200, col. 2177.
47 Quoted in Howell, 2002, 272.
48 Quoted in Howell, 2002, 401.
49 Lewis, 1978, 451.
50 Rathbone, 1924, 257.
51 Simms, 1978.
52 Quoted in Laybourn, 2000, 57.
53 Laybourn, 2000, 57.
54 Pugh, 2010, 203.
55 Pugh, 2010, 173.
56 MacDonald, 1907, 117.
57 Davidson, 1969, 191.
58 Lord Sankey, 1930 (quoted in Howell, 2002, 10).
59 Thomas, 1937.
60 Ridley, 2021, 319.
61 George V Diary, 22 February 1924 (quoted in Ridley, 2021, 320).
62 'British Labor to Fix Stand on Communism', *Chicago Tribune*, 25 June 1923.
63 'The Royal Family', *Daily Mail*, 29 June 1923.
64 Quoted in Ward, 2004, 30.
65 Webb and Webb, 1920, 108.
66 The king's confidence was not even shaken by intemperate remarks made by George Lansbury earlier that month. Lansbury told an audience at Shoreditch Town Hall: 'a few centuries ago one King ... stood up against the common people of that day and lost his head – lost it really [laughter and cheers] ... Since that day kings and queens had been what they ought to be if you had them. They never interfered with ordinary politics, and George V would be well advised to keep his finger out of the pie now.' *Manchester Guardian*, 7 January 1924. George V's private secretary noted the king's reaction: 'The King referred to recent utterances of Mr Lansbury, in which he went out of his way to express a threat and a reminder of the fate which had befallen Charles I. His Majesty was not affected by these personal attacks' (quoted in Nicholson, 1952, 384).
67 Clement Attlee to Tom Attlee (quoted in Harris, 1995, 57).
68 MacDonald Diary, 30 September 1924 (quoted in Howell, 2002, 33).
69 Quoted in Attlee, 1954, 60.
70 Morrison, 1960, 99.
71 Quoted in Laybourn, 2000, 59.

72 Howell, 2002, 28.
73 Quoted in Howell, 2002, 35.
74 Harris, 1995, 58.
75 Quoted in Howell, 2002, 35.
76 Rennie Smith Diary, 15 April 1926 (quoted in Howell, 2002, 27).
77 MacDonald Diary, 3 December 1924 (quoted in Howell, 2002, 33).
78 Harris, 1995, 60.
79 'Four Labour Members Suspended', *Manchester Guardian*, 28 June 1923.
80 Quoted in Shepherd, 2002, 239.
81 HC Deb 14 April 1926, vol. 194, cols 426–9.
82 Sidney Webb to Beatrice Webb, 30 June 1926 (quoted in Howell, 2002, 37).
83 *New Leader*, 25 May 1923.
84 Morrison, 1960, 94.
85 *New Leader*, 6 July 1923 (quoted in Wood, 1990, 106).
86 Quoted in Howell, 2002, 324.
87 Howell, 2002, 20–1.
88 HC Deb 20 March 1923, vol. 161, col. 2506.
89 Reid and Pelling, 2005, 47.
90 Beatrice Webb Diary, 15 March 1924, at https://digital.library.lse.ac.uk/objects/lse:vat325giy
91 Ernest Bevin to Hugh Dalton, 31 December 1935 (quoted in Bullock, 1960, 532).
92 Ernest Bevin to Arthur Henderson, 4 June 1926 (quoted in Howell, 2002, 187).
93 Raymond Postgate, 'Diary of the British Strike', *New Masses*, September 1926.
94 Stephens, 1981, 69.
95 Quoted in Stephens, 1981, 72.
96 In fact, the TUC's expectation was that the government would negotiate, not that they would bring it down.
97 Ernest Bevin to Arthur Henderson, 4 June 1926 (quoted in Howell, 2002, 187).
98 Quoted in Stephens, 1981, 76.
99 Pugh, 2010.
100 Pugh, 2010.
101 Laybourn, 2000, 56.
102 Howell, 2002.
103 For more on the Zinoviev Letter, see Bennett, 2018.
104 *Daily Herald*, 8 December 1923.
105 *Daily Herald*, 8 December 1923.
106 Morrison, 1960, 96.

107 'Last Session of Conference', *Daily Herald*, 16 October 1926.
108 *New Leader*, January 1923 (quoted in Bew, 2016).
109 Quoted in Ward, 1998, 308.
110 Jago, 2014.
111 Pimlott, 1985.
112 Wertheimer, 1929.
113 C.P. Trevelyan to Molly Trevelyan, 3–4 October 1927 (quoted in Howell, 2002, 325).

2 A Battle Over Peace (1931–1940)

1 These words recur with considerable frequency in the primary sources quoted by Marquand, 1977, chapters 22–25.
2 Jenkins, 1998, 289.
3 Marquand, 1977, 574.
4 Marquand, 1977, 633.
5 Marquand considers this question in Marquand, 1977, 638–41.
6 Pimlott, 1977, 13.
7 Pimlott, 1977, 15–16.
8 Pimlott, 1977, 16–17.
9 Pimlott, 1977, 16.
10 Thorpe, 1991.
11 Pimlott, 1977, 16.
12 Laski, 1936, 5.
13 Laski, 1936, 8.
14 Laski, 1936, 13, 12.
15 Pimlott, 1977, 198.
16 Durbin, 1985, 87.
17 Pimlott, 1977, 54.
18 Durbin, 1985, 90.
19 Cole, 1935, 405.
20 Pimlott, 1977, 198.
21 Pimlott, 1977, 199.
22 Pimlott, 1977, 201.
23 See, for example, Hogg, 1945.
24 Pimlott, 1985, 242.
25 Jerry H. Brookshire has pointed out that Ben Pimlott, Richard Shackleton and Keith Middlemas have all erroneously said that this change in composition took place as part of the 1931–32 reforms, rather than the earlier reforms of 1930. See Brookshire, 1986, 54, note 35.

26 Bullock, 1960, 512; Pelling, 1976, 71; Pelling, 1966, 198.
27 Brookshire, 1986, 44; Pimlott, 1977, 19.
28 The second half of this paragraph is derived from Pimlott, 1985, 243.
29 Report of the Provisional Committee of Constituency Labour Parties, October 1936 (quoted in Pimlott, 1977, 123).
30 Pimlott, 1985, 244.
31 Pimlott, 1985, 245.
32 Brookshire, 1986, 66–7.
33 See Marquand, 1977, 734–5.
34 Harris, 1995, 112.
35 There has been some discussion as to why the party took such an equivocal official line over Spain, while many on the left wanted to express much clearer support for the republicans. Accounts closer to the time suggested that the opposition leadership was inhibited by the fact that the government's policy of 'non-intervention' was supported by both the socialist government in France and by the USSR. See Jenkins, 1948, 178–81. More recently, Tom Buchanan has suggested that Labour sensitivity to losing the vote of the Catholic electorate may also have played a part in determining the party's stance. See Buchanan, 1991.
36 Harris, 1995, 150.
37 Feiling, 1946, 369.
38 Pimlott, 1985, 256–7.
39 Quoted in Jenkins, 1948, 197.
40 Quoted in Jenkins, 1948, 198.
41 Pimlott, 1977, 170.
42 The first half of this paragraph is derived from Jenkins, 1948, 201.
43 Jenkins, 1948, 201.
44 Brooke, 1992, 34.
45 Brooke, 1992, 36–7.
46 Brooke, 1992, 37–8.
47 Quoted in Brooke, 1992, 47.
48 Bullock, 1960, 652.
49 Brooke, 1992, 1.
50 Quoted in Brooke, 1992, 53.

3 In Opposition to the Wartime Government (1940–1945)

1 Tracey, 1948, 203.
2 Brooke, 1992, 74.
3 Thorpe, 2004; Brooke, 1992, 73.
4 Whiting, 2004.

5 Tracey, 1948, 204.
6 Bullock, 1967, 182–4.
7 Brooke, 1992, 172.
8 War Cabinet Minutes, 15 February 1943 (quoted in Brooke, 1992, 173).
9 NEC Minutes, 24 February 1943 (quoted in Brooke, 1992, 175).
10 Brooke, 1992, 183.
11 Pimlott, 1985, 407.
12 Brooke, 1992, 214.
13 Quoted in Brooke, 1992, 108.
14 Brooke, 1992, 107.
15 Brooke, 1992, 145.
16 Brooke, 1992, 166.
17 Shinwell, 1973, 176.
18 Labour Party Conference Report, 1946 (quoted in Brooke, 1992, 329).
19 Beer, 1965 (quoted in Brooke, 1992, 329–30).

4 'Fight, Fight and Fight Again' (1951–1964)

1 In 1953, the Bevanite MP J.P.W. Mallalieu wrote an article in *Tribune* which took the form of an interview between the author and an imaginary constituent. In it, he said that the Parliamentary Labour Party 'supported "consolidation" while the party in the country wanted a more aggressive socialist policy – "advance"'. See Harris, 1995, 515.
2 Seebohm Rowntree and Lavers, 1951.
3 G.R. Lavers, *Daily Herald*, 12 October 1951 (quoted in Kynaston, 2009, 32).
4 Butler, 1952, 108 (quoted in Kynaston, 2009, 32).
5 Kynaston, 2009, 32.
6 Detailed electoral statistics may be found in the volumes entitled *House of Commons 1951*, *House of Commons 1955*, etc., published after each general election by *The Times*.
7 Butler, 1952, 242.
8 Butler, 1952, 242.
9 Jenkin, 1952, 65.
10 For a compendium of reactions from parliamentary candidates to the 1955 election, see K.-H., 1956.
11 Crossman, 1981, 420.
12 Harold Wilson, quoted in K.-H., 1956, 477.
13 Butler, 1955, 206.
14 Brand, 1956, 312.
15 Brand, 1960, 522.

16 Brand, 1960, 522–3
17 Abrams, Rose and Hinden, 1960, 119.
18 For the significance of the Liberal Party in the general election of 1964, see Barberis, 2007, although it should be noted that the focus of the analysis differs from that developed here.
19 Crossman, 1981, 431.
20 Pimlott, 1992, 194.
21 Wilson, 1986, 150–1.
22 McKenzie, 1956, 94.
23 McKenzie, 1956, 94–5.
24 McKenzie, 1956, 93, 96.
25 McKenzie, 1956, 94–5.
26 Hanham, 1956, 378.
27 Pimlott, 1992, 196.
28 Brand, 1960, 526.
29 Pimlott, 1992, 196.
30 Harris, 1995, 450.
31 Quoted in Williams, 1979, 505–6.
32 Pimlott, 1992, 308.
33 See Pimlott, 1992, 308–9.
34 Pimlott, 1992, 309.
35 For a discussion of the 'Butskell' concept, see Williams, 1979, 312–18.
36 There is a comprehensive account of the role of the Labour Party in opposition with regard to the Suez Crisis in Rippingale, 1996, chapter 2.
37 Rippingale, 1996, 64.
38 Williams, 1979, 439.
39 Rippingale, 1996, 260.
40 Rippingale, 1996, 260.
41 Rippingale, 1996, 251.
42 Williams, 1979, 730.
43 Pimlott, 1992, 285.
44 Crossman, 1981, 1001.
45 Pimlott, 1992, 299. Pimlott develops an extended analysis of Labour's – and Wilson's – role in the Profumo affair on pp. 285–99, on which we have drawn.
46 Ostegaard, 1963, 224.
47 Brand, 1956, 292.
48 Crossman, 1981, 584.
49 Crossman, 1981, 585.
50 See Crossman, 1981, 583, 585.

51 The Manifesto Project is a large coding project which has been run by political scientists around the world since the 1980s. Researchers have scored manifestos on a left–right ideological scale, using over fifty metrics. Manifestos are coded by multiple individuals to come as close to accuracy as possible. Although by no means perfect, the Manifesto Project provides a valuable opportunity to examine the ideological movement of political parties over time, compared to each other, and in comparison to parties around the world.
52 Jacobs and Hindmoor, 2022.
53 Jacobs and Hindmoor, 2022.
54 Jacobs and Hindmoor, 2022.
55 Jacobs and Hindmoor, 2022, citing Pimlott, 1992, 276.

5 Yesterday's Men (1970–1974)

1 Wilson, 1971, 789.
2 Denham and Garnett, 2001, 193.
3 Baston, 2004, 237.
4 Foot, 1968, 155–169; text of Wilson's 1964 speech at http://www.britishpoliticalspeech.org/speech-archive.htm?speech=162
5 Campbell, 2014, 355.
6 Owen, 1991, 113; Garnett, 2016.
7 http://www.britishpoliticalspeech.org/speech-archive.htm?speech=162
8 Zeigler, 1993, 228–9; Anthony Lewis, 'All's Right with the World of Harold Wilson', *New York Times*, 4 June 1970.
9 Ponting, 1989, 215–56.
10 Zeigler, 1993, 340.
11 Curtis, 2003, 414–31.
12 Marquand, 1992, 157–8.
13 Dell, 1996, 368.
14 Alan Travis, 'Moore and That Bracelet: Who Really Took It?', *Guardian*, 20 January 2022.
15 Gilmour and Garnett, 1998, 240–2.
16 Denham and Garnett, 2001, 186.
17 Hatfield, 1978, 38.
18 Warde, 1986, 94–126.
19 Jenkins, 1972.
20 Campbell, 2014, 380.
21 Benn, 1989, 316.
22 Butler and Kitzinger, 1976, 11.
23 Jenkins, 1991, 348.

24 Benn, 1990, 57.
25 Butler and Kavanagh, 1974, 19.
26 Seyd, 1987, 24–31.
27 Benn, 1989, 507.
28 Wickham-Jones, 2004.
29 Benn, 1990, 94.
30 Denver and Garnett, 2014, 47.
31 Butler and Kavanagh, 1974, 139–41.
32 Butler and Kavanagh, 1974, 140.
33 Benn, 1990, 86.
34 Sandbrook, 2011, 619.
35 Thatcher, 1995, 239.
36 Butler and Kavanagh, 1974, 220.
37 Jenkins, 1991, 364.
38 Benn, 1990, 114–15.

6 Impossible Promises and Far-Fetched Resolutions (1979–1987)

1 Donoughue, 2008, 470.
2 Tony Benn Diary, 28 March 1979 (Benn, 1995, 466).
3 'Labour Refused to Drag MP from Bed', *Daily Telegraph*, 30 March 1979.
4 'Sick Labour MP Blameless', *Daily Mail*, 29 March 1979.
5 Quoted in Mitchell, 2018, 25.
6 Bernard Donoughue Diary, 28 March 1979 (Donoughue, 2008, 473).
7 O'Farrell, 1999, 22.
8 The former Liberal leader Jeremy Thorpe was facing trial at the Old Bailey for conspiracy to murder his secret gay lover (Bloch, 2014, 519).
9 Foot, 1986, 112.
10 See Denham and Garnett, 2001.
11 Longford, 1982, 6.
12 Boothroyd, 2001, 110.
13 Thatcher, 1993, 4.
14 Jones, 1994, 436.
15 Peter Shore, *Labour: The Wilderness Years*, BBC, Episode 1: 'Cast into the Wilderness' (1995), at https://www.youtube.com/watch?v=oIgiV8yn3xU
16 https://www.youtube.com/watch?v=RpKz54bxXuU
17 http://www.britishpoliticalspeech.org/speech-archive.htm?speech=174
18 Tony Benn, *Labour: The Wilderness Years*, BBC, Episode 1: 'Cast into the Wilderness' (1995).
19 Healey, 1989, 466.

20 Callaghan, 1987, 565.
21 'Jim Fixed Us', *Daily Telegraph*, 2 October 1979.
22 'Knives out for Jim', *Manchester Evening News*, 1 October 1979.
23 'Now Foot Faces Fire from the Left', *Western Daily Press*, 23 July 1979.
24 Benn diaries, 2 October 1979 (Benn, 1995, 482).
25 Minkin, 1992, 193.
26 Vinen, 2009, 105.
27 'Healey's Apocalyptic Warning of Western Banking Collapse', *Guardian*, 4 September 1982.
28 'Come Back Keynes, All Is Forgiven', *New Statesman*, 26 November 1982.
29 'The Life and Legacy of Michael Foot', *Tribune*, 23 July 2021.
30 Healey, 1989, 473.
31 Callaghan, 1987, 425.
32 'Come Back Keynes, All Is Forgiven', *New Statesman*, 26 November 1982.
33 'Fighting It Out', *Birmingham Post*, 26 July 1979.
34 'Unite to Fight the Tory Boneheads', *Observer*, 22 July 1979.
35 Wickham-Jones, 1996.
36 Similar efforts are discussed in Chapter 2.
37 Shaw, 2000, 115.
38 Quoted in O'Connor, 2003, 273.
39 Mullin, 1980.
40 Johnson, 2022.
41 Kogan and Kogan, 1982, 63.
42 Hayter, 2005.
43 'Labour's Left and Parliamentary Democracy', *Tribune*, 31 October 1980.
44 Minkin, 1992, 207; Jones, 1994; Longford, 1982, 23.
45 Kogan and Kogan, 1982, 98.
46 Shaw, 2000, 114.
47 Minkin, 1992, 202.
48 Silkin, 1987, 38.
49 Quoted in Mitchell, 2018, 37.
50 Quoted in Hayter, 2005, 93.
51 Weighell, 1983, 139.
52 Quoted in Kogan and Kogan, 1982, 106.
53 'More MPs to Join Jenkins', *Cambridge Evening News*, 26 January 1981.
54 'Defining the Middle Ground', *Guardian*, 11 February 1981.
55 Quoted in Hayter, 2005, 94.
56 Described extensively in Hayter, 2005.
57 Boothroyd, 2001, 112.

58 'Review: *The Wilderness Years* (BBC2)', *Independent*, 11 December 1995.
59 Butler and Butler, 2011, 164.
60 Quoted in Kogan and Kogan, 1982, 117.
61 Quoted in Heffer, 1991, 192.
62 Quoted in Hickson, Miles and Taylor, 2020, 130.
63 Foot, 1986, 122.
64 Quoted in Jones, 1994, 469.
65 Quoted in Hayter, 2005, 97.
66 Minkin, 1992, 202.
67 'Now Foot Faces Fire from the Left', *Western Daily Press*, 23 July 1979.
68 Quoted in Hickson, Miles and Taylor, 2020, 129.
69 Shaw, 2000, 117.
70 Butler and Kavanagh, 1984, 274.
71 Healey, 1989, 501.
72 Quoted in Seldon, 2022, 9.
73 Reid and Pelling, 2005, 161. The 'Wilson Report', discussed in Chapter 3, had argued for an increase in party agents.
74 Delaney, 2015, 59–74.
75 Jones, 1994, 510.
76 *The Wilderness Years*, BBC, Episode 2: 'Comrades of War' (1995).
77 Quoted in Jones, 1994, 498.
78 'Whistle-stop Foot Sounds Rallying Cry', *Manchester Evening News*, 8 June 1983.
79 Clive James, 'Campaigning Down the Drain', *Observer*, 29 May 1983.
80 'Tomato, Egg, and a Handful of Songs', *Guardian*, 8 June 1983.
81 Healey, 1989, 501.
82 Westlake, 2001.
83 'Foot Jeers at Hailsham the Munich Man', *Daily Telegraph*, 20 May 1983. See also Pugh, 2010, 374.
84 Foot volunteered for military service but was deemed physically unfit.
85 'Foot Jeers at Hailsham the Munich Man', *Daily Telegraph*, 20 May 1983.
86 Quoted in Jones, 1994, 514.
87 *The Wilderness Years*, BBC, Episode 2: 'Comrades of War' (1995).
88 *Tribune*, 26 November 1981.
89 'The Three Musketeers Take up Arms', *Guardian*, 1 August 1980.
90 'I Have Not Used the Word Socialist for Some Years Past', *Guardian*, 24 November 1981.
91 Hatherley, 2020.
92 Quoted in Bunce and Linton, 2020, 108.

93 Kogan and Kogan, 1982.
94 Hatherley, 2020, 121.
95 Messina, 1989, 152.
96 Werbner, 1991, 34–5.
97 Rees and Butt, 2004, 179.
98 Quoted in Hickson, Miles and Taylor, 2020, 143.
99 Hatherley, 2020.
100 Payling, 2014.
101 Quoted in Bunce and Linton, 2020, 112.
102 HC Deb, 24 February 1982, vol. 18, col. 877.
103 Payling, 2014, 614.
104 'Competing Should Be the Goal', *Nottingham Evening Post*, 25 July 1986.
105 Mandelson, 1987, 11.
106 Shaw, 2000, 124.
107 Quoted in Westlake, 2001, 250.
108 Gould, 1995, 179.
109 https://www.designweek.co.uk/issues/18–24-november-2019/labour-rose-design
110 Mandelson, 1987, 13.
111 Pugh, 2010, 380.
112 Gould, 1995, 193.
113 Mandelson, 1987, 12, 13.
114 Healey, 1989, 468.
115 Quoted in O'Connor, 2003, 281.
116 Heffer, 1991, 204 (emphasis in original).
117 HC Deb, 13 November 1984, vol. 457, col. 240.
118 Heffernan and Marqusee, 1992, 61.
119 Hayter, 2005, ix.
120 Crick, 2016, 340.
121 Pugh, 2010, 369.
122 Taafe and Mulhearn, 1988, 77.
123 Massey, 2020.
124 Frost and North, 2013.
125 'City in Crisis', *Liverpool Echo*, 27 September 1985.
126 'Hamilton Tells Thatcher: You've Got to Do Something', *Liverpool Echo*, 27 September 1985.
127 'Pressed into Service', *Liverpool Echo*, 3 October 1985.
128 'Secret Cabbie Convoy Foils Redundancy Protestors', *Liverpool Echo*, 30 September 1985.

129 Quoted in Massey, 2020, 300.
130 http://www.britishpoliticalspeech.org/speech-archive.htm?speech=191
131 'Kinnock Savages Militant', *Daily Telegraph*, 2 October 1985.
132 'Heffer Storms Out', *Western Daily Press*, 2 October 1982.
133 Benn, 1994a, xi.
134 Benn Diary, 1 October 1985 (Benn 1994a, 424).
135 Heffer, 1991, 213.
136 David Blunkett, quoted in Massey, 2020, 317.
137 Quoted in Massey, 2020, 309.
138 Massey, 2020, 309.
139 Massey, 2020, 303.
140 'Unite to Fight the Tory Boneheads', *Observer*, 22 July 1979.
141 Shore, 1983, 32.
142 Foot, 1986, 123.
143 Foot, 1986, 122.
144 HC Deb, 9 February 1982, vol. 17, col. 856.
145 HC Deb, 3 April 1982, vol. 21, col. 640.
146 Heffer, 1991, 196.
147 HC Deb, 14 April 1982, vol. 21, col. 1152.
148 Heffer, 1991, 195.
149 HC Deb, 3 April 1982, vol. 21, col. 639.
150 For a dissection of the 1983 manifesto, see Murphy, 2022.
151 But see Carr, 2017.
152 Quoted in Seldon, 2022, 13.
153 Seldon, 2022, 12.
154 Briefing Note for Michael Foot/Eric Heffer Visit to Brussels 10/11 February 1982: Synopsis of the Party Delegation to the EEC Commission (ESH/10/68, Labour History Archive, People's History Museum).
155 Briefing Note for Michael Foot/Eric Heffer Visit to Brussels 10/11 February 1982.
156 Speech by Neil Kinnock to the Socialist Group of the European Parliament, 15 September 1985 (KNNK16/1/9, Churchill College Archives, Cambridge).
157 Bryan Gould, 'An EEC Policy for Labour', 28 November 1985 (KNNK/8/2).
158 1987 Labour manifesto.
159 Messina, 1987, 49.
160 1983 Labour manifesto.
161 Gerald Kaufman, *Kinnock: The Inside Story*, Episode 3: 'The Pursuit of Power' (1993), at https://www.youtube.com/watch?v=8HT21AbYj_8&t=8418s
162 Quoted in Scott, 2012, 128.

163 Hayter, 2005, 90.
164 Pearce, 2002, 557.

7 Thatcher's Greatest Achievement? (1987–1997)

1 O'Farrell, 1999, 196.
2 Benn, 1994b, 317.
3 Conor Burns, 'Margaret Thatcher's Greatest Achievement: New Labour', *Conservative Home*, 11 April 2008, at https://conservativehome.blogs.com/centreright/2008/04/making-history.html
4 Labour Party, 1988, 16, 22.
5 Labour Party, 1988, 16, 22.
6 Crewe, 1989, 239–50.
7 Gould, 1998, 327.
8 Gould, 1998, 327, 326.
9 Gould, 1998, 328.
10 Oborne, 1999, 135.
11 Gould, 1998, 336.
12 David Hencke, 'Short Flays Blair's "Dark Men"', *Guardian*, 8 August 1996.
13 Campbell, 2010, 771.
14 Kavanagh, 1998, 32.
15 O'Farrell, 1999, 312.
16 Crick, 2005, 212.
17 HC Deb, 16 March 1988, vol. 129, col. 1126.
18 Young, 2008, 287.
19 HC Deb, 21 March 1988, vol. 130, col. 106.
20 HC Deb, 4 March 1996, vol. 276, cols 34–45.
21 George, 1990.
22 Jacques Delors, Speech to the Trade Union Congress, 8 September 1988, at https://ec.europa.eu/commission/presscorner/detail/en/SPEECH_%2088_66.
23 Westlake, 2001, 505–6; Stuart, 2005, 264.
24 Stuart, 2005, 259–60.
25 Young, 2008, 378.
26 Major, 1999, 590.
27 Benn, 1994a, 516.
28 Benn, 1994a, 550.
29 Hattersley, 1995, 289.
30 Adams, 1992, 458. Benn rewrote the lyrics of the eponymous song which accompanied the document: 'Miss the challenge – change your mind / Labour leads now from behind / We can run the status quo / If you doubt it OUT YOU GO.'

31 Benn, 1994a, 568.
32 Shaw, 1996, 182.
33 O'Farrell, 1999, 269, 265.
34 For a dissenting view, see Denver and Garnett, 2022, 94.
35 Benn, 2002, 95; Radice, 2004, 268.
36 Gould, 1985; Hattersley, 1987.
37 Benn, 1994a, 565.
38 Catherine Haddon, *Making Policy in Opposition: The Commission on Social Justice, 1992–1994*, Institute for Government, 2012, at https://www.institute forgovernment.org.uk/sites/default/files/publications/CSJ%20final_0.pdf
39 Sam Jones and Farah Jassat, 'Rupert Murdoch: Labour Ventures into the Lion's Den', *Guardian*, 11 July 2011.
40 Blair, 2010, 96.
41 Campbell, 2010, 217.
42 Shaw, 1996, 201.
43 Fielding, 1997, 26.
44 Kavanagh, 1998, 28.
45 Diamond, 2021, 160.
46 Hall, 1979.

8 In New Labour's Shadow (2010–2024)

1 HC Deb, 2 November 1989, vol. 159, col. 502.
2 Cunliffe et al., 2023, 74–5.
3 *The Report of the Iraq Inquiry* (July 2016), at https://www.gov.uk/government/publications/the-report-of-the-iraq-inquiry
4 Quoted in Kogan, 2019, 150–1.
5 'No Return to Boom and Bust', *Guardian*, 11 September 2008.
6 Miliband, 1961.
7 262 Labour plus forty-seven SNP and twelve Liberal Democrat MPs would produce a total of 321, one more than needed for a majority (excluding Sinn Féin). Labour would also have attracted support from one Green and four Plaid Cymru MPs.
8 Thanks to the Democratic Unionist Party, who despised Corbyn's Irish nationalism and provided confidence-and-supply to the Conservatives.
9 https://www.ipsos.com/en-uk/how-britain-voted-2017-election. See also, https://lordashcroftpolls.com/2017/06/result-happen-post-vote-survey
10 John McDonnell, Lancaster Labour Party meeting (by Zoom), 24 June 2020.
11 https://ukandeu.ac.uk/the-rally-round-the-flag-effect-and-covid-19
12 Hasan and Macintyre, 2011.

13 'Ed Miliband Confirms Labour Leadership Bid', *Guardian*, 15 May 2010.
14 Quoted in Kogan, 2019, 158.
15 Quoted in Hasan and Macintyre, 2011, 185.
16 Miliband, 2010, 55.
17 Quoted in Kogan, 2019, 164.
18 'Labour Suffered Greatly through Tony Blair', *The Big Issue*, 14 March 2014.
19 See Hattersley, 2000.
20 'Ed Miliband Is a Radical Leader for a Radical New Era', *The Observer*, 3 October 2010.
21 'John Smith's Widow Backs Ed Miliband', *The Observer*, 18 July 2010.
22 https://www.bbc.co.uk/news/uk-politics-11434981
23 'Ed Miliband Confirms Leadership Bid', *Guardian*, 15 May 2010.
24 'I'll Make Capitalism Work for the People', *Guardian*, 29 August 2010.
25 Murray, 2019, 128.
26 https://labourlist.org/2010/09/the-new-generation-ed-milibands-leadership-speech
27 Diamond, 2021, 331.
28 Beckett and Seddon, 2018, 201.
29 'Miliband Brothers Battle It out Over Iraq', *Guardian*, 29 July 2010.
30 https://www.youtube.com/watch?v=HKcS802o7U4
31 Quoted in Kogan, 2019, 163.
32 Bale, 2015, 17, 19.
33 Hasan and Macintyre, 2011, 202.
34 'Unions Hail Miliband as He Buries New Labour', *Times*, 27 September 2010.
35 'Miliband: I'm Not Blair (Really)', *Telegraph*, 1 October 2011.
36 https://www.youtube.com/watch?v=eWauZTN3brg
37 Quoted in Bale, 2015, 10.
38 Quoted in Kogan, 2019, 170.
39 Harman, 2017, 345. Quite literally, there had been a car crash when Gordon Brown unveiled Labour's 2010 election posters; an unfortunate portent.
40 Beckett and Seddon, 2018, 220.
41 'I Don't Do Personal', *Guardian*, 17 June 2015.
42 Garnett and Johnson, 2021.
43 https://twitter.com/Channel4News/status/638780593203990528
44 Quoted in Kogan, 2019, 170.
45 Hannah, 2022, 203.
46 Eagleton, 2022, 2.
47 'Keir Starmer's Ruthless Remaking of the Labour Party', *Financial Times*, 7 June 2023.

48 'Keir Starmer Appoints Adviser from Blair Years as His Chief of Staff', *Guardian*, 24 July 2021.
49 'Blair and Starmer Bask in Each Other's Reflected Glory', *Guardian*, 18 July 2023.
50 'RMT Vote Ends Historic Link with Labour', *Guardian*, 6 February 2004.
51 Hasan and Macintyre, 2011, 279.
52 It should be acknowledged that there have always been disproportionately large unions, such as Unite's predecessor the Transport and General Workers' Union (TGWU).
53 'Charlie Wheelan: The Puppet Master Who Won It for Ed', *Telegraph*, 3 October 2010.
54 Quoted in Hasan and Macintyre, 2011, 217.
55 Bale, 2015, 15.
56 Bale, 2015, 15.
57 Quoted in Kogan, 2019, 174.
58 'A Butt, a Bloody Nose, Then Night in Cells for Labour MP', *Daily Telegraph*, 24 February 2012.
59 'I Got a Bloody Nose, Says Headbutt MP', *Evening Standard*, 23 February 2012.
60 'Unite Threatens Labour with Legal Action over Falkirk Row', *Guardian*, 27 June 2013.
61 Kogan, 2019, 198.
62 Beckett and Seddon, 2018, 210–11.
63 Quoted in Kogan, 2019, 195.
64 Andy Burnham's refusal to pledge the removal of the Conservative government's cap on an individual's annual benefits was apparently deeply unpopular with GMB members and disinclined the union leadership from endorsing him, in spite of some wishing to do so (correspondence with Conrad Landin, 6 September 2023). See 'Andy Burnham Jeered at First Labour Leadership Hustings over Benefit Cap', *Guardian*, 9 June 2015.
65 Hannah, 2022, 179.
66 'Unite Members Threat to Quit if Union Turns against Trident', *Financial Times*, 17 January 2016.
67 'Jeremy Corbyn Will Come to Collective Decision on Using Nuclear Deterrent', *Telegraph*, 11 November 2019.
68 'Keir Starmer Tells Labour Frontbenchers They Should Not Join Rail Strike Pickets', *Guardian*, 20 June 2022.
69 'Keir Starmer's Stance on the Strikes Is a Betrayal of the People Who Need Labour', *New Statesman*, June 2022.
70 'Labour Risks Fresh Row as David Lammy Says Serious Party Not on Picket Lines', *Mirror*, 26 June 2022.

71 'Starmer Can't Afford to Be Blair', *Unherd*, 1 August 2022.
72 'Labour Rows Back Workers' Rights Pledge in Latest U-turn', *Independent*, 18 August 2023.
73 'Membership of Political Parties in Great Britain', House of Commons Library, at https://commonslibrary.parliament.uk/research-briefings/sn05125
74 Bale, 2015, 45.
75 See Bale, Webb and Poletti, 2020, Chapter 6.
76 Diamond, 2021, 342.
77 'Mandelson: I Try to Undermine Jeremy Corbyn Every Single Day', *Guardian*, 21 February 2017.
78 Hannah, 2022, 182.
79 Quoted in Kogan, 2019, 280.
80 https://www.itv.com/news/wales/2016-09-27/veteran-mp-paul-flynn-calls-for-labour-unity
81 https://www.bbc.co.uk/news/uk-politics-36647458
82 Quoted in Kogan, 2019, 285.
83 Hannah, 2022.
84 Ross and McTague, 2017.
85 Ross and McTague, 2017, 75.
86 Quoted in Kogan, 2019, 276.
87 Kogan, 2019, 274.
88 See Chessum, 2022, 187–9.
89 Ross and McTague, 2017, 118.
90 Ross and McTague, 2017, 119–20.
91 Thompson, 2015, 13.
92 Murray, 2019, 143.
93 'The Undoing of Ed Miliband', *Guardian*, 3 June 2015.
94 'This Could Be the Greatest Crisis the Labour Party Has Ever Faced', *Guardian*, 16 May 2015.
95 'Tony Blair Says He Wouldn't Want a Left-wing Labour Party to Win an Election', *Independent*, 22 July 2015.
96 Diamond, 2021, 332.
97 Quoted in Kogan, 2019, 248.
98 McDonnell, 2018.
99 But, see Diamond (2021) and Murphy (2023) who argue that New Labour was intellectually robust.
100 'Labour Would Rewrite Rules of UK Economy, Says John McDonnell', *Guardian*, 19 July 2019.
101 Quinn, 2018, 126.

102 Allen and Bara, 2019.
103 Based on the Manifesto Project's research, also discussed in Chapter 4.
104 https://www.gettyimages.co.uk/detail/news-photo/british-labour-party-activist-and-borough-councillor-jeremy-news-photo/1126174516?adppopup=true
105 Glasman, 2022.
106 Bolton and Pitts, 2018, 16.
107 'McDonnell: Labour Will Not Block Hard Brexit', *Independent*, 15 November 2016.
108 'Row over McDonnell's Brexit Comments Threatens Labour Truce', *Guardian*, 18 November 2016; 'Labour Split over Attitude to Brexit', *Politico*, 18 November 2016.
109 Eagleton, 2022, 75.
110 Eagleton, 2022, 79.
111 Eagleton, 2022, 79.
112 Eagleton, 2022, 82.
113 Eagleton, 2022, 82.
114 'Keir Starmer Says Brexit Can Be Stopped, Contradicting Labour Leader Jeremy Corbyn', *Independent*, 12 November 2018.
115 Quoted in Eagleton, 2022, 120.
116 HC Deb, 25 July 2019, vol. 663, col. 1464.
117 https://www.briefingsforbritain.co.uk/in-the-marginal-its-the-leavers-who-are-in-revolt
118 https://blogs.lse.ac.uk/brexit/2019/02/04/labours-path-to-vicotry-is-through-leave-voting-conservative-marginals
119 HC Deb, 25 July 2019, vol. 663, col. 1464.
120 Author (Richard Johnson) conversation with Miliband adviser.
121 https://blog.politics.ox.ac.uk/labours-eu-referendum-stance-could-lead-to-a-general-election-disaster
122 'The Reckoning', *New Statesman*, 2 June 2017.
123 Evans and Tilley, 2017.
124 Evans and Tilley, 2017.
125 https://ukandeu.ac.uk/brexit-witness-archive/john-mcdonnell
126 https://labour.org.uk/wp-content/uploads/2017/10/Chakrabarti-Inquiry-Report-30June16.pdf
127 Peter Kellner, 'Antisemitism Mattered But Did It Affect the General Election Result?', *Jewish Chronicle*, 18 December 2019.
128 Hannah, 2022, 181.
129 Balls, 2016, 336–7.

130 'Labour Will Run a Budget Surplus', *Guardian*, 24 January 2014.
131 Watts and Bale, 2019.
132 Hannah, 2022, 173.
133 Balls, 2016, 334–5.
134 Balls, 2016, 339.
135 Balls, 2016, 339.
136 Quoted in Kogan, 2019, 179.
137 'Labour in Disarray as 48 MPs Defy Whips to Vote No', *Guardian*, 21 July 2015.
138 HC Deb, 20 July 2015, vol. 598, col. 1314.
139 Beckett and Seddon, 2018, 232.
140 https://yougov.co.uk/topics/politics/articles-reports/2015/07/22/comment-corbyn-ahead-labours-leadership-contest
141 https://yougov.co.uk/topics/politics/articles-reports/2015/08/10/corbyn-pull-ahead
142 Hannah, 2022, 178.
143 Quoted in Eagleton, 2022, 87.
144 Quoted in Jones, 2020, 205.
145 Eagleton, 2022.
146 'Shadow Cabinet Decides to Abstain on Maastricht Third Reading', *Independent*, 12 May 1993.
147 Murray, 2019, 130.
148 Quoted in Kogan, 2019, 173.
149 Diamond, 2021, 331.
150 Diamond, 2021, 343.
151 Watts and Bale, 2019.
152 Quoted in Kogan, 2019, 170.
153 In contrast, Theresa May added just 2.3 million to Cameron's vote totals.

Conclusion

1 McKenzie, 1964.
2 Here we borrow the terminology, though not the line of analysis, of Drucker, 1979.
3 Ramsden, 1998.
4 For a meticulous analysis of the behaviour of the bankers in 1931, see Williamson, 1984.
5 PM speech on Net Zero, 20 September 2023, at www.gov.uk.
6 Kiran Stacey, 'Labour Figures from 1997 Victory Warn Starmer against Cautious Approach', *Guardian*, 5 October 2023.
7 Goodwin, 2006.

References

Abrams, Mark, Richard Rose and Rita Hinden. 1960. *Must Labour Lose?* London: Penguin.

Adams, Jad. 1992. *Tony Benn: A Biography*. London: Macmillan.

Allen, Nicholas and Judith Bara. 2019. 'Marching to the Left? Programmatic Competition and the 2017 Party Manifestos', *The Political Quarterly* 90(1): 124–33.

Attlee, Clement. 1954. *As It Happened*. London: Viking Press.

Bale, Tim. 2015. *Five Year Mission: The Labour Party under Ed Miliband*. Oxford: Oxford University Press.

Bale, Tim, Paul Webb and Monica Poletti. 2020. *Footsoldiers: Political Party Membership in the 21st Century*. London: Routledge.

Ball, Stuart and Anthony Seldon, eds. 2005. *Recovering Power: The Conservatives in Opposition since 1867*. Basingstoke: Palgrave Macmillan.

Balls, Ed. 2016. *Speaking Out*. London: Hutchinson.

Barberis, Peter. 2007. 'The 1964 General Election and the Liberals' False Dawn', *Contemporary British History* 21: 373–79.

Baston, Lewis. 2004. *Reggie: The Life of Reginald Maudling*. Stroud: Sutton Publishing.

Beckett, Francis and Mark Seddon. 2018. *Jeremy Corbyn and the Strange Rebirth of Labour England*. London: Biteback.

Beer, Samuel. 1965. *Modern British Politics*. London.

Benn, Tony. 1987. *Out of the Wilderness: Diaries 1963–67*. London: Hutchinson.

Benn, Tony. 1989. *Office without Power: Diaries 1968–72*. London: Arrow.

Benn, Tony. 1990. *Against the Tide: Diaries 1973–76*. London: Arrow.

Benn, Tony. 1994a. *The End of an Era: Diaries, 1980–90*. London: Arrow Books.

Benn, Tony. 1994b. *Years of Hope: Diaries, Papers and Letters 1940–1962*. London: Hutchinson.

Benn, Tony. 1995. *The Benn Diaries*. London: Hutchinson.

Benn, Tony. 2002. *Free at Last: Diaries, 1991–2001*. London: Hutchinson.
Bennett, Gill. 2018. *The Zinoviev Letter: The Conspiracy That Never Dies*. Oxford: Oxford University Press.
Bew, John. 2016. *Citizen Clem: A Biography of Attlee*. London: Riverrun.
Blair, Tony. 2010. *A Journey*. London: Hutchinson.
Bloch, Michael. 2014. *Jeremy Thorpe*. London: Little, Brown and Company.
Bolton, Matt and Frederick Pitts. 2018. *Corbynism: A Critical Approach*. Bingley: Emerald.
Boothroyd, Betty. 2001. *The Autobiography*. London: Century.
Brand, Carl F. 1956. 'The British General Election of 1955', *The South Atlantic Quarterly* 55: 289–312.
Brand, Carl F. 1960. 'The British General Election of 1959', *The South Atlantic Quarterly* 59: 521–42.
Brooke, Stephen. 1992. *Labour's War: The Labour Party during the Second World War*. Oxford: Clarendon.
Brookshire, Jerry H. 1986. 'The National Council of Labour, 1921–1946', *Albion: A Quarterly Journal concerned with British Studies*, 18: 43–69.
Buchanan, Tom. 1991. *The Spanish Civil War and the British Labour Movement*. Cambridge: Cambridge University Press.
Bullock, Alan. 1960. *The Life and Times of Ernest Bevin. Volume I: Trade Union Leader, 1881–1940*. London: Heinemann.
Bullock, Alan. 1967. *The Life and Times of Ernest Bevin. Volume II: Minister of Labour 1940–1945*. London: Heinemann.
Bunce, Robin and Samara Linton. 2020. *Diane Abbott*. London: Biteback.
Bunce, Robin and Samara Linton. 2022. 'Race and the Left', in N. Yeowell, ed. *Rethinking Labour's Past*. London: I.B. Tauris.
Butler, David and Dennis Kavanagh. 1974. *The British General Election of February 1974*. London: Macmillan.
Butler, David and Dennis Kavanagh. 1984. *The British General Election of 1983*. Basingstoke: Macmillan.
Butler, David and Gareth Butler. 2011. *British Political Facts*, 10th edition. Basingstoke: Palgrave Macmillan.
Butler, David and Uwe Kitzinger. 1976. *The 1975 Referendum*. London: Macmillan.
Butler, D.E. 1952. *The British General Election of 1951*. London: Macmillan.
Butler, D.E. 1955. *The British General Election of 1955*. London: Frank Cass.

REFERENCES

Callaghan, James. 1987. *Time and Change*. London: Collins.

Campbell, Alastair. 2010. *The Alastair Campbell Diaries: Volume One, Prelude to Power, 1994–1997*. London: Hutchinson.

Campbell, John. 2014. *Roy Jenkins: A Well-Rounded Life*. London: Jonathan Cape.

Carr, Richard. 2017. 'Responsible Capitalism', in J. Davis and R. McWilliams, eds. *Labour and the Left in the 1980s*. Manchester: Manchester University Press.

Chapple, Frank. 1985. *Sparks Fly*. London: Michael Joseph.

Chessum, Michael. 2022. *This is Only the Beginning: The Making of a New Left from Anti-Austerity to the Fall of Corbyn*. London: Bloomsbury.

Cole, G.D.H. 1935. *Principles of Economic Planning*. London: Macmillan.

Crewe, Ivor. 1989. 'Values: The Crusade that Failed', in Dennis Kavanagh and Anthony Seldon, eds. *The Thatcher Effect: A Decade of Change*. Oxford: Oxford University Press.

Crewe, Ivor and Tony King. 1995. *SDP: The Birth, Life, and Death of the Social Democratic Party*. Oxford: Oxford University Press.

Crick, Michael. 2005. *In Search of Michael Howard*. London: Simon & Schuster.

Crick, Michael. 2016. *Militant*, revised edition. London: Biteback.

Crossman, R. 1981. *The Backbench Diaries of Richard Crossman*, ed. Janet Morgan. London: Hamish Hamilton & Jonathan Cape.

Crossman, R.H.S. 1952. 'Towards a Philosophy of Socialism', in R.H.S. Crossman, ed. *New Fabian Essays*. London: Turnstile.

Cunliffe, Philip, George Hoare, Lee Jones and Peter Ramsay. 2023. *Taking Control: Sovereignty and Democracy after Brexit*. Cambridge: Polity.

Curtis, Mark. 2003. *Web of Deceit: Britain's Real Role in the World*. London: Vintage.

Davidson, J.C.C. 1969. *Memoirs of a Conservative: J.C.C. Davidson's Memoirs and Papers, 1907–37*, ed. Robert Rhodes James. London: Weidenfeld & Nicolson.

Delaney, Sam. 2015. *Mad Men and Bad Men: What Happened When British Politics Met Advertising*. London: Faber and Faber.

Dell, Edmund. 1996. *The Chancellors: A History of the Chancellors of the Exchequer, 1945–90*. London: HarperCollins.

Denham, Andrew and Mark Garnett. 2001. *Keith Joseph: A Life*. London: Acumen.

Denver, David and Mark Garnett. 2014. *British General Elections since 1964: Diversity, Dealignment and Disillusion*. Oxford: Oxford University Press.

Denver, David and Mark Garnett. 2022. 'Inevitable but Creditable Defeats? Neil Kinnock and the General Elections of 1987 and 1992', in K. Hickson, ed. *Neil Kinnock: Saving the Labour Party?* London: Routledge.

Diamond, Patrick. 2021. *The British Labour Party in Opposition and Power, 1979–2019*. London: Routledge.

Donoughue, Bernard. 2008. *Downing Street Diary*, Volume 2. London: Jonathan Cape.

Donoughue, Bernard and G.W. Jones. 2001 [1973]. *Herbert Morrison: Portrait of a Politician*. London: Phoenix Press.

Douglas, Roy. 1971. *The History of the Liberal Party, 1895–1970*. London: Sidgwick & Jackson.

Drucker, 1979. *Doctrine and Ethos in the Labour Party*. London: Allen & Unwin.

Durbin, Elizabeth. 1985. *New Jerusalems: The Labour Party and the Economics of Democratic Socialism*. London: Routledge & Kegan Paul.

Eagleton, Oliver. 2022. *The Starmer Project: A Journey to the Right*. London: Verso.

Evans, Geoffrey and James Tilley. 2017. *The New Politics of Class: The Political Exclusion of the British Working Class*. Oxford: Oxford University Press.

Feiling, Keith. 1946. *The Life of Neville Chamberlain*. London: Macmillan.

Fielding, Steven. 1997. 'Labour's Path to Power', in A. Geddes and J. Tonge, eds. *Labour's Landslide*. Manchester: Manchester University Press.

Fletcher, Nigel, ed. 2011. *How to be in Opposition: Life in the Political Shadows*. London: Biteback.

Fletcher, Nigel. 2023. *The Not Quite Prime Ministers: Leaders of the Opposition, 1783–2020*. London: Biteback.

Foot, Michael. 1984. *Another Heart and Other Pulses*. London: HarperCollins.

Foot, Michael. 1986. *Loyalists and Loners*. London: Collins.

Foot, Paul. 1968. *The Politics of Harold Wilson*. London: Penguin.

Frost, Diane and Peter North. 2013. *Militant Liverpool: A City on the Edge*. Liverpool: Liverpool University Press.

Garnett, Mark. 2016. 'Polemic, Parliament and History: Michael Foot *versus* David Owen', *Parliamentary History* 35(2): 171–88.

Garnett, Mark and Richard Johnson. 2021. 'Jeremy Corbyn's Foreign

Policy', in A. Roe-Crines, ed. *Corbynism in Perspective*. Newcastle: Agenda.

George, Steven. 1990. *An Awkward Partner: Britain in the European Community*. Oxford: Oxford University Press.

Gilbert, Martin. 1965. *Plough My Own Furrow: The Story of Lord Allen of Hurtwood*. London: Longmans, Green & Co.

Gilmour, Ian and Mark Garnett. 1998. *Whatever Happened to the Tories? The Conservatives since 1945*. London: Fourth Estate.

Glasman, Maurice. 2022. *Blue Labour: The Politics of the Common Good*. Cambridge: Polity.

Goodwin, Doris Kearns. 2006. *Team of Rivals: The Political Genius of Abraham Lincoln*. New York: Simon & Schuster.

Gould, Bryan. 1985. *Socialism and Freedom*. London: Macmillan.

Gould, Bryan. 1995. *Goodbye to All That*. London: Macmillan.

Gould, Philip. 1998. *The Unfinished Revolution: How the Modernisers Saved the Labour Party*. London: Little, Brown and Company.

Hall, Stuart. 1979. 'The Great Moving Right Show', *Marxism Today*, January.

Hanham, H.J. 1956. 'The Local Organization of the British Labour Party', *Western Political Quarterly* 9: 376–88.

Hannah, Simon. 2022 [2018]. *A Party with Socialists in It: A History of the Labour Left*, 2nd edition. London: Pluto Press.

Harman, Harriet. 2017. *A Woman's Work*. London: Allen Lane.

Harris, Kenneth. 1995 [1982]. *Attlee*, revised edition. London: Weidenfeld & Nicolson.

Harris, Robert. 1984. *The Making of Neil Kinnock*. London: Faber and Faber.

Hasan, Mehdi and James Macintyre. 2011. *Ed: The Milibands and the Making of a Labour Leader*. London: Biteback.

Hatfield, Michael. 1978. *The House the Left Built: Inside Labour Policy Making 1970–1975*. London: Victor Gollancz.

Hatherley, Owen. 2020. *Red Metropolis: Socialism and the Government of London*. London: Repeater.

Hattersley, Roy. 1987. *Choose Freedom: The Future of Democratic Socialism*. London: Penguin.

Hattersley, Roy. 1995. *Who Goes Home? Scenes from a Political Life*. London: Little, Brown and Company.

Hattersley, Roy. 2000. 'In Search of the Third Way', *Granta* 71: 229–55.
Hayter, Dianne. 2005. *Fightback: Labour's Traditional Right in the 1970s and 1980s*. Manchester: Manchester University Press.
Healey, Denis. 1989. *The Time of My Life*. London: Michael Joseph.
Heffer, Eric. 1991. *Never a Yes Man*. London: Verso.
Heffernan, Richard and Mike Marqusee. 1992. *Defeat from the Jaws of Victory: Inside Kinnock's Labour Party*. London: Verso.
Heppell, Tim and Andrew Crines. 2011. 'How Michael Foot Won the Labour Party Leadership', *Political Quarterly* 82(1): 81–94.
Heppell, Timothy, ed. 2012. *Leaders of the Opposition: From Churchill to Cameron*. Basingstoke: Palgrave Macmillan.
Hickson, Kevin, Jasper Miles and Harry Taylor. 2020. *Peter Shore: Labour's Forgotten Patriot*. London: Biteback.
Hogg, Quintin. 1945. *The Left Was Never Right*. London: Faber and Faber.
Howell, David. 2002. *MacDonald's Party: Labour Identities and Crisis, 1922–1931*. Oxford: Oxford University Press.
Jacobs, Michael and Andrew Hindmoor. 2022. 'Labour, Left and Right: On Party Positioning and Policy Reasoning', *British Journal of Politics and International Relations*, online 20 June.
Jago, Michael. 2014. *Clement Attlee: The Inevitable Prime Minister*. London: Biteback.
Jenkin, Thomas P. 1952. 'The British General Election of 1951', *The Western Political Quarterly* 5: 51–65.
Jenkins, Roy. 1948. *Mr Attlee: An Interim Biography*. London: Heinemann.
Jenkins, Roy. 1972. *What Matters Now*. London: Fontana.
Jenkins, Roy. 1991. *A Life at the Centre*. London: Macmillan.
Jenkins, Roy. 1998. *The Chancellors*. London: Macmillan.
Johnson, Richard. 2022. 'The European Labour Party: From Anti to Pro', in D. Hayter and D. Harley, eds. *The Forgotten Tribe: British MEPs, 1979–2020*. Oxford: John Harper Publishing.
Jones, Mervyn. 1994. *Michael Foot*. London: Victor Gollancz.
Jones, Nicholas. 2010. *Campaign 2010: The Making of the Prime Minister*. London: Biteback.
Jones, Owen. 2020. *This Land: The Struggle for the Left*. London: Allen Lane.
Kavanagh, Dennis. 1998. 'The Labour Campaign', in Pippa Norris and Neil Gavin, eds. *Britain Votes 1997*. Oxford: Oxford University Press.

K.-H., S. 1956. 'The General Election 1955: Some Impressions by Members of Parliament and Others', *Parliamentary Affairs* 8: 467–81.

Kilroy-Silk, Robert. 1986. *Hard Labour*. London: Chatto & Windus.

Kogan, David. 2019. *Protest and Power: The Battle for the Labour Party*. London: Bloomsbury.

Kogan, David and Maurice Kogan. 1982. *The Battle for the Labour Party*. London: Fortuna.

Kynaston, David. 2009. *Family Britain 1951–57*. London: Bloomsbury.

Labour Party. 1988. *Labour and Britain in the 1990s*. London.

Lansbury, George. 1930. *My Life*. London: Constable.

Laski, Harold J. 1936. 'The General Election, 1935', *The Political Quarterly* 7: 1–15.

Laybourn, Keith. 2000. 'Labour in and out of Government, 1923–35', in B. Brivati and R. Heffernan, eds. *The Labour Party: A Centenary History*. New York: St Martin's Press.

Lewis, Jane. 1978. 'The English Movement for Family Allowances, 1917–1945', *Social History* 11(22): 441–59.

Longford, the 7th Earl of. 1982. *Diary of a Year*. London: Weidenfeld & Nicolson.

MacDonald, J. Ramsay. 1907. *Socialism*. London: T.C. & E.C. Jack.

MacDonald, J. Ramsay. 1925. *Wanderings and Excursions*. London: Jonathan Cape.

McDonnell, John, ed. 2018. *Economics for the Many*. London: Verso.

McKenzie, R.T. 1956. 'The Wilson Report and the Future of Labour Party Organization', *Political Studies* 4: 93–7.

McKenzie, R.T. 1963. *British Political Parties*, 2nd revised edition. London: Mercury.

McKenzie, R.T. 1964. *British Political Parties: The Distribution of Power within the Conservative and Labour Parties*, 2nd edition. London: Heinemann.

Major, John. 1999. *The Autobiography*. London: HarperCollins.

Mandelson, Peter. 1987. 'Marketing Labour: Personal Reflections and Experience', *Contemporary Record* 1(4): 11–13.

Marquand, David. 1977. *Ramsay MacDonald*. London: Jonathan Cape.

Marquand, David. 1992. *The Progressive Dilemma*, 2nd edition. London: Heinemann.

Massey, Christopher. 2020. 'The Labour Party's Inquiry into Liverpool

District Labour Party and Expulsion of Nine Members of the Militant Tendency, 1985–1986', *Contemporary British History* 34(2): 299–324.

Messina, Anthony. 1987. 'Post-War Protest Movements in Britain: A Challenge to Parties', *Review of Politics* 49(3): 410–28.

Messina, Anthony. 1989. *Race and Party Competition*. Oxford: Clarendon Press.

Miliband, Ed. 2010. 'Ed Miliband', in T. Hampson, ed. *The Labour Leadership*. London: The Fabian Society.

Miliband, Ralph. 1961. *Parliamentary Socialism: A Study in the Politics of Labour*. London: Allen & Unwin.

Minkin, Lewis. 1992 [1991]. *The Contentious Alliance: Trade Unions and the Labour Party*. Edinburgh: Edinburgh University Press.

Mitchell, Austin. 2018. *Confessions of a Political Maverick*. London: Biteback.

Morrison, Herbert. 1960. *An Autobiography*. London: Oldhams Press.

Mortimore, Roger and Andrew Blick. 2018. *Butler's British Political Facts*. Basingstoke: Palgrave.

Mullin, Chris. 1980. *How to Select or Reselect Your MP*. London: Campaign for Labour Party Democracy.

Murphy, Colm. 2022. 'What Did the 1983 Manifesto Ever Do for Us', in N. Yeowell, ed. *Rethinking Labour's Past*. London: I.B. Tauris.

Murphy, Colm. 2023. *Futures of Socialism: Modernisation, the Labour Party, and the British Left, 1973–1987*. Cambridge: Cambridge University Press.

Murphy, J.T. 1948. *Labour's Big Three*. London: Bodley Head.

Murray, Andrew. 2019. *The Fall and Rise of the British Left*. London: Verso.

Newman, Michael. 1993. *Harold Laski: A Political Biography*. Basingstoke: Palgrave Macmillan.

Nicholson, Harold. 1952. *George V*. London: Legend.

O'Connor, Kristine Mason. 2003. *Joan Maynard: Passionate Socialist*. London: Politico's.

O'Farrell, John. 1999. *Things Can Only Get Better: Eighteen Miserable Years in the Life of a Labour Supporter*. London: Black Swan.

Oborne, Peter. 1999. *Alastair Campbell: New Labour and the Rise of the Media Class*. London: Aurum Press.

Ostegaard, Geoffrey. 1963. 'The Transformation of the British Labour Party', *The Indian Journal of Political Science* 24: 217–38.

Owen, David. 1991. *Time to Declare*. London: Michael Joseph.

Paton, John. 1936. *Left Turn: The Autobiography of John Paton*. London: Secker & Warburg.
Payling, Daisy. 2014. 'Socialist Republic of South Yorkshire: Grassroots Activism and Left-Wing Solidarity in 1980s Sheffield', *Twentieth Century British History* 25(4): 602–27.
Pearce, Edward. 2002. *Denis Healey*. London: Little, Brown and Company.
Pelling, Henry. 1966. *A History of British Trade Unionism*. London: Macmillan.
Pelling, Henry. 1976. *A Short History of the Labour Party*, 5th edition. New York: Macmillan.
Pimlott, Ben. 1977. *Labour and the Left in the 1930s*. Cambridge: Cambridge University Press.
Pimlott, Ben. 1985. *Hugh Dalton*. London: Jonathan Cape.
Pimlott, Ben. 1992. *Harold Wilson*. London: HarperCollins.
Ponting, Clive. 1989. *Breach of Promise: Labour in Power 1964–1970*. London: Hamish Hamilton.
Pugh, Martin. 2010. *Speak for Britain: A New History of the Labour Party*. London: The Bodley Head.
Quinn, Thomas. 2018. 'Revolt on the Left: Labour in Opposition', in N. Allen and J. Bartle, eds. *None Past the Post: Britain at the Polls 2017*. Oxford: Oxford University Press.
Radice, Giles. 2004. *Diaries, 1980–2001*. London: Weidenfeld & Nicolson.
Ramsden, John. 1998. *An Appetite for Power: A New History of the Conservative Party*. London: HarperCollins.
Rathbone, Eleanor. 1924. *The Disinherited Family*. London: Edward Arnold & Co.
Rees, Phil and Faisal Butt. 2004. 'Ethnic Change and Diversity in England, 1981–2001', *Area* 36(2): 174–86.
Reid, Alastair and Henry Pelling. 2005. *A Short History of the Labour Party*, 12th edition. Basingstoke: Palgrave Macmillan.
Ridley, Jane. 2021. *George V*. London: Chatto & Windus.
Rippingale, Simon. 1996. 'Hugh Gaitskell, the Labour Party and Foreign Affairs, 1955–63', unpublished dissertation, University of Plymouth.
Ross, Tim and Tom McTague. 2017. *Betting the House: The Inside Story of the 2017 Election*. London: Biteback.
Sandbrook, Dominic. 2011. *State of Emergency: The Way We Were, Britain, 1970–74*. London: Penguin.

Sandbrook, Dominic. 2019. *Who Dares Wins: Britain, 1979–1982*. London: Penguin.

Scott, Len. 2012. 'Selling or Selling out Nuclear Disarmament? Labour, the Bomb, and the 1987 General Election', *International History Review* 34(1): 115–37.

Seebohm Rowntree, B. and Lavers, G.R. 1951. *Poverty and the Welfare State: A Third Social Survey of York Dealing Only with Economic Questions*. London: Longmans, Green & Co.

Seldon, Anthony. 2022. 'Neil Kinnock Reflects', in K. Hickson, ed. *Neil Kinnock: Saving the Labour Party?* London: Routledge.

Self, Robert. 2006. *Neville Chamberlain: A Biography*. London: Routledge.

Seyd, Patrick. 1987. *The Rise and Fall of the Labour Left*. London: Macmillan.

Shaw, Eric. 1996. *The Labour Party since 1945*. Oxford: Blackwell.

Shaw, Eric. 2000. 'The Wilderness Years', in B. Brivati and R. Heffernan, eds. *The Labour Party: A Centenary History*. Basingstoke: Palgrave Macmillan.

Shepherd, John. 2002. *George Lansbury: At the Heart of Old Labour*. Oxford: Oxford University Press.

Shinwell, Emanuel. 1973. *I've Lived Through It All*. London: Victor Gollancz.

Shore, Peter. 1983. 'The Purpose of Labour's Economic Programme', in G. Kaufman, ed. *Renewal: Labour's Britain in the 1980s*. Harmondsworth: Penguin.

Silkin, John. 1987. *Changing Battlefields: The Challenge to the Labour Party*. London: Hamilton.

Simms, Madeleine. 1978. 'Parliament and Birth Control in the 1920s', *Journal of the Royal College of General Practitioners* 28: 83–8.

Squires, Michael. 1990. *Saklatvala*. London: Lawrence & Wishart.

Stephens, Mark. 1981. *Ernest Bevin: Unskilled Labourer and World Statesman*. London: TGWU.

Stuart, Mark. 2005. *John Smith: A Life*. London: Politico's.

Taafe, Peter and Tony Mulhearn. 1988. *Liverpool: A City That Dared to Fight*. London: Fortress.

Taverne, Dick. 2014. *Against the Tide*. London: Biteback.

Thatcher, Margaret. 1993. *The Downing Street Years*. London: HarperCollins.

Thatcher, Margaret. 1995. *The Path to Power*. London: HarperCollins.

Thomas, J.H. 1937. *My Story*. London: Hutchinson.

REFERENCES

Thompson, Helen. 2015. 'Post-Crisis, Post-Devolution Politics, and the Mansion Tax', *Political Quarterly* 86(1): 9–15.

Thorpe, Andrew. 1991. *The General Election of 1931*. Oxford: Oxford University Press.

Thorpe, Andrew. 2004. 'Smith, Hastings Bertrand Lees- (1878–1941)', *Oxford Dictionary of National Biography*. Oxford: Oxford University Press.

Tilley, James and Geoffrey Evans. 2017. 'The New Politics of Class after the 2017 General Election', *The Political Quarterly* 88(4): 710–15.

Tracey, Herbert. 1948. 'Labour and the Second World War', in Herbert Tracey, ed. *The British Labour Party: Its History, Growth, Policy, Leaders, Vol. I*. London: Caxton.

Vinen, Richard. 2009. *Thatcher's Britain: The Politics and Social Upheaval of the Thatcher Era*. London: Simon & Schuster.

Ward, Paul. 1998. *Red Flag and Union Jack: Englishness, Patriotism, and the British Left, 1881–1924*. Woodbridge: Boydell Press.

Ward, Paul. 2004. *Britishness since 1870*. London: Routledge.

Warde, Alan. 1986. *Consensus and Beyond: The Development of Labour Party Strategy since the Second World War*. Manchester: Manchester University Press.

Watts, Jake and Tim Bale. 2019. 'Populism as an Intra-Party Phenomenon: The British Labour Party under Jeremy Corbyn', *British Journal of Politics and International Relations* 21(1): 99–115.

Webb, Sidney and Beatrice Webb. 1920. *A Constitution for the Socialist Commonwealth of Great Britain*. London: Longmans, Green & Co.

Weighell, Sid. 1983. *On the Rails*. London: Orbis.

Werbner, Pnina. 1991. *Black and Ethnic Leaderships*. London: Routledge.

Wertheimer, Egon. 1929. *Portrait of the Labour Party*. London: G.P. Putnam's Sons.

Westlake, Martin. 2001. *Kinnock: The Biography*. London: Little, Brown and Company.

Whiting, R.C. 2004. 'Greenwood, Arthur (1880–1954)', *Oxford Dictionary of National Biography*. Oxford: Oxford University Press.

Wickham-Jones, Mark. 1996. *Economic Strategy and the Labour Party*. London: Palgrave Macmillan.

Wickham-Jones, Mark. 2004. 'The New Left', in Raymond Plant, Matt Beech and Kevin Hickson, eds. *The Struggle for Labour's Soul*. London: Routledge.

Williams, Philip. 1979. *Hugh Gaitskell*. London: Jonathan Cape.

Williamson, Philip. 1984. 'A Bankers' Ramp? Financiers and the British Political Crisis of August 1931', *English Historical Review* 99(393): 770–806.

Wilson, 1986. *Memoirs: The Making of a Prime Minister 1916–64*. Weidenfeld & Nicolson and Michael Joseph.

Wilson, Harold. 1971. *The Labour Government 1964–70: A Personal Record*. London: Weidenfeld & Nicolson.

Wood, Ian. 1990. *John Wheatley*. Manchester: Manchester University Press.

Young, Hugo. 2008. *The Hugo Young Papers: Thirty Years of British Politics Off the Record*. London: Allen Lane.

Zeigler, Philip. 1993. *Wilson: The Authorised Life of Lord Wilson of Rievaulx*. London: Weidenfeld & Nicolson.

Index

Abbott, Diane 128, 170, 171, 174, 188, 195
Abel-Smith, Brian 88
Abrams, Mark 75
Alternative Economic Strategy (AES) 104
Anderson, Sir John 63
Ashworth, Jonathan 193–4
Asquith, H.H. 9
Attlee, Clement 11, 13, 23–4, 32, 33, 45, 46, 52, 53, 54, 55, 56, 57, 61, 64, 69, 73, 79, 93, 101, 104, 115, 176, 199, 205
Axelrod, David 184

Baldwin, Stanley 19, 23, 24, 28, 41, 42
Balls, Ed 167, 171, 174, 185, 193, 194, 196
Bank of England 38, 67, 95, 163, 166
Barker, Sara 50
Beckett, Francis 171, 173, 178
Beer, Samuel 67
Benn, Tony 51, 101–3, 104–5, 106, 107, 108, 110–11, 115, 119, 121, 122, 123, 128, 134, 135, 137, 142, 157, 158, 159, 160, 168, 170–1
Bevan, Aneurin (Nye) 50, 51, 55, 71, 72, 79–80, 83, 95, 200
Beveridge Report 63, 64, 66, 161
Bevin, Ernest 16, 21, 27, 28, 29, 47, 48, 52, 53, 57, 63, 64, 82, 176
Blair, Tony 143, 146, 148, 149–50, 152, 156, 157, 159, 161, 162, 163–4, 165, 166, 170, 172, 173, 175, 176, 185, 188, 190, 199, 203
Blunkett, David 135
Bonar Law, Andrew 9, 24
Boothroyd, Betty 113
Bragg, Billy 142, 145
Brailsford, H.N. 25
Bromley, John 18
Brooks, Stephen 57, 65, 66
Brookshire, Jerry 49
Broughton, Alf 112
Brown, Gordon 149–50, 152, 159, 162–3, 167, 169, 170, 171–2, 174, 176, 185, 188, 191
Bullock, Alan 49
Burnham, Andy 170, 171, 174, 194
Butler, David 70, 73–4, 124
Butler, Richard Austen 84
'Butskell' concept 83, 202

Callaghan, James 93, 95, 101, 111, 112, 113, 114–15, 116–17, 120, 126, 136
Cameron, David 138, 156, 165, 180, 192
Campaign for Labour Party Democracy (CLPD) 117–19, 120, 183
Campaign for Nuclear Disarmament (CND) 81, 140, 156, 179
Campaign for Social Democracy (CSD) 107
Campaign Group 122
Campbell Adamson, William 108–9
Campbell, Alastair 149, 162, 202–3
Campbell, John 101

INDEX

Castle, Barbara 98, 111, 129
Chakrabarti, Shami 192
Chamberlain, Neville 4, 16, 53, 54, 55, 56, 61
Churchill, Winston 16, 27, 56, 60, 61–2, 64, 200
Chuter Ede, James 61, 64
Citrine, Walter 48, 53
Clarke, Charles 134, 149
Clarke, Kenneth 152
Clause IV (*see* Labour Party constitution)
Clegg, Nick 156
Clinton, Bill 164
Clynes, J.R. 9–10, 119
Cole, G.D.H. 27, 43, 44
Collins, Ray 178
Commonwealth 83, 85
Communist Party of Great Britain 10, 15, 19, 21, 34, 53, 55, 102
Confederation of British Industry (CBI) 109
Cooper, Jack 76
Cooper, Yvette 174
Corbyn, Jeremy 7, 119, 158, 168, 169, 171, 173–5, 179, 181–3, 184, 185, 186, 187–9, 190, 191–2, 194, 196–7, 200, 201–2
Cortes, Manuel 172, 178
Cousins, Frank 80–1, 82, 89
COVID-19 pandemic 169, 180, 203
Cowley, Jason 190
Cripps, Sir Stafford 44, 45, 46, 50, 54–5
Cromer, Lord 96, 109
Crosland, Tony 71, 72, 100, 111
Crossman, Richard 73, 86, 88
Cruddas, Jon 185
Cunningham, Jack 151
Cryer, Bob 115

Dacre, Paul 162
Daily Herald 16
Daily Mail 126, 154, 162
Dalton, Hugh 33, 43, 45, 46–7, 50, 51, 52, 54, 56, 65
Dalyell, Tam 137
Davies, John 97
Dawes Plan 17, 27
de Gaulle, Charles 85
Deakin, Arthur 79–80
Delors, Jacques 153
devaluation (of sterling) 93
devolution 160
Diamond, Patrick 171, 185, 196
Diego Garcia 95
Dimbleby, David 1
Duffy, Terry 120, 131–2
Duncan Smith, Iain 200

Eden, Sir Anthony 53, 83, 84
education 20, 64, 65, 66, 71, 88, 116, 163, 167
electoral reform 32
European Economic Community (EEC) 84–5, 86, 100–2, 105, 107, 138–40, 152–3
and 1975 referendum 101–2, 107
European Exchange Rate Mechanism (and 'Black Wednesday') 154, 155, 156
European Free Trade Area (EFTA) 84
European Union (EU) 156, 169, 182, 183, 186, 187, 188, 189, 191, 195, 197, 200
and 2016 'Brexit' referendum 169, 182, 183, 187, 191, 192, 194, 195
Evans, Geoffrey 191
Evans, Moss 131
expenses scandal (2009) 163, 204

Fabian Society 12, 20, 43, 108, 170
Falklands conflict 136–7
financial crisis (2007–8: and 'austerity') 167, 193, 204, 205

INDEX

Flannery, Martin 123
Fletcher, Nigel 2
Flynn, Paul 182
Foot, Michael 111, 113, 116–17, 120, 121, 122, 124–6, 135, 136–7, 203
Forster, E.M. 16
Fyfe, Hamilton 16

Gaitskell, Hugh 43, 45, 69, 74, 75, 79, 80, 81, 82, 83–4, 85, 86, 88, 100, 117, 119, 137 143, 145
general elections:
    1922 9, 23, 30, 31, 32
    1923 13, 17, 31
    1924 18, 31
    1929 11, 31, 41
    1931 39–40, 42, 43, 45, 51
    1935 41, 42, 44, 50, 52
    1945 67, 78, 168, 186, 190, 194
    1951 68, 70, 72–3, 75, 103
    1955 72–4, 76, 87, 88, 90, 91
    1959 74–5, 79, 80, 87, 89, 90, 91, 103, 142, 143, 145, 200
    1964 5, 72, 75, 76, 82, 87, 89, 90, 91
    1966 92, 96
    1970 1, 92, 93, 95–6, 97, 101, 102, 103, 106, 110
    1974 (Feb) 96, 98, 105–6, 107, 108–11, 186, 198
    1974 (Oct) 199
    1979 112, 114, 115, 123, 124
    1983 113, 119, 124–7, 131, 138–9, 142, 145, 153, 161, 186, 192
    1987 130–1, 140, 142, 144, 145, 153, 157, 201
    1992 143, 151
    1997 143, 146, 148, 149, 150, 152, 154, 157, 160–1, 162, 164, 186, 193, 199
    2010 165, 167, 189, 190, 196
    2015 168, 184, 189, 190, 191
    2017 168, 169, 183, 185–6, 190, 194, 195
    2019 169, 183, 185, 188, 189, 191
General Strike (1926) 10, 25, 27–9
George V 16, 17, 22, 33
Giddens, Anthony 164
Glasman, Maurice 187
Gorbachev, Mikhail 140
Gould, Bryan 129–30, 131, 139, 154, 158, 160
Gould, Philip 145–6, 147, 148–9
Greater London Council (GLC) 128–9
Greenwood, Arthur 20, 37, 46, 52, 54, 55, 56, 58, 61, 63, 64
Greenwood, Tony 119
Greene, Ben 50
Griffiths, Jim 61, 64
Guild socialism 44

Hailsham, Lord (Quintin Hogg) 126
Hain, Peter 183
Halifax, Lord 56
Hamilton, John 133–4, 135
Hanham, H.J. 78
Hardie, Keir 18
Harman, Harriet 12, 173, 194
Harrison, Walter 101
Hart, Judith 137, 139
Hatherley, Owen 128
Hattersley, Roy 111, 120, 157–8, 160, 171
Hayter, Dianne 132, 141
Hayward, Ron 115
Healey, Denis 108, 111, 114–15, 116–17, 120, 121, 122, 123, 124, 127, 134, 140
Heath, Edward 92, 96–8, 99, 102, 105, 107, 108, 109, 135, 201
Heffer, Eric 124, 132, 134–5, 137, 140, 157
Henderson, Arthur 13, 15, 28, 39

Herbison, Peggy 76
Heseltine, Michael 151, 155–6
Hilary, John 188
Hindmoor, Andrew 89–90
Hitler, Adolf 52–3, 54, 126
Hodge, Margaret 182
Hodges, Frank 15
Hoey, Kate 150
Holland, Stuart 104–5, 150
House of Lords 26
Howard, Michael 151
Howell, David 12, 26
hunger marches 52

immigration 94, 107, 166
Independent Labour Party (ILP) 7, 12, 16, 18–19, 20, 26, 53, 55
Industrial Relations Act (1971) 98, 106
Institute for Public Policy Research (IPPR) 161
International Monetary Fund (IMF) 114
In Place of Strife 95, 98
Iraq War 166, 171–2, 173, 174, 181, 196
Irish nationalists 25

Jacobs, Michael 89–90
Jay, Douglas 43, 45
Jenkins, Clive 123
Jenkins, Roy 6, 83–4, 95, 100, 101–2, 103, 110, 111, 120–1, 127
Johnson, Boris 169, 182, 188, 189, 192–3
Jones, Jack 102, 131
Jones, Mervyn 125
Joseph, Sir Keith 112–13, 138
Jowitt, William 64
Joyce, Eric 176–7

Kaufman, Gerald 138, 140
Kavanagh, Dennis 124

Kendall, Liz 174
Kenny, Paul 173, 176
Kenyan Asians 94
Keynes, John Maynard 27
Keynesianism 37, 45, 57, 110, 115, 117, 159
Kinnock, Glenys 140
Kinnock, Neil 113, 122, 124, 125, 129, 130, 134–5, 138, 139, 140, 141, 142, 145, 146, 148, 149, 152, 154, 157, 158, 159, 160, 161, 164, 171, 200
Kitson, Alex 138
Kogan, David 185
Kosovo 166

Labour governments:
 1924 17–18, 29, 34
 1929–31 34, 36–9, 47, 48
 in 1940–5 coalition 35–6, 47, 51, 57, 58, 60–7
 1945–51 51, 59, 67, 68–71, 79, 82, 104
 1964–70 93–6, 97, 99
 1974–9 114–17
 1997–2010 166, 170–7
Labour Party conferences:
 1923 22
 1925 21–2, 27
 1926 32
 1927 33
 1931 37
 1933 48
 1934 44, 45
 1936 50
 1937 50
 1940 56–7, 58, 60
 1952 51, 72
 1960 72, 81, 89
 1962 85
 1964 93, 94
 1970 103
 1976 114–15

1979 115, 118, 138
1980 118, 138
1981 Wembley special conference 120–1, 167, 175
1981 138
1985 134
1987 144
1989 159
1990 159
1991 159
1999 145
2011 173
Labour Party constitution 11, 12–13, 14, 30, 117, 161
  Clause IV 13–14, 68–9, 75, 87, 88, 91, 161–2, 163, 194, 199
Labour Representation Committee 10, 18
Labour's Programme 1973 103–4, 105, 117, 186
Lamont, Norman 155
Lammy, David 180
Lange, David 120
Lansbury, George 16, 18, 19–20, 23, 25, 32, 46, 52, 176
Lansman, Jon 120, 183
Laski, Harold 42–3, 65
Lavers, G.R. 70
Laws, David 93
Lawson, Nigel 151–2
Lawther, Will 79
Laybourne, Keith 22
League of Nations 20, 46
Lees-Smith, Hastings 61
Lestor, Joan 115, 122
Lever, Harold 102
Liberal Party 9, 10, 17, 24, 26, 29, 31–2, 39, 41–2, 44, 54–5, 72–3, 75–6, 106, 108, 112, 126, 200
Liberal Democrats 93, 149
Livermore, Spencer 185
Livingstone, Ken 128, 161
Lloyd George, David 9, 32

local government 13, 20, 34, 113, 127–9, 133–5, 150, 151

Maastricht Treaty 155, 195
McCluskie, Sam 138
McClusky, Len 177, 195
MacDonald, Ramsay 10, 11, 12, 14, 16, 17, 18–19, 20, 22, 23–4, 25, 26, 27, 33, 36–7, 39, 41, 115, 119, 134, 201
McDonnell, John 129, 170, 174, 182, 183, 185–6, 187, 191, 194
McKenzie, Robert 77, 78, 81, 199, 204
Maclean, Neil 23
Macmillan, Harold 86, 172, 200
Major, John 143, 146, 151, 154, 155, 156, 157, 163, 195, 199
Mandelson, Peter 129–30, 131, 141, 147, 170, 174, 182, 196, 202–3
Maudling, Reginald 93, 94
Maxton, James 18, 25
Maxwell-Fyfe, David 78
May, Sir George 38
May, Theresa 168, 184, 192, 195
Maynard, Joan 118, 132
means test 52
Michels, Roberto 191
Mikardo, Ian 103
Miliband, David 167, 170, 171–2, 174, 176
Miliband, Ed 119, 167–8, 169, 170, 171–2, 173, 174, 176, 177–8, 180, 181, 183, 184, 185, 188, 189, 193, 194, 196, 200
Miliband, Ralph 167
Militant Tendency 113, 131, 132–4, 150
Milne, Seumas 187
minimum wage 11, 14, 20–1
Mitchell, Austin 120
Momentum 183
Mond, Sir Alfred 26

Morrison, Herbert 11, 13, 24, 25, 32, 43, 45, 56, 63, 64, 66, 128, 129
Mosley, Sir Oswald 17, 33, 37
Mullin, Chris 118–19
Murdoch, Rupert 162
Murray, Andrew 171, 184, 195
Mussolini, Benito 53, 200

National Council of Labour (NCL) 48–9, 51
National Executive Committee (NEC) 7, 13, 15, 19, 20, 21, 22, 27, 30, 35, 43, 46, 48, 50, 51, 53, 55, 56–7, 58, 65, 76, 77, 79, 85, 103, 114, 118, 121, 123, 129, 131, 132, 133, 135, 136, 138, 139, 141, 157, 159, 183, 184, 201
National Health Service (NHS) 69, 88, 116
nationalisation (*see also* Labour Party constitution, Clause IV) 44–5, 62, 65, 66, 67, 68–9, 70, 71, 75, 81, 87, 88, 91, 97, 103, 105, 107, 116, 117, 159, 161, 169, 174, 186, 199, 204
Miners' Federation of Great Britain 26, 79
National Union of Mineworkers (NUM) 107, 109, 113, 117, 132, 155–6, 162
New Statesman 16
Nigeria 94–5
North Atlantic Treaty Organization (NATO) 81
nuclear disarmament 81, 87, 89, 91, 126, 129, 138, 140, 159, 179–80

Oborne, Peter 147
O'Farrell, John 142, 145, 150, 159–60
opposition parties, role of 3–4, 24, 102

Osborne, George 193
Owen, Dr David 94, 95, 120–1, 129

pacifism 35, 46–7
Parry, Bob 134
Pearce, Edward 141
Pelling, Henry 14, 49
pensions 12, 62, 64, 88–9, 116
Pethick-Lawrence, Frederick 61
Phillips, Morgan 76, 79
Pimlott, Ben 40, 41, 45, 49, 78, 79, 87, 90
poll tax (Community Charge) 4, 150–1
Ponsonby, Arthur 25, 26, 33
Poplarism 19–20
Postgate, Raymond 28
Powell, Enoch 94, 97, 101, 108, 109
Private Finance Initiative (PFI) 164
Profumo affair 86
Pugh, Martin 22, 29, 131

Radice, Giles 120, 160
Rathbone, Eleanor 21
Rees, Merlyn 111
republicanism 22–3
Rhodesia 94
Rodgers, William 120–1, 127

Saklatva, Shapurji 15
Sawyer, Tom 135
Scanlon, Hugh 102, 131
Scargill, Arthur 132, 156
Scottish National Party (SNP) 112, 168, 190
Section 28 151
Seddon, Mark 171, 173, 178
'Selsdon Man' 97–8, 135
Shaw, Eric 124
Shaw, George Bernard 16
Shaw, Tom 24
Shinwell, Manny 13, 65, 66
Shore, Peter 102, 122, 124, 129, 135

Short, Clare 148, 149
Sierra Leone 166
Silkin, Jon 120, 121
Skeffington, Arthur 76
Smith, Elizabeth 171
Smith, John 146, 147, 149, 150, 152, 154, 155, 156, 158, 160, 161, 164, 166, 171, 195, 203
Smith, Owen 182–3, 187
Smith, Rennie 24
Snowden, Philip 11, 20, 24, 36, 37–8, 51
Social Contract 107, 111
Social Democratic Party (SDP: and SDP-Liberal Alliance) 93, 113, 123, 126–7, 131, 142
Socialist League 44, 45, 53
Soviet Union 15, 17, 54, 55, 81, 140
Starmer, Sir Keir 169–70, 174, 175, 180, 187–8, 195, 197, 202, 203
Stephen, Campbell 19
Straw, Jack 126
Suez Crisis (1956) 83–4, 86, 136
Sunak, Rishi 192, 202, 203

Taverne, Dick 105–7
Taylor, Ann 112
Thatcher, Margaret (and 'Thatcherism') 4, 92, 109, 112–13, 115, 117, 126, 128, 129, 132, 133, 135, 136, 137, 143, 144–5, 146, 147, 150–1, 152, 153, 154, 155, 157, 159, 160, 161, 163–4, 165, 175, 199, 201, 203
Thomas, Jimmy 22
Thompson, Heen 184
Thornberry, Emily 180
Thorpe, Andrew 40–1
Tiffin, Jock 80
Tilley, James 191
Titmus, Richard 88
Townsend, Peter 88
trade unions 7–8, 11, 15, 17–18, 21, 26–9, 33, 34, 38, 48, 49, 50, 53, 58, 70, 80, 81, 82, 95, 97, 98, 99, 102, 107, 116, 118, 119, 120–1, 123, 127, 131–2, 138, 144, 150, 158, 167, 168, 175, 176, 177, 178, 179–80, 183, 195
Trade Union Congress (TUC) 16, 20, 27, 28, 29, 43, 48–9, 85, 115, 153
Trevelyan, Sir Charles 33
Tribune (newspaper) 119, 126–7
Tribune Group 122
Trickett, Jon 187
Truss, Liz 169, 192, 193, 200
Tuffin, Alan 121
tuition fees 149, 161, 174

unemployment 36–8, 40, 41, 42, 51–2, 95, 100, 135–6
United States (and 'special relationship') 83, 94, 140, 166, 199
Upper Clyde Shipbuilders (UCS) 102

Vansittart, Sir Robert 54
Vietnam War 94

Wake, Egerton 32
Wallhead, Richard 18
Watson, Sam 79
Webb, Beatrice 23, 26, 27
Webb, Sidney 11, 13, 23
Weighell, Sid 120
welfare state 69, 70, 71, 88, 97, 100, 145, 166, 167, 169, 174, 186, 194
Wells, H.G. 16
Westland Affair 146, 154
Wheatley, John 13, 18, 22
Wigg, George 86
Williams, Len 76, 79
Williams, Philip 84

INDEX

Williams, Shirley 111, 120–1, 126–7
Williamson, Tom 79
Wilson, Harold 69, 73, 75, 76–7, 78, 81, 82, 86, 87, 90, 92, 93, 94, 95, 96, 97–8, 99, 100–11, 115, 119, 126, 147, 205
'Winter of Discontent' (1978–9) 115–16, 180, 197

Wolff, Michael 130
Wood, Sir Kingsley 63, 64
Wood, Stuart 185
Woolton, Lord 64, 78

Yesterday's Men 1, 92

Zinoviev Letter 31, 200